About the Sidran Foundation

The Sidran Foundation is a publicly-supported, non-profit organization devoted to advocacy, education, and research in support of people with psychiatric disabilities. The foundation is particularly interested in providing support and advocating empowerment for people who have survived psychological trauma, and has developed rsources in this area. The Sidran Press is publisher of a number of books and informational brochures on psychological trauma topics, including **Soldier's Heart: Survivors' Views of Combat Trauma,** a compilation of original prose, poetry, and art that is written by veterans with combat-induced trauma disorders and **Managing Traumatic Stress Through Art: Drawing from the Center,** a unique workbook designed especially for trauma survivors that introduces inventive ways to understand, manage, aand transform the aftereffects of trauma. In addition, Sidran has compiled an extensive database of trauma support and treatment resources and conducts educational workshops. For more information, or for a catalogue of books, contact The Sidran Press, 2328 W. Joppa Rd., Suite 15, Lutherville, MD 21093. Phone (410) 825-8888; Fax (410) 337-0747.

Risking Connection:
A Training Curriculum for Working with Survivors of Childhood Abuse

Karen W. Saakvitne, Ph.D., Sarah Gamble, Ph.D.,
Laurie Anne Pearlman, Ph.D. and Beth Tabor Lev, Ph.D.

The Sidran Foundation and Press is developing a basic trauma training curriculum especially designed for staff in public mental health settings. Developed with the support of the Departments of Mental Health in the states of Maine and New York, the curriculum will soon be available through Sidran to all interested states, agencies, and individuals. The authors of the curriculum are affiliated with the Trauma Research, Education, and Training Institute, Inc. (TREATI) of South Windsor, CT. It is being prepared with editorial and clinical input from helping professionals and trauma survivors with extensive experience in state mental health systems, clinical treatment of traumatic stress conditions, curriculum design, and the law.

The flexible format curriculum will consist of five half-day modules focusing on:
- Understanding trauma is the first step;
- Using connections to develop treatment goals with survivor clients: the R.I.C.H. guideline;
- Keeping a trauma framework when responding to crises and life-threatening behaviors;
- Working with dissociation and staying grounded: self-awareness as a tool for clients and helpers; and
- Vicarious traumatization and integration: putting it all together.

These modules are intended for mental health staff with all levels of experience working with trauma survivor clients, and with a broad range of background training and experiences (mental health workers, nurses, social workers, psychiatrists, etc.).

For more information about the curriculum, please contact Esther Giller, Sidran Foundation and Press, 2328 W. Joppa Road, Suite 15, Lutherville, MD 21093, <esther@sidran.org>.

Sidran

Secondary Traumatic Stress

Secondary Traumatic Stress

Second Edition

Self-Care Issues for Clinicians, Researchers, and Educators

EDITED BY

B. Hudnall Stamm, Ph.D.

SIDRAN PRESS

2328 W. Joppa Road, Ste. 15
Lutherville, Maryland 21093
(410) 825-8888
www.sidran.org

The views expressed by individual contributors to this book do not necessarily represent the policies and opinions of The Sidran Press or The Sidran Foundation for Mental Illness. Contributor's comments about therapy should not be considered medical advice. The editors and publisher of this volume recommend that readers follow the advice of a physician who is directly involved in their care or the care of a member of their family.

International Standard Book Number: 1-886968-07-1

Printed in the United States of America

Library of Congress Cataloging-in-Publication Data

Secondary traumatic stress : self-care issues for clinicians,
     researchers, and educators / edited by B. Hudnall Stamm. — 2nd ed.
          p.   cm.
     Includes bibliographical references and index.
     ISBN 1-886968-07-1 (paper : alk. paper)
     1. Post-traumatic stress disorder—Treatment.
     2. Psychotherapists—Job stress.   I. Stamm, B. Hudnall, 1958–   . [DNLM: 1. Stress
        Disorders, Post-Traumatic—therapy.   2. Burnout, Professional—prevention & control.
     3. Counseling.   WM 170 S445 1999]
RC552.P67.S39   1999
616.85'21—dc21
DNLM/DLC
     for Library of Congress   99-22834
                                                                              CIP

Contents

Part One: Setting the Stage

Chapter 1
Compassion Fatigue: Toward a New Understanding of the
    Costs of Caring   3
Charles R. Figley, Ph.D.

Chapter 2
Secondary Exposure to Trauma and Self-Reported Distress
    Among Therapists   29
Kelly R. Chrestman, Ph.D.

Chapter 3
The Risks of Treating Sexual Trauma: Stress and Secondary
    Trauma in Psychotherapists   37
Nancy Kassam-Adams, Ph.D.

Preface
to the
Second Edition

The better part of a decade has passed since I first committed to paper the words that formed the genesis of this book and which appear in the preface to the 1995 edition. They are, for me, as interesting and baffling as when I first wrote them. I am a scientist and I value my ability to think logically. However, at times as I go about my work in the traumatic stress field, it is difficult for me to differentiate between my feelings and my thoughts. I am caught reflecting on the ebb and flow of hope and frustration that is so much a part of our work.

When I was completing the first edition of this book, AIDS was rampaging through the world. Now rather than learning how to die *from* AIDS, many are struggling to learn to live *with* AIDS. There is no cure, but there is hope. During that same time, the new South Africa emerged from the odium of apartheid; the Roman Catholic and Episcopal churches and the governments of Canada and Australia apologized for their role in the genocide of indigenous peoples; the PLO and Israel agreed to extend Palestinian self-rule into the West Bank; there was the return of home rule to the countries of the former Soviet Union; and a peace agreement was reached in Northern Ireland. The O. J. Simpson trial brought to the world's attention the horror of family violence and, while producing mixed feelings about the guilt or innocence of Simpson, brought consensus against family violence and racism.

Concomitantly, there has been a global rise in the number of children who were soldiers. Eighty-three percent of the men of Liberia were killed in a civil war that had its roots in American slavery 200 years earlier. As the world watched in awe while the Truth and Reconciliation Commission heroically staggered forward toward healing in South Africa, warfare continued in the eastern South African province of KwaZulu-Natal. During the Northern Ireland peace process, a bomb blast that killed 28 people tore at the hearts of the people in Omagh and around the world. Between April and July of 1996 Hutu extremists killed as many as 800,000 people. In 1995 when I wrote about the spice basket from Burundi, we could speak in terms of the loss of a village. Now we speak in terms of loss of a people. To our growing horror, the loss of a culture or a nation or a people is not limited to tribes in Africa. Who among us has not stood and held our breath willing the Dayton Peace Accord success in the Balkans. Around the globe, eyes are trained each day to CNN world news and we pray for coverage of peace rather than violence wrought by despair.

Why do we move forward only to see new horrors arise? Why does terror overwhelm our best efforts to gain a foothold in the light? It is naïve to hope for a cure for terror. Nonetheless, I think we have to get up each day and do something. Somehow, we are existentially bound to go out and do business with the world. How we are in relationship with others is a direct reflection of our relationship with the deepest knowledge of our spirits. We move forward as individuals and as groups only to discover a dark area, one that frightens us or allows for unique self-expression, and we may falter as individuals and as groups.[1]

[1] I am indebted to Dr. Mark Agnew (Anchorage, Alaska) and Dr. Peter Petschauer and Amy C. Hudnall (Department of History, Appalachian State University), from whose probing e-mails these words emerged.

Most of us have current and historical understanding of light and dark: of light shining in the darkness or the darkness that does not understand the light. I would submit that when we align ourselves with the uncomprehending and incomprehensible darkness, we lose our vision and simultaneously find that it is too difficult to continue the journey in the light. Perhaps this is the best understanding I can offer of what it means to suffer secondary traumatic stress. By perceiving the light in the dark, by knowing there is hope when those we seek to help feel hopeless, we are both heroes and at risk. How shall we differentiate between our heroic and our dark times?

I wrote this poem in the fall of 1994 as a question to myself when I was between the light and the dark. For me, it represented my interior battlefields though it can easily be applied to the struggles of war. It still stands as a harsh condemnation of my own arrogance in believing that I act heroically and a sharp reminder of how important it is that I continue to try.

O that I would go to battle not this day.
There is no glory there.
Only the blackness of eternal loss
and hope that is despair.

There is no glory for the should.
The battle steals away
the splendor of the soul in light
and takes its power for the fight.

O that I would go to battle not this day.
There is no hope in that field.
There is no glory for the dead,
whose souls are given for the fight,
who will walk empty from that night.

O that I would go to battle not this day.
That I could turn this enemy with joy in my voice,
calling it to join with me
to see the unity of light and dark.

As if we could see who was whom.

Am I the light?
Should I so presume to wonder if I could
walk this path with clarity of vision?
Am I the light?
Should I so presume?

Perhaps not.
I would not so stand here on this field
if I were of the light.
Never would I have turned
from the truth long enough to see this path.

O that I would go to battle not this day.
Run
Run. It is not a beauteous sight.
It is not glory.
It is not what we believed.

O that I would go to battle not this day.
That I could reach across this field
to the other who stands and prays
"O that I would go to battle not this day."

I know as I hear the sharpening of the sword
that no one has the heart for this.
There is no joy in the battle
There is no joy in the fight.

O that we could go to battle not this day.
That we would reach to the other and say,
Unite for the time that we may,
to stand in the light
and know the futility of the battle.

O that I would go to battle not this day.
But I will fight on.
I know no other way.
It is finished.
There is no place to be
but in the battle deceived.

I move, only to discover a frightening dark place and falter.
Can I presume to make a difference? Or, must I stay in the bat-

tle deceived? I have to believe that I can make a difference; that I can honor that existential obligation to chose light. I also must remember that the darkest of my incomprehensible darkness is my own deception. A deception that tells me the world is all darkness or that I, alone, am the light.

Discernment comes from my hope and from my community.

This book was, and in this second edition, continues to be, about learning to live well with the joy and sorrow of caring. I believe that for those of us called to perceive the darkness and the light the world looks very different than it does to others. For we see clearly the darkness. Together, we must stay rooted, looking with hope toward the horizon for dawn's first light. This book is dedicated to that watch.

B. Hudnall Stamm
Saint Valentine's Day 1999
Mink Creek, Idaho
www.isu.edu/~bhstamm

Preface
to the
First Edition

B. Hudnall Stamm

After much contemplation, and consulting with several colleagues, I have decided to include a very personal essay about my motivation for doing trauma work and particularly to supporting the caregivers who do trauma work. While this essay is not traditional scientific writing, perhaps it reflects the very demand that Secondary Traumatic Stress makes on us: to depart from believing in the illusion that we are protected from other's pain by scientific postures and our "white coats." I would not suggest that we leave objectivity behind, but that we recognize that our personal passions drive our desires to do this work and our training and good supervision—of our clinical work, or research, or our teaching—help us keep our balance and objectivity. Objectivity and flintiness are not a guarantee of our training. Nor should they be. The capacity for compassion and empathy seems to be at the core of our ability to do the work and at the core of our ability to be wounded by the work (Figley, in this volume).

These ideas are at the crux of my desire to bring together the chapters in this book. My ideas are not scientific but are born of that passion that fuels science. And I believe they convey much of what we are discovering as a caregiving group: trauma can be terrifying and fear can be debilitating, but these experiences can present opportunities. Engaging the power of trauma will change us, and it has the power to harm us when we engage it in such close quarters. But, engaging it can bring us to the edge of the human condition and offer us opportunities to move beyond the common distractions of life, which frees us to deal with the unspeakable which is happening in our very experience.

Those of you who are reading this likely have strong wills and have applied these wills to your academic, clinical, and personal endeavors. You are to be commended for this. The ear or eye that conceives the truth is that of an individual and should never be ignored or belittled. However, I would submit that there is a point where individual will is no longer sufficient. At these times, I find myself awash in the tension between the individual and the community. In these cases, without losing the value of individual introspection, my recognition of being in pain and overwhelmed makes me aware that the solutions I have are a spent force. Trauma work reminds me of my individual limits; I come face to face with the fact that the world is full of death, hate, violence, and evil.

In the past half-decade, my family has been involved in documenting the establishment of the Wind River Indian Reservation in Wyoming. From 1878-1900, as a result of the U.S. government policies, the total Shoshone Indian population declined by over 30% while the Arapahoe Indians saw a nearly 15% drop. In 1873 the government food rations were estimated to be 2,300 calories per person per day. By 1893 the rations were 250 calories per person per day. Concomitantly, game supplies on reservation were nearly depleted from hunting pressure and the inhabitants were forbidden to hunt off reservation (Stamm, 1994; Stamm & Stamm, 1995).

Nearly a decade ago, my community sheltered an 18-year-old who had been caught in one of the wars in South America. Because he was an altar boy in the Roman Catholic Church, at age 14, he witnessed the murder of his family members, was arrested, and then tortured for information about the Church's activities.

On my bookshelf is a beautiful spice basket from Africa. It was a thank-you gift I received after teaching a Trauma Self-Care workshop. It was given to me by a former African relief worker who had left her post in fear for her life and the lives of her children. The village where she worked had been the repository of knowledge about how to make these traditional baskets. I was taken aback by the generosity of her gift but my heart was doubly moved when she told me that there would be no more baskets. All of the people in the village had been killed in the bloody battles raging in their area. For me, this basket is a daily reminder of the beauty that is falling under the sword in our world.

When I take in the meanings of these experiences, my will does not sustain me. The need to reach beyond myself to see the hope that exists in the world is overwhelmingly clear.

So where is the hope amid this much suffering? I believe it is in the nurturance of the individual within the sustenance of community. My experiences have shown me how communities, when well cared for, sustain their members during these times of failed self-sufficiency. The deepening community that results can bring about healing and positive individual transformations for all of its members. My respect for the leaders of these communities and for their commitment to reach beyond the limited capacity of their individual abilities is enormous. But the individual leaders are not the community. It is the collective wisdom of the group that sustains their ability to lead. The leaders may bring the vision but it is the community which gives the empowerment to reach the vision. Interdependency *is* the process. Interdependency does not substitute the group for the individual but weaves the individual with the group in such a way as to increase the individual's and the group's tolerance for the task of living. One's individual commitment to participating in the process of one's community is the only thing that can sustain and transform the community as it changes to meet the needs of its individual members, the needs of the member's family and friends, and even the world. T. S. Eliot wrote:

What life have you if you have not life together?
There is no life that is not in community.

So, I charge us all—as teachers, clinicians, and researchers, as we go about the work of healing—to build strong sustaining communities. Ones that will prepare us to follow our individual paths. I believe that together, we can change the world for the better. To move forward, we must look with eyes that are willing to see, listen with ears that are willing to hear, think with intellects which are not bound to unproductive ways; and feel with souls that are willing to bear the transient pain of change. I believe this is a task too difficult to be done entirely alone; that it can only be done, not by the community, but in the context of community. The individual heart sees truth, but it is the revelation of it to society as a whole which leads to change.

I would submit that the journey is full of joy, hope, laughter, and expectation. I believe that together we can change the world, but we must know what we are doing. Together, supported with our clinical knowledge, research, study, patience, tolerance, and respect for the dignity of each person, we can create a new vision of society. While we will certainly not eliminate trauma nor likely eliminate the hatred, evil, or violence that feeds it, we may learn to transform our encounters with these things into opportunities for growth for ourselves and for those whom we seek to heal.

Introduction
to the
Second Edition

You can't describe it unless you've seen it.
You can't explain it unless you've done it.
You can't imagine it unless you've been there.
Then it never goes away.

Bill Blessington, Retired Reporter
Chugiak, Alaska

There is a soul weariness that comes with caring. From daily doing business with the handiwork of fear. Sometimes it lives at the edges of one's life, brushing against hope and barely making its presence known. At other times, it comes crashing in, overtaking one with its vivid images of another's terror with its profound demands for attention; nightmares, strange fears, and generalized hopelessness.

When I first tried to write about this phenomenon, I looked toward the diagnosis of posttraumatic stress disorder for guidance. For acceptability, like any good scholar, I tried to build a case for the extension of a known phenomenon to justify the existence of one that I believed existed but for which there was yet very little quantitative evidence. Nonetheless, the phenomenon was both more and less than the extension of the post-traumatic stress disorder diagnosis. The name that we drew from this connection to posttraumatic stress disorder—secondary traumatic stress—is a harsh name. It is not a name one wants associated with their ability to care. As I have worked with providers and particularly, with administrators, I find that the name is off-putting. Likewise vicarious traumatization. Try telling an administrator that you want to work with one of his or her caregivers because they have become vicariously traumatized. "Well if there is something wrong with them, I don't want them on my staff." Another name is countertransference. This one defines quite nicely part of the phenomenon but applies more generally to working with people with all kinds of problems, not only working with people who have been traumatized (Stamm, 1997). In the title of this book, I use the term self-care. That, too, is a misnomer. Self-care implies somehow that (a) the person should take care of keeping the problem from happening, and (b) if it does happen, it is the individual's fault. We know that is not true. Certainly, an element of self-care is important, and for many, when organizations cannot or will not help, it is the only alternative by default. However, it is neither the answer nor the source of the problem. Burnout is quite the acceptable term. Administrators know it, they fear it (it costs money), and they want to prevent it. But what we are talking about is not burnout, although burnout may be comorbid. Compassion Fatigue. In 1993, Charles Figley and I discussed using the term compassion fatigue in place of secondary traumatic stress precisely because of its more palatable nature. A physician friend commented at the time, "It sounds like something good. You get it because you care, it is noble." Although I had helped with the development of the Compassion Fatigue Self-Test (Figley & Stamm, 1996), in 1995 I dropped this term because of its use by the media in regard to public apathy regarding homeless people. In 1999, the media use the term less and I find that I am using it more. There are two rea-

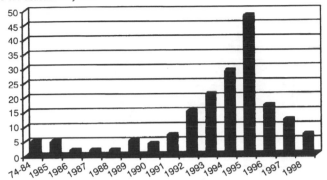

Figure 1: Publication by Year

sons for that. First, it is a term that many frontline workers use to think about themselves. Second, there is something to the labeling aspect of it. Even with this, I am not entirely satisfied with any of the terms we use.

So, what is in a name? Apparently not the field. For, despite our struggle with nomenclature to resolve to a set of common terms, the field has produced a remarkable amount of work in the past 7 years. From a handful of papers written by a few people, there are nearly 200 published papers (see Figure 1). Since 1996, 13 dissertations were catalogued, 10 in 1997. Nineteen ninety-five was a banner year, when the original version of this book (Stamm, 1995), Figley (1995), and Pearlman & Saakvitne (1995) were all published. Of the 48 publications in 1995, 28 were chapters in this book or in Figley (1995). These books, along with Wilson (1994) and Paton and Violanti (1996) account for 25% of the published literature on the topic.

It is instructive to review the pattern of publications. Since 1992, the majority of papers focus on the theory of indirect exposure, not on particular groups of people who are at risk for exposure. The two major groups that have been identified are emergency services personnel and health care/social service providers. Emergency service providers were identified early but the volume of literature has remained relatively constant over the past 15 years with a slight increase at 1995. Providers

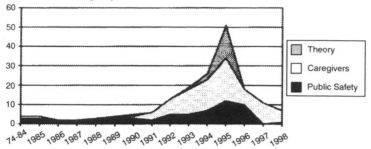

Figure 2: Publication Target by Year

Note 1 From 1992-1997 there were 13 "other" publications including teachers, clergy, transportation operators, and jurors.
Note 2 Theory papers are not independent from caregivers/public safety.

such as therapists, nurses, physicians, and child protective services workers were identified later but there has been more literature published on these groups (see Figure 2).

Thirteen other papers about work-related exposure were published during this time, three about the risks related to conducting research on traumatized individuals and three about the risks involved in teaching and training about trauma. The remaining papers relate to clergy and missionary work, to being a corrections officer or on a jury, and to exposure due to work as a reporter or train engineer. In all, there is a growing global literature developing. Drawing from the published literature and from the over 500 pages of e-mail regarding STS that I have received in the past three years, I plotted a global representation of the areas where I know research and/or interventions are happening. Work is progressing in more than 22 countries on more than 30 work specialties.

Other papers about work-related exposure might have been included here but are not. It is not difficult to identify work-related risks but it is very hard to differentiate between direct and indirect exposure. The most confusing differentiations are those where the helper/worker is exposed due to both the work activity and the environment in which the work takes place. Consider, for example, emergency service personnel. Are they

Figure 3 Published and Unpublished STS Research & Interventions

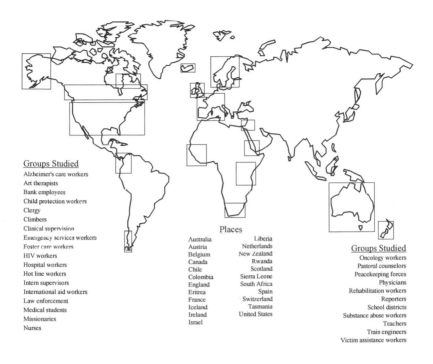

Groups Studied
Alzheimer's care workers
Art therapists
Bank employees
Child protection workers
Clergy
Climbers
Clinical supervision
Emergency services workers
Foster care workers
HIV workers
Hospital workers
Hot line workers
Intern supervisors
International aid workers
Law enforcement
Medical students
Missionaries
Nurses

Places

Australia	Liberia
Austria	Netherlands
Belgium	New Zealand
Canada	Rwanda
Chile	Scotland
Colombia	Sierra Leone
England	South Africa
Eritrea	Spain
France	Switzerland
Iceland	Tasmania
Ireland	United States
Israel	

Groups Studied
Oncology workers
Pastoral counselors
Peacekeeping forces
Physicians
Rehabilitation workers
Reporters
School districts
Substance abuse workers
Teachers
Train engineers
Victim assistance workers

potentially traumatized because they are exposed to the other's trauma as a helper, or because they are working in horrific environments which most of us would find challenging? Similarly, consider relief aid workers. In their role as helpers, they (a) hear horrible stories and see the results of torture, famine, disease, and war. They also (b) live in circumstances which may include deprivation and more often than not, direct risks to their safety. By virtue of (a) they may be vicariously or secondarily traumatized. By virtue of (b) they may be directly exposed. Drawing a distinction is both semantically difficult and ethically impractical. There is also the problem of being vicariously or secondarily exposed due to a friend or family member's experience (e.g. Figley, 1998; Stamm, Varra, & Sandberg, 1992). Nonetheless, in this book I have chosen to focus on exposure due to some work (either paid or volunteer) activity that places one in the path of another's traumatic material.

Is STS a Disorder?

Another very difficult epistemological issue is whether compassion fatigue/secondary traumatic stress/vicarious traumatization is a disorder. In the first edition of this book, I argued for its inclusion as a disorder (where appropriate), under the rubric of posttraumatic stress disorder. However, I also observed, and still believe, that reactions following indirect exposure because of another's trauma do not have to be a disorder. Moreover, if pathology should develop following exposure, I would submit that posttraumatic stress disorder is only one of the possible idioms of distress (cf. Stamm & Friedman, in press). In fact, the early psychometric investigations of the Compassion Fatigue Self-Test alerted us to look for depression-like symptoms (Figley & Stamm, 1996). The complete spectrum of traumatic stress continues to elude our best efforts to understand it as a holistic phenomenon. Likewise, secondary traumatic stress eludes us. In another paper (Stamm & Friedman, in press), I have written about a variety of possible idioms of distress, which may include somatic reactions, dissociation, depression, complex PTSD, and substance abuse.

Sidestepping the issue of diagnosis, many of the newer studies try to address STS in a holistic manner. Meldrum and colleagues (Meldrum, King, & Spooner, 1999) address STS in mental health case managers as a work stress issue, not strictly as an issue of psychological pathology. Sidran Press and The Traumatic Stress Institute are completing a trauma training curriculum which not only improves patient care, it is an STS primary prevention program (Saakvitne, Gamble, Pearlman, & Tabor Lev, in press). A recent qualitative study based on content analysis derived the following themes related to STS (a) struggling with changing beliefs, (b) intrapsychic struggles, (c) struggling with the therapeutic relationship, (d) work-related struggles, (e) struggling with social support, (f) struggling with power issues, and (g) struggling with physical illness (Arvay, 1998). In her study of train engineers' reactions to "person-under-train" events, Margiotta (1999) is measuring acute and delayed reactions, as well as a variety of physical health and social support issues. Although this study is retrospective, and primarily should be classified as direct rather than indirect exposure, it may help to tease out the types of experiences people have following work-related events.

It Is Personal and Professional

STS is not purely about work-related pathology. It leaks into the most private areas of our lives. The link between structural and functional social support and hardiness (King, King, Keane, Fairbank & Adams, 1998) speaks to the importance of understanding STS and changes in our activities of daily living. Rudolph's model (Rudolph, 1996; Rudolph, Stamm & Stamm, 1997) includes balancing personal and professional resources. It is predicated on the concept that revering—as personal or organizational heroes—the image of self-sacrificing, dedicated workers who never give a care to their own needs is potentially dangerous. When helpers do not have sufficient time to meet their personal needs for rest, family care, self-care, and professional development, they are at an increased risk for draining or damaging their social support and for developing the negative effects of helping.

Throughout this book, the theory of prevention of STS suggests that we spend time with our social support networks. What happens when the quality of support we feel in our relationships with our families, friends, and co-workers is fragile? A study in Canada is investigating this fragility. Alksnis (1999) questions the advice, observing that the advice is based on the assumption that the relationships themselves are not negatively affected by the trauma work that the practitioner does. For trauma workers, the boundaries between individual and organizational domains, between work and personal spheres are frangible (Stamm, Rudolph, & Bober, 1997). Whether or not the personal sphere is supportive, if we take an ecological perspective, we need to look at the workplace as a health promoting or diminishing environment. The workplace also serves as a recovery environment as much as the therapist office, community clinic, or hospital (Bober, 1996). To this end, we have included a new chapter in this book, Rudolph & Stamm, which addresses administrative and policy guidelines suggested by the other chapters in this book.

Hanging in the Balance

As a field, we have established that there are risks associated with being in harm's way as an act of compassion. Yet here we are in the trauma field, doing the work we set out to do. While nearly any of us could recount incidents of distress brought about by another's traumatic exposure, there is an element of satisfaction in our work that is very powerful. I first conceived of the idea that there was an important aspect to balance between the positive and negative aspects of helping in 1995 (Stamm, in press). I did not bring these thoughts to fruition until the end of 1997. The prompt was the request to consult on a project that involved bank employees who were trained as volunteers to debrief other employees following bank robberies (Ortlepp, 1997).

Thus, the languishing project on Compassion Satisfaction evolved to a new concept and a new measure (Stamm, in press). Beyond the idea that it is necessary to track what is right as well as what is wrong, there are several compelling psychometric reasons for tracking both fatigue and satisfaction. The most obvious reason is to reduce the risks of reporting bias. Moreover, as I began working with groups of providers in general research and prevention programs, I discovered that people were sometimes insulted by the implication that there might be something wrong with them. By offering items that were both positive and negative, I not only got better data, my participants were happier.

From a single test has grown a large website with an ever-increasing number of documents pertaining to traumatic exposure (http://www.isu.edu/~bhstamm/ts.htm). Many people ask about the measures that we use for assessing quality of life and traumatic stress symptoms. My colleagues and I believe that even if people experience highly stressful events, they may also have positive experiences. Because of that, we try very hard to make sure to understand the balance between personal resources (social support, belief systems, financial and community resources) and the stressful experiences a person has had. At minimum, we would include a measure of a person's history of exposure to extremely stressful events (e.g., The Stressful Life Experience Screening by Stamm et al., 1996), a measure of secondary exposure (e.g., The Compassion Fatigue and Satisfaction Test, Stamm, in press), and a measure of quality life (e.g., Life Status Review, Stamm, Rudolph & Varra, 1998).

What Is New in This Edition

This revised edition of *Secondary Traumatic Stress: Self-Care Issues for Clinicians, Researchers, and Educators* contains a number of new features yet retains the core of the previous edition. The body of the book, chapters 1–15, remains largely unchanged. However, additional material directed toward updating and increasing the utility of the book has been added in before and after the core chapters.

A new preface. With this edition, I continued my previous position of sharing some of the personal passion that drives me to do this work. For me, the new preface represents a higher level of trust and respect both for the work we do, and for my willingness to share my personal reflections on the work. When I wrote the original preface, I was quite unsure about committing those thoughts to publication. Although I had written similar things, I had never published anything like it before. Frankly, I questioned my motivation for including it, and more than that, questioned how it would affect my reputation as a researcher. Interestingly, of the hundreds of e-mails I have received about this book, the majority are comments thanking me for including the essay. Many of you told me that it spoke to your motivation as clinicians, researchers, and educators. I hope that this new preface will be a step further into that journey of balancing our personal and our professional spheres.

Introduction to the Second Edition. This introduction is largely about what we have learned since the original publication of this book. Originally, we were working with very little data and a great deal of theory. As the review of the published literature shows, there is now a growing amount of data upon which to expand our theory. We have not progressed to the point of randomized clinical trials or sophisticated tests. However, thanks in large part to the contribution of our recently graduated doctoral colleagues, there are a number of new quantitative studies. One paper in preparation even provides suggestions for protection of researchers doing research on traumatic stress and secondary traumatic stress (Sherrod, 1999). I have tried to highlight some of the studies about which I have knowledge to assist in coordinating our efforts and in focusing our continuing work.

Compassion Fatigue and Satisfaction Test. The newly revised version of the Compassion Fatigue Self-Test has been included in Chapter 1. The new test has three subscales: (a) Burnout, (b) Compassion Fatigue, and (c) Compassion Satisfaction. There is a copyright release on the measure, so that the measure may be copied and used freely. In addition, updated information may be found at the website http://www.isu.edu/~bhstamm/tests.htm.

Technology Updates on Chapter 11: Creating Virtual Community. Four years is a lifetime on the Internet. This chapter has been revised to reflect changes in technology. Where appropriate, the text has been revised and new web sites are included.

A new chapter on Moderating STS through Administrative & Policy Action by Rudolph & Stamm. This chapter grew from our work with administrators and policy advocacy. You will find a practical explanation of the policy process and suggestions for becoming involved in positive ways. There are sample policy interventions based on the content of the chapters of this book.

An Annotated Bibliography. This bibliography contains nearly 200 references to published materials in the STS field.

An Index. This new feature should make using this book more efficient. The index provides a comprehensive list of topics allowing for easy referencing across chapters.

REFERENCES

Alksnis, C. (1999). *The effects of working in a rape crisis center.* Unpublished raw data (Location protected).

Arvay, M. J. (1998). *Narratives of secondary traumatic stress: Stories of struggle and hope.* Unpublished doctoral dissertation, University of Victoria, Victoria, British Columbia, Canada.

Bober, T. E., Hess, M., Templeton, G. A., & Pearlman, L. A. (1996) *Vicarious trauma: Creating a resilient workplace.* Workshop presented at the 11th Annual International Society for Traumatic Stress Studies Conference, San Francisco, CA.

Figley, C. R. (1998). *Burnout in families: The systemic costs of caring.* Boca Raton, FL: CRC Press.

King, L., King, D., Fairbank, J., & Adams, G. (1998). Resilience-recovery factors in post-traumatic stress disorder among female and male veterans: Hardiness, post war social support, and additional stressful life events. *Journal of Personality and Social Psychology, 74* (2) 420–434.

Margiotta, S. M. (1999). *Effects of 'person-under-train' incidents on locomotive engineers.* Unpublished doctoral dissertation. Smith College School for Social Work, Northampton, MA.

Meldrum, L., King, R., & Spooner, D. (1999). *Secondary traumatic stress among Australian mental health case managers.* Work, Stress and Health '99: Organization of Work in a Global Economy. APA-NIOSH Joint Conference, March 11–13, 1999, Baltimore, MD.

Ortlepp, K. (1999). *Non-professional trauma debriefers in the workplace: Individual and organizational antecedents and consequences of their experiences.* Doctoral dissertation. University of the Witwatersrand, Johannesburg, South Africa.

Rudolph, J. M. (1996). *Compassion fatigue: A concern for mental health policy, providers, and administration.* Masters thesis. University of Alaska Anchorage.

Rudolph, J. M., Stamm, B. H., & Stamm, H. E. (1997). *Compassion fatigue: A concern for mental health policy, providers and administration.* Poster presented at the 13th Annual Conference of the International Society for Traumatic Stress Studies, Montreal, PQ, Canada.

Saakvitne, K. W., Gamble, S. G., Pearlman, L. A., & Tabor Lev, B. (in press). *Risking connection: A training curriculum for working with survivors of childhood abuse.* Lutherville, MD: Sidran Press.

Sherrod, N. B. (1999). *Secondary traumatic stress: Suggestions for trauma researchers.* Unpublished manuscript. University of Missouri-Columbia.

Stamm, B. H. (in press). Measuring compassion satisfaction as well as fatigue: developmental history of the compassion fatigue and satisfaction test. In C. R. Figley (Ed.), *Treating compassion fatigue.* Philadelphia: Brunner/Mazel. Test available online at http://www.isu.edu/~bhstamm/tests.htm.

Stamm, B. H. (1997). Work-related secondary traumatic stress. *PTSD Research Quarterly,* 8(2), Spring. http://www.dartmouth.edu/dms/ptsd/RQ_Spring_1997.html.

Stamm, B. H. (August, 1998). Improving care with technology: Reducing Military Caregiver Stress. In R. Ax (Chair), *Federal telehealth—Issues and initiatives.* Presented at the 106th Annual Convention of the American Psychological Association, San Francisco, CA.

Stamm, B. H. & Friedman, M. J. (in press). Cultural diversity in the appraisal and expression of traumatic exposure. In A. Shalev, R. Yehuda, & A. McFarlane, *International handbook of human response to trauma.* New York: Plenum.

Stamm, B. H., Rudolph, J. M., & Boeber, T. (1997). *Prevention of secondary traumatic stress: Individual and institutional responses.* Symposium at the 13th Annual Conference of the International Society for Traumatic Stress Studies, Montreal, PQ, Canada.

Stamm, B. H., Rudolph, J. M., Dewane, S., Gaines, N., Gorton, K., Paul, G., McNeil, F. Bowen, G., & Ercolano, M. (1996). Psychometric review of Stressful Life Experiences Screening. In B. H. Stamm (Ed.), *Measurement of stress, trauma, and adaptation* (Lutherville, MD: Sidran Press). Available online at http://www.isu.edu/~bhstamm/tests.htm.

Stamm, B. H., Rudolph, J. M., Smith, A., & Varra, E.M. (1998, November). *Life status review: Monitoring biopsychosocial risk factors in traumatic stress.* Presented at the Fourteenth Annual Meeting of the International Society for Traumatic Stress Studies, Washington, DC, USA. Available online at http://www.isu.edu/~bhstamm/tests.htm.

Stamm, B. H., Varra, E. M., & Sandberg, C. T. (1993). *When it happens to another: Direct and indirect trauma.* Presented at the 9th Annual Conference of the International Society for Traumatic Stress Studies, San Antonio, TX.

Introduction
to the
First Edition

This book is a book of ideas. Over the past several years, I have been privileged to participate in ongoing interactions with many of the contributors as we have become more and more clear about the potential costs of caring for others, or what can be termed in the broadest sense, Secondary Traumatic Stress (STS). One of the single most important contributions toward capturing the attention of traumatologists was the paper "Vicarious Traumatization: A Framework for Understanding the Psychological Effects of Working with Victims" (McCann & Pearlman, 1990), published only five years ago in the *Journal of Traumatic Stress*. That article described the experiences of respected clinicians and resonated with others. Working with people who have been traumatized changes a person—for better or for worse, the other's traumatic material touches the lives of caregivers. As early as 1978 (Figley, 1978), and again in 1983 (Figley, 1983a, 1983b), Figley wrote that caring for people who had been traumatized left marks on the victim's family members. These and other early contributions sounded the warning: Family, friends, and professionals were susceptible to "catching" traumatic stress from those in whom they invested their empathy and energy.

Perhaps, as Figley argues (Figley, 1983a, 1983b, 1995, in this volume), it is necessary for this to occur. If we are not engaged with others sufficiently to understand their pain and their experiences, then how could we truly be with them? But, when we do engage with them empathically, it seems that there are grave risks. This begs the question as to whether or not it is worthwhile to put oneself at risk. A resounding "yes" echoes from the fact that The International Society for Traumatic Stress Studies has grown from a few forward-thinking individuals to over 1,800 members in more than 30 countries in just a decade. If we are to engage in this potentially dangerous work, how can we protect ourselves? What puts us at risk? Who needs to "take care"? Only clinicians? Experience has shown that other caregivers, such as public safety officers, can suffer Secondary Traumatic Stress (for example, Mitchell & Bray, 1990; Mitchell & Everly, 1993; Stamm, Varra & Sandberg, 1993; Varra, 1995; Varra & Stamm, 1992). Moreover, as McCammon writes in this book, even teaching about trauma can put both the student and the teacher at risk.

The body of literature about Secondary Traumatic Stress is small but growing rapidly. It is as if we have been doing a massive triage at the disaster site of humanity. First we attended to those who were most obviously in pain: the veterans and the rape victims. Then we began to address others who were in pain as we discovered that there were a multitude of events that could traumatize people. Finally, as we take a psychological deep breath, we discover that the caregivers have been wounded in the fray. Two major works about caregivers appeared this year, one by Figley (1995) and one by Pearlman and Saakvitne (1995). Pearlman and Saakvitne's work is a carefully woven, research-based, theoretical book addressing the issues of the clinician. Figley's book is an edited collection of compelling papers describing and defining the phenomenon as we now know it.

Both will no doubt change the frequency and texture of the thinking on this topic over the next few years.

This book assumes that STS exists. The authors begin with this premise—that engaging emphatically with another's traumatic material carries risks. From this, it addresses the question: What might we do? Contributors were recruited based on their previous work with STS and offered an opportunity to write about whatever they chose—they were literally invited to "get on their soapboxes." Authors were encouraged to think theoretically and broadly, even radically. In effect, this is a "think-tank" book. Even the breadth of the articles is intended to spark controversy and thinking. All of us who participated in this project expect that our ideas will undergo metamorphosis over the next few years. And we all hope these papers will help encourage and guide the field of STS as it gathers strength.

Perhaps James Munroe puts it best in his contribution to this volume when he raises the ethical dilemma of how we are to proceed in the absence of empirically demonstrated effective means of prevention. This book does not pronounce absolutes but offers considered opinions based on personal and clinical experience, and whenever possible, on quantitative evidence. The astute reader will notice that there is a chorus of important points that emerge from the collective voice of the authors—primarily, (a) do not do this work alone and (b) monitor your responses to the work through your own careful attendance to your process and through supervision by your trusted colleagues. This is a good standard of practice, regardless of whether it is applied in the consulting room, the classroom, or in research.

STRESS, TRAUMATIC STRESS, AND TRAUMATIC STRESS DISORDERS

For the past one-and-a-half decades, traumatic stress, virtually embodied as Post Traumatic Stress Disorder, has been conceived as a medical diagnosis that has required experiencing "an event that is outside the range of usual human experience and that would be markedly distressing to almost anyone" (American Psychiatric Association [APA], 1987, p. 250). Because caregiving is an event that many people will encounter at some time in their life, it is not likely that most experiences of caregiving can be described as "outside the range of usual human experience." However, a powerful witness is arising in the literature that suggests being exposed to another's traumatic material has the potential of producing traumatic stress in the caregiver (see for example, Figley, 1995; McCann & Pearlman, 1990; Pearlman & Saakvitne, 1995).

A great deal of the ambiguity present in the DSM-III-R definition of traumatic stress and indirect exposure as a stressor was removed by restructuring the traumatic stress diagnoses for the DSM-IV. The old PTSD rubric allowed for traumatization even if one was not the direct target of the event (see Figley, in this volume). However, under the new rubric for PTSD (or the newly-defined Acute Stress Disorder) this has become much more explicit. According to the DSM-IV guidelines, a person must have "experienced, *witnessed, or been confronted* with an event or events that involve actual or threatened death or serious injury, or a threat to the physical integrity of oneself or *others*" [italics added for emphasis] (APA, 1994, p. 426). Thus, the focus shifts from the exclusionary perspective of identifying the direct target of the event, or at least one closely linked to such a "target" (like a family member), to the possibility of being indirectly included in the confrontation regardless of relationship to the event target. Part two of criterion A makes this even more explicit as the DSM-IV abandons the solitary focus on the event. The second element of the criterion—"the person's response involved intense fear, helplessness, or horror" (APA, 1994, p. 426)—provides the key to understanding exposure to another's experience as a traumatic stressor.

No longer is pathological traumatic stress addressed from the event-only perspective. Instead, the new DSM rubrics suggest it is necessary to consider the ecology of the entire system and focus on the interaction *between the person and the event*. It is this bi-fold nature of the definition—if the caregiver reacts with intense fear, helplessness, or horror—then the possibility of caregiving as an etiology of pathology exists.

Regardless of whether or not the DSM-IV criteria for association with a traumatic stress *disorder* is met or not, many of the experiences that are commonly reported by caregivers are similar to those which are associated with stress reactions and PTSD. Those reports can include recurrent and intrusive recollections; recurrent distressing dreams; flashbacks and dissociative experiences; psychological distress at exposure to symbols of the event or the person being cared for; and physiological manifestations such as difficulty with sleep, irritability, difficulty concentrating, etc. (cf., APA, 1987, 1994; McCann & Pearlman, 1990; all chapters in this volume).

Thus, the term *stressful experience,* (Stamm, 1993; Stamm, Varra & Sandberg, 1993) can be used to recognize the person-event interaction at the broadest and most encompassing level, without necessarily imposing the status of a disorder. Two other terms originated by Figley (1985) can be updated to reflect the changes made in the DSM-IV (1994). The term *traumatic stress reaction* refers to "the natural and consequent behaviors and emotions [;]...a set of conscious and unconscious actions and behaviors associated with dealing with the stressors" or memories of the experience (Figley, 1985, p. xix, in this volume). *Traumatic Stress Disorder* (Figley, 1985) can be used to describe experiences that are so traumatically stressful and place such high demands on the person for change that the person's psychosocial resources are challenged sufficiently to create pathology.

In sum, I would suggest envisioning traumatic stress not merely as diagnosable pathology, but as part of the larger concept of stress, which can include the important concept of Secondary Traumatic Stress. Moreover, it can include, but *is not lim-*

ited to, the mental disorders of Acute Stress Disorder and PTSD. Stressful experiences, including caregiving, can be conceived as an individual's experience in relation to the event, in which elements of the event in combination with that specific individual's resources create a situation in which the experience itself is stress-producing. Subsequently, one's beliefs—of faith in life, in others, in self—are disorganized, restructured, or at least challenged (Stamm, 1993, 1995).

Perhaps one of the keys to understanding the differentiation between a traumatically stressful experience and a stressful experience is the level of demand for re-orientation. Experience-induced re-orientation is stressful, but may or may not cause a diagnosable traumatic stress mental disorder. From my research, I believe that the greater the demand and/or the fewer the resources the person has with which to make the change, the greater the potential for the stress to be traumatic or even pathological (Stamm, 1993, 1994, 1995; Stamm, Varra & Sandberg, 1992). Figure 1 below is a simplified graphic of this theoretical assumption. While the graphic is drawn in a linear form to represent the continuous nature of stress, and for simplicity's sake, no attribution should be made about stress as a linear concept.

Thus, I propose that caregiving can be a stressful experience that may produce a situation ripe for a traumatic stress response that may or may not lead to a traumatic stress disorder. In addition, I assume that stress reactions are not always ultimately injurious. Challenges to one's sense of self and the world are catalysts and the paths that emerge are as varied as the people that experience the challenges.

While no book can ever address the full context of even a single experience, the point of this book is to create a window to the larger picture of the *Self*-changing nature of caregiving. People live in a context; stressful events are not isolated from the person who lives in them. The shift away from the DSM-III-R event-centered definition to the person-event interaction as specified in the DSM-IV clearly recognizes the importance of

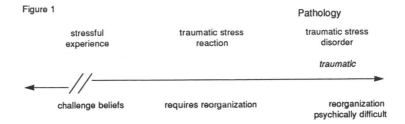

Figure 1

contextualizing stressful experiences. The articles in this book attempt to raise the question of stressful experiences in an ecological perspective so that we might learn to use what we know to prevent the abortive-growth process of the pathology of PTSD and to enhance the possibility of positive developmental growth in the face of the inviolate changes of trauma.

THE CHAPTERS IN THIS BOOK

The book begins with a summary paper by Charles R. Figley in which he raises the issues of Compassion Fatigue—or as he puts it, the costs of caring. Figley draws on his nearly 20 years of clinical experience and research to provide a compelling case for Compassion Fatigue. Following Figley's paper are two brief chapters that review new research asking questions about the exact nature of the cost of doing trauma work. Both Kelly R. Chrestman and Nancy Kassam-Adams provide data supporting the positive gains and potential risks involved in doing trauma therapy. These brief reports are the only "pure" research chapters in this book. Both are included, and in summary form, because of their timely nature and because of the interesting questions that they raise. Clearly this is an exciting, emerging field in which to do research.

The next three chapters (Laurie Anne Pearlman; Dena J. Rosenbloom, et al.; and Don Catherall) offer suggestions for ways in which trauma therapists can create safe environments in which to work. The clinical groups from which these chapters originate—The Traumatic Stress Institute and The Phoenix Institute—are well-known for their employee-supportive environments. Both clinics have cultures in which Secondary Traumatic Stress has been a consideration for many years. These three chapters draw on the theory and practice of these successful clinics.

Susan L. McCammon's paper introduces ideas that are beginning to take hold in clinical training and university settings. The melodic title of "Painful Pedagogy" belies the potential struggle that lies underneath the convoluted issues of teaching about trauma. Many of the people who are attracted to the field have trauma histories. Many of them struggle with these histories in training situations. This is intensified in a large classroom that is not a supervised setting or a training clinic. Drawing on her years of university teaching experience as well as her public safety personnel training courses, Dr. McCammon offers multiple suggestions about framing material and creating safe environments in which to teach trauma material.

Chrys J. Harris and Jon G. Linder raise a beguilingly simple issue. How do we communicate when we are under stress? They point out that our ability to understand and our ability to make ourselves understood have a major impact on our ability to be mentally healthy in challenging situations. In very pragmatic terms, Harris and Linder offer simple and constructive suggestions to assist the reader in understanding their primary and secondary methods of communication.

The primary care provider is likely to see far more of the sequelae of trauma than any therapist. Unfortunately, current medical school training rarely provides trauma-related training to the primary care provider. Lyndra J. Bills, who is trained both as an internist and a psychiatrist, offers a systematic approach with which the primary care provider can diagnose trauma. While this may not appear to be an STS issue, consider the ongoing stress on the primary care provider when he or she sees the patient returning time and again with persistent and untreatable conditions. Often the physician has no training to help the patient. Far too often these patients are shuffled from physican to physician with little or no truly helpful treatment. Teaching the physician about trauma-based medicine supports the physician's need for competency and authority in a very positive way.

One of the more sweeping approaches to addressing Secondary Traumatic Stress is presented by Michael R. Terry in "*Kelengakutelleghpat*." This paper outlines a region-wide, community-based intervention program that includes everyone in the community as part of the healing community. This unique paper, which tells the story of an Arctic Alaska Native community, changes the traditional white western perception of treatment—both physical and mental health—and reframes it in an entirely different way.

Recognizing that not all people will be able to create elaborate treatment communities in which to practice, Frederick Pearce and I offer an alternative strategy for developing professional community. We draw on the emerging technology-based global community and its potential resources that can help reduce the isolation of caregivers.

The last four chapters directly address ethical issues related to Self Care and STS. Clearly all chapters in this book speak to ethical concerns, but these four papers cut right to the heart of the issue. James F. Munroe's systematic paper follows the ethical guidelines of the American Psychological Association; although, as Munroe points out, it applies equally well to others. Mary Beth Williams and John F. Sommer continue in their tradition of framing *standards of practice* guidelines for therapy from a distinctly Self-Care and ethical perspective. The final two papers are particularly challenging. The first, by Jonathan Shay, applies his strong background in the classics (see Shay, 1994) to the issues of Self Care—reframing as it were—all of philosophy or at least all of Self-Care! The final chapter in this book is likely to be the most provocative. Sandra L. Bloom argues from a feminist-theoretical perspective that we have collectively created violence and that this violence is like an infection that is destroying our humanity. Dr. Bloom raises issues that challenge our thinking and bear consideration and research.

In sum, four kinds of chapters are here: (a) those setting the stage (Figley, Chrestman, Kassam-Adams); (b) those that offer models to protect therapists (Pearlman, Rosenbloom et al., Catherall); (c) those that extend the issues of STS and Self-Care beyond therapy (McCammon, Harris & Linder, Bills, Terry, Stamm & Pearce); and (d) those that address the ethical dilemmas raised by Self Care (Munroe, Williams & Sommer, Shay, Bloom). The thoughts collected here offer a wealth of directions from which future clinicians, teachers, and researchers can go forth to expand our understanding of the costs of caring.

REFERENCES

American Psychiatric Association. (1987). *Diagnostic and statistical manual of mental disorders* (3rd ed., rev.). Washington, D.C.: American Psychiatric Association.

American Psychiatric Association. (1994). *Diagnostic and statistical manual of mental disorders* (4th ed.). Washington, D.C.: American Psychiatric Association.

Figley, C. R. (1978). Psychosocial adjustment among Vietnam veterans: An overview of the research. In C. R. Figley (Ed.), *Stress disorders among Vietnam veterans: Theory, research, and treatment*. New York: Brunner/Mazel.

Figley, C. R. (1983a). Catastrophe: An overview of family reactions. In C. R. Figley & H. I. McCubbin (Eds.), *Stress and the family: Coping with catastrophe* (v. 2). New York: Brunner/Mazel.

Figley, C. R. (1983b). The family as victim: Mental health implications. In P. Berner (Ed.), *Proceedings of the VIIth world congress of psychiatry*. London: Plenum.

Figley, C. R. (1985). Introduction. *Trauma and its wake: The study and treatment of PTSD*. New York: Brunner/Mazel.

Figley, C. R. (Ed.) (1995). *Compassion fatigue: Coping with secondary traumatic stress disorder in those who treat the traumatized*. New York: Brunner/Mazel.

McCann, L. & Pearlman, L. A. (1990). Vicarious traumatization: A framework for understanding the psychological effects of working with victims. *Journal of traumatic stress*, *3* (1), 131-149.

Mitchell, J. T. & Bray, G. (1990). *Emergency services stress*. Englewood Cliffs: Prentice Hall.

Mitchell, J. T. & Everly, Jr., G. S. (1993). *Critical incident stress debriefing*. Ellicott City, MD: Chevron Publishing Corporation.

Pearlman, L. A. & Saakvitne, K. W. (1995). *Trauma and the therapist: Countertransference and vicarious traumatization in psychotherapy with incest survivors*. New York: W. W. Norton.

Shay, J. (1994). *Achilles in Viet Nam: Combat trauma and the undoing of character*. New York: Atheneum.

Stamm, B. H. (1995). A process approach to community, spirituality, trauma and loss. Trauma, Loss, and Dissociation Conference, Washington, D.C.

Stamm, B. H. (1994). Contextualizing death and trauma: A preliminary attempt. In C. R. Figley (Ed.), *Death and trauma*. Manuscript submitted for publication.

Stamm, B. H. (1993). Conceptualizing Traumatic Stress: A Metatheoretical Structural Approach. Dissertation, Laramie, WY: University of Wyoming.

Stamm, B. H., Varra, E. M. & Sandberg, C. T. (1993). When it happens to another: Direct and indirect trauma. Ninth Annual Conference of the International Society for Traumatic Stress Studies, San Antonio, TX.

Varra, E. M. & Stamm, B. H. (1992). Vicarious traumatization: Emotional support providers of sexual/physical assault victims. The First World Conference on Traumatic Stress, Amsterdam, The Netherlands.

Varra, E. M. (1995). Mediating factors of vicarious trauma in friends and family members of assault and abuse victims. Master's Thesis, Laramie, WY: University of Wyoming.

Notes From the Field:
Charles R. Figley

Back in 1993 it became clear to me that advances in the treatment of PTSD and other anxiety disorders lagged far behind advances in knowledge and assessment. As a result, we started the Active Ingredient Project to focus attention on finding and applying the most efficient treatment approaches to unwanted traumatic stress reactions. That project continues. Today we know much, much more about the trauma induction and reduction process. We know, among other things, that exposure is a key ingredient to any effective treatment of this kind. So is relaxation (e.g., self-soothing methods) and desensitization.

Our intention back in 1993 was clear. After we begin to identify and assemble the most effective methods for eliminating traumatic stress reactions, we would first focus on traumatologists—those who study, assess, and help the traumatized.

Most recently, we developed the Compassion Fatigue Specialist Certification Program, with the first course offered in January 1999. This Program was developed through the hard work of Eric Gentry, Anna Baranowsky, and Kathy Dunning.

This Program is the most recent addition to our Traumatology Institute Certification Program. The Institute was established by the Florida Board of Regents last year and incorporates the Florida State University Psychosocial Stress Research Program. The Institute offers the following: Field Traumatologist (non-mental health professionals), Certified Traumatologist, and Master Traumatologist. The Institute has sites in Miami and outside Washington, DC. Other sites are in various stages of development. Those interested in certification, training, or establishing an Institute training site should call 850-644-1966 or visit our web site at http://www.cpd.fsu.edu/pet/trauma.htm.

In addition to the books like this one, several articles are now being published in TRAUMATOLOGYe. It can be accessed at http://www.fsu.edu/~trauma/.

Notes from the Field: Laurie Anne Pearlman
What Is Vicarious Traumatization?

———

What is vicarious traumatization? I have answered that question hundreds of times (and even sometimes when no one was asking). I first knew what vicarious traumatization was experientially, before it had a name, before I had a framework. The first year I worked full-time as a trauma therapist, I found the holidays dull and empty. That had never happened to me before. When I was a child, my mother had a knack for making occasions like birthdays and Thanksgiving special. She decorated cakes, sewed matching outfits for my dolls and me, and served us tea from tiny porcelain cups. She made me feel I was special because our family got to celebrate all of the Jewish and Christian holidays. I have developed and sustained special traditions and celebrations for holidays and other occasions my whole life. Yet here I was in a funk at Thanksgiving, my personal favorite. Inexplicable.

And the funk didn't even seem to pass. I found myself enjoying all of life, except work, a little less. Yet I didn't think I was depressed. Violent imagery was intruding upon my consciousness when I wanted to have fun. A deep sense of sorrow pervaded my days, and my clients' stories ran around in my mind at night. Eventually, thanks to an organizational structure that included "feelings time," supervision, case conferences, and seminars—time to talk about our work—I learned that I wasn't alone in feeling "weird," not like myself. As we talked my colleagues at the Traumatic Stress Institute and I recognized the commonality of our responses and, through lengthy discussion, we developed the concept of vicarious traumatization.

We began talking to other trauma therapists and then other trauma workers about it. We began writing about it (McCann & Pearlman, 1990; Pearlman & Saakvitne, 1995). People responded with tears and thanks. "Yes!" "That's what's going on for me." We began doing research on it (Pearlman & Mac Ian, 1995). Others did research and wrote about vicarious traumatization and related concepts, such as secondary traumatic stress and compassion fatigue (Figley, 1995; Follette, Polusny, & Milbeck, 1994; Schauben & Frazier, 1995; Stamm, 1995).

By now, many of us have spoken and written about how VT can affect us (in all of the same ways, if less intensely, that direct trauma affects its victims). We have thought about what contributes to VT (both who the helper is and where and with whom s/he works). We have thought about how we can address it (through self-care, self-awareness, balance among work, play, and rest, and connection with other people). We have talked about transforming VT (by challenging negative beliefs, developing community, and investing in our own spirituality).

Armed with all of this knowledge and with a history of conducting many VT workshops and research studies, in January 1999 I went to Rwanda. My dearest friend and colleague, Ervin Staub, and I are trying to help people there heal in the aftermath of the 1994 genocide. We spent two weeks in Rwanda meeting people, hearing their stories, learning how they are living now. We met primarily with helpers, many of whom are themselves survivors, and all of whom are traumatized. The whole society is reeling. We observed their daily heroism, manifest not only by getting out bed each morning, but also by their devotion to helping others.

One day, while we were there, Ervin said, "What will it be like if we get really engaged with Rwanda?" It is happening. It has happened. I think about the people there every day. The genocide is now real to me. I listened to people who hid in cellars and car trunks. I worked with young women whose husbands and children were murdered. The sister of one of our colleagues was given up to the killers by her husband's family.

Upon our return, both of us have found life a little colorless. I have been glad to return to my familiar routines and surroundings, my clients and colleagues. Yet, I haven't had the same kind of engagement with my work, my friends, or my life that I had before I went to Rwanda. At first I thought, well, I guess I need a vacation. And I probably have culture shock. And I'm tired. Of course, I had the flu for a week after I returned. Maybe that's it. After a couple of weeks, I had an astounding realization: "I think I have VT!" Despite my immersion in this concept for years, my own VT came as a surprise.

How often does it happen to each of us that we awaken to a new realization about ourselves that we might have known all along? How often does it happen to every trauma worker that we both know and don't know what our work does to us? Knowing about our own VT is like that unsettling experience of feeling like you're waking up from a bad dream, and then realizing in a few moments that you're still asleep, and then waking up again. And again. We need to keep returning our attention to our experience—internal and external—to assess where we are in the VT process. Because it is a process, it is not an event, a diagnosis, or even an experience. It's fluid, ever-changing, always shadowing us. As long as we are engaging empathically with trauma survivors and feeling responsible to help in some way, we are going to experience VT.

Once I realized I was suffering from VT, I began to do some of the things that I know can help (see Saakvitne, Pearlman, &

the Staff of the Traumatic Stress Institute, 1995). I began talking to people about it. At lunch the other day with a colleague, Dena Rosenbloom, with whom I co-authored a chapter in this volume (Rosenbloom, Pratt, & Pearlman, 1995), I realized I felt like Woody Allen when I heard myself say, "How can I enjoy life when people are suffering?" And the idea of a vacation doesn't appeal. I would feel too guilty lying on the beach, thinking about Anne and Michael and Beatrice, some of the incredibly brave and resilient Rwandan helpers who are out in the community working on healing and reconciliation even as I write.

Before I went to Rwanda, my beloved colleague, Beth Stamm, invited me to write something about VT for this revised edition. It felt like a work assignment; I declined. When I returned from Rwanda, I realized I wanted to write to everyone to try to remind you, as I myself have been reminded, that we are not the masters of our VT. We must learn to live with it, and that means honoring and acknowledging it, treating it with respect, and working with it.

I am working to transform my VT by following my passion, strengthening connections, and creating meaning. My current passion is to find ways to take contemporary knowledge about traumatic stress to greater numbers of people. I'm working to do so through a variety of projects, of which the Rwanda project is one. The development of a trauma training curriculum through Sidran Press (Saakvitne, Gamble, Pearlman, & Tabor Lev, in press) is another.

Beginning to reconnect with friends and colleagues has begun to help me reconnect with me. Talking with colleagues here at the Traumatic Stress Institute about the trip, the project, the research, and the people I encountered in Rwanda has been very helpful. Talking with Ervin and others about my VT is essential.

I am still struggling toward meaning. Why didn't I try to do something, anything, before or during the genocide in Rwanda? Where was the United States? Are my efforts to help now of any use? What if I had invested this time, thought, and energy five years ago, before the genocide? What can be done now in other parts of the world where war is ongoing, where genocide is a possibility? How can we live with ourselves if we don't act?

What are the risks of really connecting with the people in Rwanda, of building relationships? And relationships have already begun to form. People were grateful for our presence, for what we had to offer, and even simply for our awareness and concern. The potential rewards of the work are evident. These relationships will become part of me and will provide meaning and connection, and thus part of the antidote to my VT. The process of struggling to find meaning, to make sense of what happened and to find meaning the work, is another crucial part of transforming my VT.

REFERENCES

Figley, C. R. (Ed.). (1995). *Compassion fatigue: Coping with secondary traumatic stress disorder in those who treat the traumatized.* New York: Brunner/Mazel.

Follette, V. M., Polusny, M. M., & Milbeck, K. (1994). Mental health and law enforcement professionals: Trauma history, psychological symptoms, and the impact of providing services to child sexual abuse survivors. *Professional Psychology, 25*(3), 275–282.

McCann, I. L., & Pearlman, L. A. (1990). Vicarious traumatization: A framework for understanding the psychological effects of working with victims. *Journal of Traumatic Stress, 3*(1), 131–149.

Pearlman, L. A., & Mac Ian, P. S. (1995). Vicarious traumatization: An empirical study of the effects of trauma work on trauma therapists. *Professional Psychology: Research and Practice, 26*(6), 558–565.

Pearlman, L. A., & Saakvitne, K. W. (1995a). *Trauma and the therapist: Countertransference and vicarious traumatization in psychotherapy with incest survivors.* New York: W. W. Norton.

Rosenbloom, D. J., Pratt, A. C., & Pearlman, L. A. (1995). Helpers' responses to trauma work: Understanding and intervening in an organization. In B. H. Stamm (Ed.), *Secondary traumatic stress: Self-care issues for clinicians, researchers, and educators.* Lutherville, MD: Sidran Press.

Saakvitne, K. W., Gamble, S. G., Pearlman, L. A., & Tabor Lev, B. (in press). *Risking connection: A training curriculum for working with survivors of childhood abuse.* Lutherville, MD: Sidran Press.

Saakvitne, K. W., Pearlman, L. A., & the Staff of the Traumatic Stress Institute. (1996). *Transforming the pain: A workbook on vicarious traumatization.* New York: W. W. Norton.

Schauben, L. J., & Frazier, P. A. (1995). Vicarious trauma: The effects on female counselors of working with sexual violence survivors. *Psychology of Women Quarterly, 19*(1), 49–64.

Stamm, B. H. (Ed.). (1995). *Secondary traumatic stress: Self-care issues for clinicians, researchers, and educators.* Lutherville, MD: Sidran Press.

PART ONE

SETTING THE STAGE

Compassion Fatigue: Toward a New Understanding of the Costs of Caring

Charles R. Figley

Charles R. Figley was the 1994 recipient of the Lifetime Achievement Award from the International Society for Traumatic Stress Studies. Figley's impact on the field can be seen in his community involvement and in his nearly 20 years of writing. During those years, by his actions and words, he has called our attention to both the direct and indirect victims of trauma. His most recent book, Compassion Fatigue: Coping with Secondary PTSD Among Those Who Treat the Traumatized, *is a landmark contribution to the STS literature. In this chapter, Figley outlines the logic of his thinking and helps the reader understand the context from which STS can arise.*

The work of helping traumatized people is gratifying. Helpers discover early in their careers that traumatized people are relieved by a caring professional who understands and respects their pain, engenders hope in recovering from it, goes about the task with confidence, and quickly succeeds. Being a helper, however, also brings risks: Caring people sometime experience pain as a direct result of their exposure to other's traumatic material. Unintentionally and inadvertantly, this secondary exposure to trauma may cause helpers to inflict additional pain on the originally traumatized. This situation—call it Compassion Fatigue, Compassion Stress, or Secondary Traumatic Stress—is the natural, predictable, treatable, and preventable unwanted consequence of working with suffering people. While this is an old problem, the terms are new, and this paper discusses the emergence of information that forms the basis of our understanding of Compassion Fatigue and Compassion Stress.

This chapter and book recognize that something specific *must be done* to counteract the challenges of Compassion Stress and Fatigue. Furthermore, we now know, finally, that something *can be done* to help caring professionals. Among other things, we can help professionals to recognize their shortcomings—their special vulnerability to Compassion Stress and Fatigue—and help them cope more effectively with the cost of caring. There is no doubt that traumatic events will continue to occur and affect hundreds of thousands of people each year. These traumatized people require the services of professionals who are well prepared to help and, in turn, to help themselves. Therefore, we need to keep these caring professionals at work and satisfied.

CONCEPTUAL CLARITY

The field of traumatology (i.e., the study and treatment of traumatized people) has made great progress in the last decade (Figley, 1995). However, the field itself has a very, very long history with many factors creating the field. One contribution has been the much greater awareness of the number of various traumatic events and their extraordinary impact on so many people. Another has been the development of scholarly synthesis and the politics of mental health professions (cf. Scott, 1993). According to many professionals, traumatology reached a milestone in 1980 with the publication of the American Psychiatric Association's *Diagnostic and Statistical Manual of Mental Disor-*

ders *(Third Edition,) (DSM-III)* (American Psychiatric Association [APA], 1980). The DSM-III includes the diagnosis of Post Traumatic Stress Disorder (PTSD), which views common symptoms experienced by a wide variety of traumatized persons as a psychiatric disorder; one that can be accurately diagnosed and treated. PTSD, therefore, represents the latest in a series of terms that describes the harmful biopsychosocial effects of emotionally traumatic events. Though a subsequent revision of the DSM-III modified the symptom criteria somewhat (APA, 1987), the popularity of the concept with professionals working with traumatized people (including lawyers, therapists, emergency professionals, and researchers) grew, as did the accumulation of empirical research that validated the disorder. Thus the PTSD diagnosis has been applied widely in mental health research and practice to people traumatized by one of many types of traumatic events and has influenced case law and mental health compensation.

This PTSD concept brought order to the research in traumatology (Figley, 1988a, 1992a, 1992b) and the body of literature has grown significantly since 1980. For example, in a review of trauma-related articles cited in *Psychological Abstracts*, Blake, Albano, and Keane (1992) identified 1,596 citations between 1970 and 1990. Most of these papers, however, lack conceptual clarity. They rarely consider the contextual and circumstantial factors in the traumatizing experience, nor do they adopt the current PTSD nomenclature. Rather, nearly all of the hundreds of reports focusing on traumatized people *exclude* those who were traumatized *indirectly or secondarily* and focus on those who were directly traumatized (i.e., the "victims"). Yet, descriptions of what constitutes a traumatic event (i.e., Category A [criterion] in the DSM-III and DSM-III-R descriptions of PTSD) clearly indicate that mere knowledge of another's traumatic experiences can be traumatizing.

People are traumatized either directly or indirectly. According to the DSM-IV diagnosis of PTSD (APA, 1994), the essential feature of Post Traumatic Stress Disorder is the development of characteristic symptoms following exposure to an extreme traumatic stressor involving direct personal experience of an event that involves threatened death, actual or threatened serious injury, or other threat to one's physical integrity; or witnessing an event that involves death, injury, or a threat to the physical integrity of another person; or *learning about unexpected or violent death, serious harm, or threat of death or injury experienced by a family member or other close associates* (criterion A1, p. 425) [italics added for emphasis].

Therefore, people can be traumatized without actually being physically harmed or threatened with harm. Simply *learning about* the traumatic event(s) carries traumatic potential. The DSM-IV (APA, 1994) also notes that "events experienced by others that are learned about include, but are not limited to, violent personal assault, serious accident, or serious injury experienced by a family member or close friend; learning about the sudden, unexpected death of a family member or close friend; or learning that one's child has a life threatening disease" (p. 424).

This has led to a conceptual conundrum in the field, although few have identified it. I have noted (Figley, 1976, 1982, 1983a, 1983b), for example, that the number of "victims" of violent crime, accidents, and other traumatic events are grossly underestimated because they count only those directly in harm's way and exclude family and friends of the victims. In one presentation (1982) and subsequent publications (1983a, 1983b), I also stated there is a phenomenon I called "secondary catastrophic stress reactions," meaning that the empathic induction of a family member's experiences results in considerable emotional upset. For example, fathers, especially in more primitive societies, appear to exhibit symptoms of pregnancy out of sympathy for those of their wives (i.e., *couvade* phenomenon) (cf. Hunter & Macapline, 1963); some spouses appear to share the psychiatric illnesses of their spouses (*folie a deux*) (Andur & Ginsberg, 1942; Gralnick, 1939). There are parallels with other phenomenon reported in the medical and social science literature. These include copathy (Langlin, 1970), identification (Brill, 1920; Freud, 1949), sympathy (Veith, 1965) and hyperarousal. Apparently, something connected to an emotional arousal associates with an empathic and sympathetic reaction, similar to the ways "mass hysteria" or psychogenic illness appears to sweep though groups of people, including children (cf., Colligan & Murphy, 1979).

Caring for traumatized people presents other risks as well. The process of dispensing care can exhaust the care-giver. I believe (Figley, 1995)

> we become emotionally drained by [caring so much]; we are adversely affected by our efforts. Indeed, simply being a member of a family and caring deeply about its members makes us emotionally vulnerable to the catastrophes which impact them. We too become 'victims,' because of our emotional connection with the victimized family member (p. 12).

In another treatise, I suggested (Figley, 1985) that families and other interpersonal networks (e.g., friends, work groups, clubs, and the client-therapist relationship) are powerful systems for promoting recovery following traumatic experiences. Yet at the same time, these same systems and their members are "traumatized by concern."

IDENTIFICATION OF TRAUMA

There are several kinds of trauma that can occur. (a) *Simultaneous trauma* takes place when all members of the system are directly affected at the same time, such as a natural disaster. (b) *Vicarious trauma* happens when a single member is affected out of contact from the other members (e.g., war, coal mine accidents, hostage situations, distant disasters). (c) *Intrafamilial trauma* or abuse takes place when a member causes emotional injury to another member. (d) *chasmal* or *secondary trauma* strikes when the traumatic stress appears to "infect" the entire system after first appearing in only one member. This latter phenomenon most closely parallels what we are now calling Secondary Traumatic Stress (STS) and Secondary Traumatic Stress Disorder (STSD).

Richard Kishur, a former masters student of mine, re-analyzed a large data set of a study of New York City crime victims and their supporters (family members, neighbors, friends). Borrowing from the transmission of genetic material or "crossing-over" that takes place between like pairs of chromosomes during meiotic cell division, Kishur (1984) coined the term *"Chasmal Effect."* To him, this term best accounted for why there was such a strong correlation between the quality of symptoms of crime victims and the supporters of these victims:

> it is clear that a pattern of effects emerge(s) in both victim and supporter. The crime victims, as well as their supporters, suffer from the crime episodes long after the initial crisis has passed. Symptoms of depression, social isolation, disruptions of daily routine, and suspicion or feelings of persecution affect the lives of these persons (Kishur, 1984, p. 65).

Yet, even in the absence of precise, conceptual tools, the literature is replete with implicit and explicit descriptions of this phenomenon. Some of the most cogent examples are reports by traumatized people who complain that family and friends discourage them from talking about their traumatic experiences after a few weeks because it is so distressing to the *supporters* (Figley, 1983b, 1989; Stanton & Figley, 1978).

To my dismay, I have seen many colleagues and friends abandon clinical work or research with traumatized people because of their inability to deal with the pain of others: "the same kind of psychosocial mechanisms within families that make trauma 'contagious,' that create a contact for family members to infect one another with their traumatic material, operate between traumatized clients and the therapist" (Figley, 1989, p. 144). I also believe that those most vulnerable to this contagion are those who "begin to *view themselves as saviors, or at least as rescuers*" (Figley, 1989, pp. 144-145).

In summary, there has been widespread, though sporadic, attention in the medical, social science, family therapy, and psychological literature to the phenomenon we refer to as compassion stress/fatigue or secondary traumatic stress/disorder. At the same time, in spite of the clear identification of this phenomenon as a form of traumatization in all three versions of the DSM, nearly all attention has been directed to people in harm's way, but not to those who care for and worry about them. They, too, become traumatized as a result of their caring.

WHY ARE THERE SO FEW REPORTS OF SECONDARY TRAUMA?

Although the focus of traumatology is nearly timeless, the field is quite young. Beaton and Murphy (1995) note that perhaps the field is in a "pre-paradigm state," as defined by Kuhn (1970). Kuhn, in his classic treatise on theory development, reasoned that paradigms follow the evolution of knowledge, which, in turn, influence the development of new knowledge. Prevailing paradigms are viewed, suddenly, as anomalies when new information and paradigm shifts occur. This certainly applies to the prevailing, limiting view of PTSD and the need to recognize that the process of attending to the traumatic experiences and expression may be traumatic itself. Thus, knowledge about experiencing, re-experiencing, and reacting to traumatic material evolved in fits and starts. After more than a decade of application of the concept and two revisions of the DSM, however, it is time to consider the least studied and understood aspect of traumatic stress: Secondary Traumatic Stress.

WHY STSD?

A wide variety of sources confirms (e.g., Ochberg, 1988; Wilson & Raphael, 1993) that the most important and frequent remedies for people suffering from traumatic and post-traumatic stress are personal, rather than clinical or medical. This includes the naturally occurring social support of family, friends, and acquaintances, and professionals who care (cf. Flannery, 1992; Figley, 1988; Solomon, 1989).

Yet, little is written about the "cost of caring" (Figley, 1982, 1989). It is important to know how these supporters become upset or traumatized as a result of their exposure to victims. By understanding this process we cannot only prevent additional subsequent traumatic stress among supporters, we can also increase the quality of care for victims by helping their supporters.

Scholars and clinicians require a conceptualization that accurately describes the indices of traumatic stress for *both* those in harm's way and for those who care for them and become impaired in the process. Alternative theoretical explanations for the *transmission of trauma* that *results* in this impairment are discussed in the latter part of this paper.

DEFINITION OF SECONDARY TRAUMATIC STRESS AND STRESS DISORDER

Here we define secondary traumatic stress as the natural, consequent behaviors and emotions resulting from *knowledge about* a traumatizing event experience by a significant other. It is the stress resulting from *helping or wanting to help* a traumatized or suffering person.

There is a fundamental difference between the sequela or pattern of response, during and following a traumatic event, for people exposed to primary stressors and those exposed to secondary stressors. Moreover, not only are family and friends of people exposed to primary stressors (i.e., "victims") vulnerable to *secondary* traumatic stress and stress disorders, so are mental health professionals and other helpers.

Therefore, STSD is a syndrome of symptoms nearly identical to PTSD except that exposure to a traumatizing event experienced by one person becomes a traumatizing event for the second person. Thus, the STSD symptoms are directly connected to the person experiencing primary traumatic stress (illustrated in Table 1). Table 1 depicts and contrasts the symptoms of PTSD with the symptoms of STSD. At the same time, we suggest that perhaps PTSD should stand for *Primary* Traumatic Stress Disorder, rather than *Post* Traumatic Stress Disorder, since every stress reaction is "post" by definition.

CONTRASTS BETWEEN STS AND OTHER CONCEPTS

Secondary traumatic stress phenomenon has been called different names over the years. Indeed, we will suggest that Compassion Stress and Compassion Fatigue are appropriate substitutes! Most often these names are associated with the "costs of caring" (Figley, 1982) for others in emotional pain.

Among the few dozen references in this general area, this phenomenon is called secondary victimization (Figley, 1982, 1983a, 1985a, 1989), co-victimization (Hartsough & Myers, 1985), and secondary survivor (Remer & Elliott, 1988a, 1988b). McCann and Pearlman (1990) suggest that "vicarious traumatization" is an accumulation of memories of clients' traumatic material that affects and is affected by the therapist's perspective of the world.

Miller, Stiff, and Ellis (1988) coined the term "emotional contagion," to describe an affective process in which "an indi-

TABLE 1. Comparison of the sympsoms of PTSD with the Symptoms of STSD.

PRIMARY	SECONDARY
A. Stressor	**A. Stressor**
1. Experienced, witnessed, or been confronted with an event or events that involve actual or threatened death or serious injury, or a threat to the physical integrity of oneself or others	1. Experienced, witnessed, or been confronted with an event or events that involve actual or threatened death or serious injury, or a threat to the physical integrity of oneself or others;
2. the person's response involved "intense fear, helplessness or horror"; an event such as a. serious threat to self b. sudden destruction of one's environment	2. the person's response involved "intense fear, helplessness or horror"; an event such as a. serious threat to traumatized person TP b. sudden destruction of TP's environment
B. Reexperiencing Trauma Event	**B. Reexperiencing Trauma Event**
1. Recollections of event	1. Recollections of event/TP
2. Dreams of the event	2. Dreams of the event/TP
3. Sudden reexperiencing of event	3. Sudden reexperiencing of event/ TP
4. Distress over reminders of event	4. Reminders of TP/ event distressing
C. Avoidance/Numbing of Reminders	**C. Avoidance/Numbing of Reminders**
1. Efforts to avoid thought/feelings	1. Efforts to avoid thought/feelings
2. Efforts to avoid activities/ situations	2. Efforts to avoid activities/situations
3. Physiologic amnesia	3. Physiologic amnesia
4. Diminished interest in significant activities	4. Diminished interest in significant activities
5. Detachment, estrangement from others	5. Detachment, estrangement from others
6. Diminished affect	6. Diminished affect
7. Sense of foreshortened future	7. Sense of foreshortened future
D. Persistent Arousal	**D. Persistent Arousal**
1. Difficulty falling/staying asleep	1. Difficulty falling/staying asleep
2. Irritability or outbursts of anger	2. Irritability or outbursts of anger
3. Difficulty concentrating	3. Difficulty concentrating
4. Hypervigilance for self	4. Hypervigilance for TP
5. Exaggerated startle response	5. Exaggerated startle response
6. Physiologic reactivity to cues	6. Physiologic reactivity to cues

(Symptoms under one month duration are considered normal, acute, crisis-related reactions. Those not manifesting symptoms until six months or more following the event are delayed PTSD or STSD.)

vidual observing another person experiences emotional responses parallel to that person's actual or anticipated emotions"
(p. 254). Other terms that appear to overlap with STS or STSD
include partners of rape survivors and war veterans (Verbosky &
Ryan, 1988); generational effects of trauma (Danieli, 1985; Mc-
Cubbin, Dahl, Lester & Ross, 1977); the need for family "detoxification" from war-related traumatic stress (Rosenheck &
Thompson, 1986); and the "savior syndrome" (NiCarthy, Merriam & Coffman, 1984). Perhaps the most important concepts
that parallel compassion fatigue, however, are "burnout" and
"countertransference."

COUNTERTRANSFERENCE AND SECONDARY STRESS

Countertransference is connected with psychodynamic therapy
and often appears to be an emotional reaction to a client by a
therapist. Though there are many definitions, countertransference in the context of psychotherapy is the distortion of judgment on the part of the therapist due to the therapist's life experiences and is associated with her or his unconscious, neurotic
reaction to the client's transference (Freud, 1959). More recently,
Corey (1991) defined countertransference as the process of seeing oneself in the client, of over-identifying with the client, or
of meeting needs through the client.

In the recent book, *Beyond Transference: When the Therapist's
Real Life Intrudes* (Gold & Nemiah, 1993), contributors recount
how personal events in the lives of therapists impact the quality
and characteristics of therapies. Yet, the most compelling part of
the book focused on how *clients themselves*, not the therapist's reaction, are so stressful and difficult to handle. Countertransference was once viewed simply as the therapist's conscious and
unconscious response to the patient's transference, especially if it
connected with the past experiences of the therapist. Johansen
(1993) suggests that a more contemporary view of counter-

transference is that it includes all of the emotional reactions of the therapists toward the patient—irrespective of the source. This includes, for example, the life stressors—past or present— experienced by the therapist. But it also includes the therapist's absorption of the traumata expressed by the client. This, unfortunately, is rarely discussed in the literature and is, of course, the major focus of this book and others (e.g., Figley, 1995).

A recent study (Hayes, Gelso, VanWagoner & Diemer, 1991) found that five qualities of therapists appear to help therapists, in varying degrees, to manage countertransference effectively. There are anxiety management, conceptualizing skills, empathic ability, self-insight, and self-integration. The study surveyed 33 expert therapists regarding the importance of five factors, subdivided into 50 personal characteristics, which composed their five-item, Likert-response-type Countertransference Factors Inventory (CFI). Although all five are important, expert therapists rated *self-integration* and *self-insight* as the most important factors in managing countertransference.

In a follow-up study, VanWagoner, Gelson, Hayes, and Diemere, (1991) surveyed 93 experienced counseling professionals using the CFI to rate the factors for either (a) therapists in general or (b) an excellent therapist in particular. The following picture of an excellent therapist, in contrast to therapists generally, was viewed by the sample as: (a) having more insight into and explanations for their feelings; (b) having greater capacity for empathy for, and understanding of, the client's emotional experience; (c) being more able to differentiate between the needs of self and client; (d) being less anxious with clients; and (e) being more adept at conceptualizing "client dynamics" in both the client's current and past contexts (p. 418).

One could argue, then, that secondary traumatic stress includes but is not limited to what these researchers and other professionals view as countertransference. First, it is assumed that countertransference happens only within the context of psychotherapy. Second, countertransference is a reaction by the therapist to the transference actions on the part of the client. Third, countertransference is a negative consequence of therapy and should be prevented or eliminated. However, Secondary Traumatic Stress or STSD is a natural consequence of caring between two people: one has been traumatized initially and the other is affected by the first's traumatic experiences. These effects are not necessarily a problem, but more a natural by-product of caring for traumatized people. This notion of a natural by-product will be discussed later.

BURNOUT AND SECONDARY STRESS

Some view the problems faced by workers with job stress as simply burnout. According to Pines and Arnson (1988, 1989) burnout is "a state of physical, emotional, and mental exhaustion caused by long term involvement in emotionally demanding situations." A 1993 literature search of the *Psychological Abstracts* listed over 1,100 articles and over 100 books since the term was coined by Freudenberger (1975) and carefully explicated by Maslach (1976). The most widely used measure of burnout is the Maslach Burnout Inventory (MBI) developed by Maslach and Jackson (1981). It measures three aspects: emotional exhaustion (e.g., "I feel emotionally drained from my work."); depersonalization (e.g., "I worry that the job is hardening me emotionally."); and reduced personal accomplishment (e.g., "I feel I'm not positively influencing other people's lives in my work."). More recently, Pines and Arnson (1988) developed the Burnout Measure (BM) which measures physical exhaustion (e.g., feeling tired or rundown), emotional exhaustion (e.g., feeling depressed, hopeless), and mental exhaustion (e.g., feeling disillusionment, resentment toward people). Emotional exhaustion appears to be the key factor in common between the two measures of burnout. Burnout has been defined as a collection of symptoms associated with *emotional exhaustion*:

(a) burnout is a process (rather than a fixed condition) that begins gradually and becomes progressively worse (Cherniss, 1980; Maslach, 1976, 1982); (b) the process includes (1) gradual exposure to job strain (Courage & William, 1986), (2) erosion of idealism (Freudenberger, 1986; Pines, Aronson & Kafry, 1981), and (3) a void of achievement (Pines & Maslach, 1980); and (c) accumulation of intensive contact with clients (Maslach & Jackson, 1981).

In a comprehensive review of the empirical research focusing on the *symptoms* of burnout, Kahill (1988) identified five categories: (a) physical symptoms (fatigue and physical depletion/exhaustion; sleep difficulties; specific somatic problems such as headaches, gastro-intestinal disturbances, colds, flu); (b) emotional symptoms (e.g., irritability, anxiety, depression, guilt, sense of helplessness); (c) behavioral symptoms (e.g., aggression, callousness, pessimism, defensiveness, cynicism, substance abuse); (d) work-related symptoms (e.g., quitting the job, poor work performance, absenteeism, tardiness, misuse of work breaks, thefts); and (e) interpersonal symptoms (e.g., perfunctory communication with, inability to concentrate/focus on, withdrawal from clients/co-workers, and then dehumanize, intellectualize clients.)

In addition to depersonalization, burnout has been associated with a reduced sense of personal accomplishment and discouragement as an employee (cf. Maslach & Jackson, 1981). From a review of the research literature, it appears that the most salient factors associated with the symptoms of burnout include client problems: chronicity, acuity, and complexity that is perceived to be beyond the capacity of the service provider (Freudenberger, 1974, 1975; Maslach, 1976, 1982; Maslach & Jackson, 1981). Moreover, Karger (1981) and Barr (1984) note that service providers are caught in a struggle between promoting the well-being of their clients while, at the same time, struggling with policies and structures in the human service delivery system that tend to stifle empowerment and well-being.

Often child protection workers, for example, are forced to handle several dozen cases simultaneously, follow policies and procedures that monitor and protect the child, while at the same time dealing with extremely hostile parents. The turnover rate among these workers is very high, with the assumption that it is due to the heavy case load, not the nature of the work and its emotional toll.

In contrast to burnout, which emerges gradually and is a result of emotional exhaustion, STS can emerge suddenly and without much warning. In addition to a faster onset of symptoms, Figley (1995) notes that STS includes a sense of helplessness and confusion; a sense of isolation from supporters; and the symptoms are often disconnected from real causes. Yet, STS has a faster rate of recovery from symptoms. The Compassion Fatigue Self-Test for Psychotherapists was designed to help therapists differentiate between burnout and STS and will be discussed later. This measure is found in Table 1 and is discussed elsewhere in some detail (Figley, 1995; Figley & Stamm, in press).

WHY COMPASSION STRESS AND COMPASSION FATIGUE?

Thus, STS and STSD are the latest and most exact descriptions of what has been observed and labeled over hundreds of years. But the most friendly term for this phenomenon, and one that I will use here, is the concept of *compassion fatigue* (Joinson, 1992). *Webster's Encyclopedic Unabridged Dictionary of the English Language* (New York: Gramercy, 1989) defines compassion as a "feeling of deep sympathy and sorrow for another who is stricken by suffering or misfortune, accompanied by a strong desire to alleviate their pain or remove its cause" (p. 299). Its antonyms include mercilessness and indifference. From my very informal research, the terms Compassion Stress and Compassion Fatigue are favored by nurses (Joinson first used the term in print in 1992 in discussing burnout among nurses), emergency

Compassion Satisfaction/Fatigue Self-Test for Helpers

Helping others puts you in direct contact with other people's lives. As you probably have experienced, your compassion for those you help has both positive and negative aspects. This self-test helps you estimate your compassion status: How much at risk you are of burnout and compassion fatigue and also the degree of satisfaction with your helping others. Consider each of the following characteristics about you and your **current** situation. Write in the number that honestly reflects how frequently you experienced these characteristics in the last week. Then follow the scoring directions at the end of the self-test.

0 = Never	1 = Rarely	2 = A Few Times	3 = Somewhat Often	4 = Often	5 = Very Often

Items About You

__ 1. I am happy.

__ 2. I find my life satisfying.

__ 3. I have beliefs that sustain me.

__ 4. I feel estranged from others.

__ 5. I find that I learn new things from those I care for.

__ 6. I force myself to avoid certain thoughts or feelings that remind me of a frightening experience.

__ 7. I find myself avoiding certain activities or situations because they remind me of a frightening experience.

__ 8. I have gaps in my memory about frightening events.

__ 9. I feel connected to others.

__ 10. I feel calm.

__ 11. I believe that I have a good balance between my work and my free time.

__ 12. I have difficulty falling or staying asleep.

__ 13. I have outburst of anger or irritability with little provocation.

__ 14. I am the person I always wanted to be.

__ 15. I startle easily.

__ 16. While working with a victim, I thought about violence against the perpetrator.

__ 17. I am a sensitive person.

__ 18. I have flashbacks connected to those I help.

__ 19. I have good peer support when I need to work through a highly stressful experience.

__ 20. I have had first-hand experience with traumatic events in my adult life.

__ 21. I have had first-hand experience with traumatic events in my childhood.

__ 22. I think that I need to "work through" a traumatic experience in my life.

__ 23. I think that I need more close friends.

__ 24. I think that there is no one to talk with about highly stressful experiences.

__ 25. I have concluded that I work too hard for my own good.

__ 26. Working with those I help brings me a great deal of satisfaction.

__ 27. I feel invigorated after working with those I help.

__ 28. I am frightened of things a person I helped has said or done to me.

__ 29. I experience troubling dreams similar to those I help.

__ 30. I have happy thoughts about those I help and how I could help them.

__ 31. I have experienced intrusive thoughts of times with especially difficult people I helped.

__ 32. I have suddenly and involuntarily recalled a frightening experience while working with a person I helped.

__ 33. I am pre-occupied with more than one person I help.

__ 34. I am losing sleep over a person I help's traumatic experiences.

__ 35. I have joyful feelings about how I can help the victims I work with.

__ 36. I think that I might have been "infected" by the traumatic stress of those I help.

__ 37. I think that I might be positively "inoculated" by the traumatic stress of those I help.

__ 38. I remind myself to be less concerned about the well being of those I help.

__ 39. I have felt trapped by my work as a helper.

__ 40. I have a sense of hopelessness associated with working with those I help.

___ 41. I have felt "on edge" about various things and I attribute this to working with certain people I help.
___ 42. I wish that I could avoid working with some people I help.
___ 43. Some people I help are particularly enjoyable to work with.
___ 44. I have been in danger working with people I help.
___ 45. I feel that some people I help dislike me personally.

Items About Being a Helper and Your Helping Environment
___ 46. I like my work as a helper.
___ 47. I feel like I have the tools and resources that I need to do my work as a helper.
___ 48. I have felt weak, tired, run down as a result of my work as helper.
___ 49. I have felt depressed as a result of my work as a helper.
___ 50. I have thoughts that I am a "success" as a helper.
___ 51. I am unsuccessful at separating helping from personal life.
___ 52. I enjoy my co-workers.
___ 53. I depend on my co-workers to help me when I need it.
___ 54. My co-workers can depend on me for help when they need it.
___ 55. I trust my co-workers.
___ 56. I feel little compassion toward most of my co-workers.
___ 57. I am pleased with how I am able to keep up with technology.
___ 58. I feel I am working more for the money/prestige than for personal fulfillment.
___ 59. Although I have to do paperwork that I don't like, I still have time to work with those I help.
___ 60. I find it difficult separating my personal life from my helper life.
___ 61. I am pleased with how I am able to keep up with helping techniques and protocols.
___ 62. I have a sense of worthlessness/disillusionment/resentment associated with my role as a helper.
___ 63. I have thoughts that I am a "failure" as a helper.
___ 64. I have thoughts that I am not succeeding at achieving my life goals.
___ 65. I have to deal with bureaucratic, unimportant tasks in my work as a helper.
___ 66. I plan to be a helper for a long time.
This form may be freely copied as long as (a) authors (B.H. Stamm & C.R. Figley) are credited, (b) no changes are made, and (c) it is not sold.

Scoring Instructions
Please note that research is ongoing on this scale and the following scores should be used as a guide, not confirmatory information.
1. Be certain you respond to all items.
2. Mark the items for scoring:
   a. Put an x by the following 26 items: 1–3, 5, 9–11, 14, 19, 26–27, 30, 35, 37, 43, 46–47, 50, 52–55, 57, 59, 61, 66.
   b. Check the following 16 items: 17, 23–25, 41, 42, 45, 48, 49, 51, 56, 58, 60, 62–65.
   c. Circle the following 23 items: 4, 6–8, 12, 13, 15, 16, 18, 20–22, 28, 29, 31–34, 36, 38–40, and 44.
3. Add the numbers you wrote next to the items for each set of items and note:
   a. *Your potential for Compassion Satisfaction (x):* 118 and above = extremely high potential; 100–117 = high potential; 82–99 = good potential; 64–81 = modest potential; below 63 = low potential.
   b. *Your risk for Burnout (check):* 36 or less = extremely low risk; 37–50 = moderate risk; 51–75 = high risk; 76–85 = extremely high risk.
   c. *Your risk for Compassion Fatigue (circle):* 26 or less = extremely low risk, 27–30 = low risk; 31–35 = moderate risk; 36–40 = high risk; 41 or more = extremely high risk.

workers, and other professionals who experience STS and STSD in the line of duty. Thus the terms can be used interchangeably by those who feel uncomfortable with STS and STSD. The discomfort, for some, might be their concern that such labels are derogatory. The stress and even the fatigue of compassion, in the line of duty as nurses or therapists, better describes the causes and manifestations of their duty-related experiences.

Elsewhere I (Figley, 1995) present two models to account for how and why some people develop Compassion Fatigue, while others do not. At the heart of the theory are the concepts of empathy and exposure. If we are not empathic with, or if we are not exposed to, the traumatized, there should be little concern for Compassion Fatigue. Throughout, authors discuss the special vulnerabilities of professionals—especially therapists—who work with traumatized people on a regular basis. These trauma workers are more susceptible to Compassion Fatigue. This special vulnerability is due in part to a number of reasons associated with the fact that trauma workers are always knee-deep in the extreme intensity of trauma-inducing facts. And as a result, no matter how hard they try to resist it, trauma workers are drawn to this intensity. Beyond this natural by-product of therapeutic engagement, there appears to be four additional reasons why trauma workers are especially vulnerable to compassion fatigue:

1. *Empathy Is a Major Resource for Trauma Workers to Help the Traumatized.* Empathy is important in assessing the problem and formulating a treatment approach because the perspectives of the clients—including the victim's family members must be considered. Yet as noted earlier, research on secondary traumatic stress and secondary traumatic stress disorders suggests that empathy is a key factor in the *induction* of traumatic material from the primary to the secondary "victim." Thus, the process of empathizing with a traumatized person helps us understand that person's experience of being traumatized, but in the process we may be traumatized as well.

2. *Many Trauma Workers Have Experienced Some Type of Traumatic Event in Their Lives.* Since trauma specialists focus on the context of a wide variety of traumatic events, it is inevitable that they would work with the traumatized who experienced events that were similar to those experienced by the trauma worker. There is a danger of over-generalizing the trauma worker's experiences and methods of coping to the victim and over-promoting these methods. For example, a crime-related traumatization may be very different from experiences of the trauma worker, yet the counselor may assume that they are sufficiently similar and not listen as carefully. Also, the counselor may suggest what worked well for him or her, but which would be ineffective—or at worst—inappropriate for the victim.

3. *Unresolved Trauma of the Worker Will Be Activated by Reports of Similar Trauma in Clients.* It is also possible that trauma workers who are survivors from previous traumatic events may harbor unresolved traumatic conflicts. Their issues may be provoked as a result of the traumatic experiences for a client. Cerney (1995), Yassen (1995), and others confirm the power of past traumatic experiences on current functioning.

4. *Children's Traumata Are Also Provocative for Caregivers.* Police, fire fighters, EMTs, and other emergency workers report that they are most vulnerable to compassion fatigue when dealing with the pain of children (see Beaton & Murphy, 1995). Moreover, trauma workers are more likely than other practitioners to be exposed to childhood trauma because children so often are either the focus of trauma counseling or the important players.

Implications for Training and Educating the Next Generation of Professionals

The previously referenced book (Figley, 1995) more fully explicates the role of trauma in the lives of professionals. That book reviews in detail the scholarly and practical literature to identify what we know and have known about Compassion Fatigue (i.e., STSD). Each of the contributors suggests their own theories, concepts, and methods of assessment and treatment. Few discuss the implications for trauma worker education, however.

As an educator, as well as a researcher and practitioner, I am concerned about the next generation of trauma workers. Though we need to know much, much more about Compassion Fatigue—who gets it when and under what circumstances; how it can be treated and prevented—we know a great deal already. We know enough to realize that Compassion Fatigue is an occupational hazard of caring service providers—be they family, friends, or family counselors.

Recognizing this we, as practicing professionals, have a special obligation to our students and trainees to prepare them for these hazards. A place to start is incorporating stress, burnout, and Compassion Fatigue into our curriculum and especially into our supervision in practica.

We can use the relatively protected environment of our educational centers and the clients that seek help there as opportunities for discussing these issues. Some fundamental principles for *preventing* Compassion Fatigue might be useful as noted above. In addition, training programs could (a) institute policies that require *processing all clinical material that appears to be upsetting* to either the individual worker or other team members (including a supervisor); (b) recognize that upsetting clinical material *is and should be discussed* confidentially with confidants (spouse/partner)—by following proscribed ethical procedures—but also recognize that the confidant, could, in turn, become upset, and (c) experiment with various methods for avoiding Compassion Fatigue without sacrificing clinical effectiveness.

We must do all that we can to insure that trauma workers are prepared. As noted elsewhere (Figley, 1995), we have a "duty to inform" them about the hazards of this work. At the same time, however, we need to emphasize that this work is most rewarding: one can see the immediate transformation from sadness, depression, and desperation of people suffering the shock of highly stressful events to hope, joy, and a renewed sense of purpose and meaning of life. This transformation is equally possible for professionals who recognize that they are suffering from Compassion Fatigue. We hope that this chapter and others here and elsewhere (e.g., Figley, 1995) will help facilitate this transformation in those both in harm's way and the professionals they seek for help.

REFERENCES

American Psychiatric Association. (1980). *Diagnostic and statistical manual of mental disorders* (3rd ed.). Washington, D.C.: American Psychiatric Association.

American Psychiatric Association. (1987). *Diagnostic and statistical manual of mental disorders* (3rd ed., rev.). Washington, D.C.: American Psychiatric Association.

American Psychiatric Association. (1994). *Diagnostic and statistical manual of mental disorders* (4th ed. draft). Washington, D.C.: American Psychiatric Association.

Andur, M. & Ginsberg, T. (1942). Folie a deux. *Medical bulletin of the veterans administration*, *14*, 230–263.

Barr, D. (1984). Burnout as a political issue. *Catalyst*, *4* (4), 68–75.

Beaton, R. & Murphy, S. A. 1995. Working-people in crisis: Research implications. In C. R. Figley (Ed.), *Compassion fatigue: Coping with secondary PTSD among those who treat the traumatized*. New York: Brunner Mazel.

Blake, D. D., Albano, A. M. & Keane, T. M. (1992). Twenty years of trauma: Psychological abstracts 1970 through 1989. *Journal of traumatic stress*, *5* (3), 477–484.

Brill, A. (1920). The empathy index and personality. *Medical record*, *97*, 131–134.

Cherniss, C. (1980). *Staff burnout: Job stress in the human services*. Beverly Hills, CA: Sage.

Colligan, M. J. & Murphy, L. R. (1979). Mass psychogenic illness in organizations: An overview. *Journal of occupational psychology*, *52*, 77–90.

Corey, G. F. (1991). *Theory and practice of counseling psychotherapy*. Belmont, CA: Brooks Cole.

Courage, M. M. & Williams, D. M. (1986). An approach to the study of burnout in professional care providers in human service organizations. *Journal of social service research, 10* (1), 7–22.

Danieli, Y. (1985). The treatment and prevention of long term effects and intergenerational transmission of victimization: A lesson from Holocaust survivors and their children. In C. Figley (Ed.), *Trauma and its wake: Study and treatment of PTSD*. New York: Brunner/Mazel.

English, O. S. (1976). The emotional stress of psychotherapeutic practice. *Journal of the American academy of psychoanalysis, 4,* 191–201.

Figley, C. R. (1975). Interpersonal adjustment and family life among Vietnam veterans: A general bibliography. *Congressional record*, February 19.

Figley, C. R. (1978). Psychosocial adjustment among Vietnam veterans: An overview of the research. In C. R. Figley (Ed.), *Stress disorders among Vietnam veterans: Theory, research, and treatment*. New York: Brunner/Mazel.

Figley, C. R. (1982). Traumatization and comfort: Close relationships may be hazardous to your health. Keynote address for Families and Close Relationships: Individuals in Social Interaction, Conference at Texas Tech University, Lubbock, TX.

Figley, C. R. (1983a). Catastrophe: An overview of family reactions. In C. R. Figley & H. I. McCubbin (Eds.), *Stress and the Family: Coping with Catastrophe* (v. 2). New York: Brunner/Mazel.

Figley, C. R. (1983b). The family as victim: Mental health implications. In P. Berner (Ed.), *Proceedings of the VIIth world congress of psychiatry*. London: Plenum.

Figley, C. R. (1985a). The role of the family: Both haven and headache. In M. Lystad (ed.), *Role stressors and supports for emergency workers* (DHH publication # 85–1408 [Adm], 84–94). Washington, D.C.: U.S. Government Printing Office.

Figley, C. R. (1985b). From victim to survivor: Social responsibility in the wake of catastrophe. In C. R. Figley (Ed.), *Trauma and its wake: The study and treatment of PTSD*. Brunner/Mazel: New York.

Figley, C. R. (1986). Traumatic stress: The role of the family and social support system. In C. R. Figley (Ed.), *Trauma and its wake: The study and treatment of post-traumatic stress disorder* (v. 2). New York: Brunner/Mazel.

Figley, C. R. (1988a). Toward a field of traumatic stress. *Journal of traumatic stress, 1* (1), 3–16.

Figley, C. R. (1988b). A five-phase treatment of PTSD in families. *Journal of traumatic stress, 1* (1), 127–139.

Figley, C. R. (1988c). Victimization, trauma, and traumatic stress. *Counseling psychologist, 16* (4), 635–641.

Figley, C. R. (1989). *Helping traumatized families*. San Francisco: Jossey-Bass.

Figley, C. R. (1992a). Posttraumatic stress disorder, part I: Empirically based conceptualization and symptom profile. *Violence update, 2* (7), 1; 8–11.

Figley, C. R. (1992b). Posttraumatic stress disorder, part IV: Generic treatment and prevention approaches. *Violence update, 3* (3).

Figley, C. R. (1993). Compassion stress and the family therapist. *Family therapy news,* (February), 1–8.

Figley, C. R. (1994). Coping with stressors on psychoanalytic psychotherapy. In J. Strachey (Ed. and Trans.), *The standard edition of the complete works of Sigmund Freud* (v.2). 139–151. London: Hogarth.

Figley, C. R. (Ed.) (1995). *Compassion fatigue: Coping with secondary traumatic stress disorder in those who treat the traumatized.* Brunner/Mazel: New York.

Figley, C. R. & Stamm, B. H. (in press). Review of the Compassion Fatigue Self-Test. In B. H. Stamm (Ed.), *Measurement of trauma, stress, and adaptation*. Lutherville, MD: Sidran Press.

Freudenberger, H. J. (1974). Staff burnout. *Journal of social issues, 30* (1), 159–165.

Freudenberger, H. J. (1975). Staff burnout syndrome in alternative institutions. *Psychotherapy, 12* (1), 73–82.

Freudenberger, H. J. (1986). The issues of staff burnout in therapeutic communities. *Journal of psychoactive drugs, 18* (2), 247–251.

Gold, J. H. & Nemiah, J. C. (Eds.). (1993). *Beyond transference: When the therapist's real life intrudes*. Washington, D.C.: American Psychiatric Press.

Gralnick, A. (1939). Folie a deux: The psychosis of association. *Psychiatric quarterly, 15,* 277–279.

Hartsough, D. & Myers, D. (1985). *Disaster work and mental health: Prevention and control of stress among workers*. Washington, D.C.: National Institute of Mental Health, Center for Mental Health Studies of Emergencies.

Hayes, J. A., Gelso, C. J., Van Wagoner, S. L., & Diemer, R. A. (1991). Managing countertransference: What the experts think. *Psychological reports, 69*, 138–148.

Hunter, R. & Macalpine, I. (1963). *Three hundred years of psychiatry, 1535–1860.* London: Oxford University Press.

Johansen, K. H. (1993). Countertransference and divorce of the therapist. In J. H. Gold. & J. C. Nemiah (Eds.), *Beyond transference: When the therapist's real life intrudes.* Washington, D.C.: American Psychiatric Press.

Joinson, C. (1992). Coping with compassion fatigue. *Nursing, 22* (4), 116–122.

Kahill, S. (1988). Interventions for burnout in the helping professions: A review of the empirical evidence. *Canadian journal of counseling review. 22* (3), 310–342.

Karger, H. (1981). Burnout as alienation. *Social service review, 55* (2), 268–283.

Kishur, R. (1984). Chiasmal effects of traumatic stressors: The emotional costs of support. Master's thesis, West Lafayette, Indiana: Purdue University.

Kuhn, T. (1970). *The structure of scientific revolutions* (2nd ed.). Chicago: University of Chicago Press.

Laughlin, H. P. (1970). *The ego and its defenses.* New York: Appleton-Century-Crofts.

Maslach, C. (1976). Burn-out. *Human behavior, 5* (9), 16–22.

Maslach, C. (1982). *Burnout: The cost of caring.* Englewood Cliffs, NJ: Prentice Hall.

Maslach, C. & Jackson, S. E. (1981). The measurement of experienced burnout. *Journal of occupational behavior, 2* (2), 99–113.

Maslach, C. & Jackson, S. E. (1984). Patterns of burnout among a national sample of public contact workers. *Journal of health and human resources administration, 7* (2), 189–212.

McCann, L. & Pearlman, L. A. (1990). Vicarious traumatization: A framework for understanding the psychological effects of working with victims. *Journal of traumatic stress, 3* (1), 131–149.

McCubbin, H. I., Dahl, B. B., Lester, G. R., & Ross, B. (1977). *The POW and his children: Evidence for the origin of second generational effects of captivity.*

Miller, K. I., Stiff, J. B., & Ellis, B. H. (1988). Communication and empathy as precursors to burnout among human service workers. *Communication monographs*, *55* (9).

NiCarthy, G., Merriam, K., & Coffman, S. (1984). *Talking it out: A guide to groups for abused women*. Seattle: Seal Press.

Ochberg, F. M. (1988). *Post-traumatic therapy and victims of violence*. New York: Brunner/Mazel.

Pines, A. M. (1993). Burnout. In L. Goldberger & S. Breznitz (Eds.), *Handbook of stress: Theoretical and clinical aspects* (2nd ed.). New York: Free Press.

Pines, A. M. & Aronson, E. (1981). *Burnout*. Schiller Park, IL: M.T.I. Teleprograms.

Pines, A. M. & Aronson, E. (1988). *Career burnout: Causes and cures*. New York: Free Press.

Pines, A., Aronson, E., & Kafry, D. (1981). *Burnout: From tedium to personal growth*. New York: Free Press.

Pines, A. & Maslach, C. (1980). Combating staff burnout in child care centers: A case study. *Child care quarterly*, *9*, 5–16.

Remer, R. & Elliot, J. (1988a). Characteristics of secondary victims of sexual assault. *International journal of family psychiatry*, *9* (4), 373–387.

Remer, R. & Elliot, J. (1988b). Management of secondary victims of sexual assault. *International journal of family psychiatry*, *9* (4), 389–401.

Rosenheck, R. & Thompson, J. (1986). "Detoxification" of Vietnam war trauma: A combined family-individual approach. *Family process*, *25*, 559–570.

Scott, W. J. (1993). *The politics of readjustment: Vietnam veterans since the war*. New York: Aldine De Gruyter.

Solomon, Z. (1989). A three year prospective study of PTSD in Israeli combat veterans. *Journal of traumatic stress*, *2* (1), 59–73.

Stanton, M. D. & Figley, C. R. (1978). Treating the Vietnam veteran within the family system. In C. R. Figley (Ed.), *Stress disorders among Vietnam veterans: Theory, research, and treatment*. New York: Brunner/Mazel.

Van Wagoner, S. L., Gelso, C. J., Hayes, J. A., & Diemer, R. A. (1991). Countertransference and the reputedly excellent therapist. *Psychotherapy: Theory, research and practice*, *28*, 411–421.

Veith, I. (1965). *Hysteria: The history of a disease*. Chicago: University of Chicago Press.

Verbosky, S. J. & Ryan, D. A. (1988). Female partners of Vietnam veterans: Stress by proximity. *Issues in mental health nursing, 9,* 95–104.

Webster's Encyclopedic Unabridged Dictionary of the English Language. (1989). New York: Gramercy.

Wilson, J. P. and Raphael, B. (1993). *International handbook of traumatic stress syndromes.* New York: Plenum.

2

Secondary Exposure to Trauma and Self Reported Distress Among Therapists

Kelly R. Chrestman

This chapter is one of two brief reports of research on therapists who treat traumatic stress clients. Kelly Chrestman discusses the implications of her research in which she found that therapists who had higher caseloads of trauma clients reported more trauma-related symptoms and less interactions with family and friends. This is a sobering finding that challenges those of us who work with trauma. However, Chrestman also found that experience and quality of life variables were mediators for increased symptom reporting. Moreover, the increased symptoms were not necessarily representative of phobic avoidance but representative of increased awareness of true danger. If this is the case, it seems particularly important for us to identify the potential dangers to clinicians and ways of positively mediating unwanted affects.

Vicarious traumatization (McCann & Pearlman, 1990), contact victimization (Courtois, 1988), or secondary post traumatic stress reaction (Dutton & Rubenstein, 1995; Figley, 1995) are terms which have been used to describe disruptive and painful psychological effects which may develop in mental health professionals who work with survivors of traumatic events. These effects have been distinguished from more general concepts, such as countertransference and burnout, in that the secondary post-traumatic stress reaction is a response to characteristics of disclosed traumatic events which the therapist has not experienced directly (Danieli, 1985). Secondary traumatization in therapists has been hypothesized to include symptoms which have been observed in trauma survivors themselves including intrusive imagery related to the client's traumatic disclosures (Courtois, 1988; Danieli, 1988; Herman, 1992; McCann & Pearlman, 1990), avoidant responses (Blank, 1985; Courtois, 1988; Dutton, 1992; Haley, 1974), physiological arousal (McCann & Pearlman, 1990; Dutton & Rubenstein, 1995; Figley, 1995), other somatic complaints (Herman 1992a, 1992b), distressing emotions (Blank, 1985; Courtois, 1988; Herman, 1992a, 1992b; Margolin in Herman 1992b; Scurfield, 1985), addictive or compulsive behaviors (Crews, Polusny, Milstein, Arkowitz & Follette, 1992; Dutton & Rubenstein, 1995; Figley, 1995; Herman, 1992b; McCann & Pearlman, 1990), and functional impairment (Dutton & Rubenstein, 1995; Figley, 1995; Herman, 1992b; McCann & Pearlman, 1990). Overall distress is hypothesized to be mediated by risk and resiliency factors which include the therapist's personal characteristics, characteristics of the client and the trauma, the therapist's attempts to cope, and the environment in which the therapy takes place (Dutton & Rubenstein, 1995; Figley, 1995).

To test this model a survey methodology was employed and questionnaires were mailed to therapists belonging to the International Society for Traumatic Stress Studies (ISTSS), the International Society for the Study of Multiple Personality and Dissociation (ISSMP&D), and the American Association of Marital and Family Therapists (AAMFT). Response packets consisted of a variety of questionnaires designed or selected to assess personal and professional history, psychological symptoms, cognitive schemata, coping behaviors, and behavior changes. In short, it was predicted that therapists reporting secondary exposure to trauma would endorse more distress/symptoms on measures of trauma specific responses, and more negatively valenced cognitions on measures of cognitive schemata than therapists who do not report secondary exposure. It was also expected that relevant personal and contextual variables would mediate the relationship between secondary exposure and negative outcome.

EMPIRICAL EVIDENCE

Results supported these expectations for the most part. First, a predictable relationship between secondary exposure and psychological distress change was demonstrated. Specifically, secondary exposure to trauma was associated with increased symptoms of intrusion and avoidance on the Impact of Event Scale (Horowitz, Wilner & Alvarez, 1979) and increased symptoms of dissociation and sleep disturbance on the Trauma Symptom Checklist (Elliot & Briere, 1991). While scores did not reflect symptomatology in the clinical range, they indicated a level of distress which was significantly different from therapists who did not experience secondary exposure.

Second, several variables appeared to have a mediational relationship between secondary exposure and therapist distress. Specifically, increased professional experience was associated with decreased avoidance, dissociation, anxiety, and sexual abuse trauma symptoms; increased income was associated with decreases in all symptom measures; utilization of additional training, as assessed by number of CEUs obtained, was associated with decreased avoidance; increased percentages of trauma clients in the caseload was associated with increased levels of dissociation, anxiety, sexual abuse trauma symptoms, and intrusion; higher percentages of time spent in general clinical activities relative to other activities was associated with increased avoidance; and higher percentages of time spent in research activities was associated with decreased avoidance.

Third, there were no significant differences in cognitive schemata when assessed directly through the World Assumptions Scale (Janoff-Bulman, 1989). However, therapist behaviors related to safety schemata endorsed on a modified form of the Behavior Change Checklist (Mac Ian & Pearlman, 1992) changed relative to the amount of time spent with trauma clients. In this sample, as the percent of clients in the caseload increased, therapists decreased their children's activities away from home, decreased so-called "risky" behavior, felt less comfortable when seeing clients in the office alone, increased checking of doors, and increased listening for noises. These behaviors are clearly related to safety of self and significant others and can be construed as representative of the impact of secondary exposure on safety-related cognitions of therapists.

Other behaviors which varied with the percent of trauma clients in the caseload included talking to family or friends about work and attending professional activities. Those with higher ratios of trauma clients talked less to family and friends about work and attended more professional conferences and activities. These behaviors may represent an attempt to protect significant others from exposure to secondary trauma by restricting disclosure and by seeking other forums for discussion of trauma therapy. They also reflect a therapist's sense of isolation or alienation related to the extreme nature of his or her work. Seeking out other trauma therapists through conferences and professional activities may represent an attempt to identify with similar others and to regain a sense of community.

In summary, therapists experiencing secondary exposure were more likely to report slight increases in trauma-related symptomatology and to report increased efforts to protect themselves and their families from harm. As professional experience, income, and post-graduate training increased, symptom reports decreased. Other risk factors associated with increased symptoms were higher ratios of clinical versus non-clinical activities and higher percentages of trauma clients in the caseload. Thus, the increase in symptomatology appears to be related to both the percentage of time spent in clinical activities generally and time spent with trauma clients specifically.

IMPLICATIONS

It should be noted that mean symptom scores do not fall in the clinical range. Further, changes in safety behaviors may represent increased awareness of true danger rather than phobic avoidance as the behavior changes are not associated with extreme measures of avoidance on the symptom measures.

This is not to say that most trauma therapists are immune to secondary trauma. Many therapists reported episodes of extreme distress from which they recovered, but which were overwhelming to them for a short period of time. For these therapists, more extreme distress after secondary exposure to trauma appeared to be an acute, rather than chronic phenomena from which they were able to recover with accessing unusual means of coping.

In addition, though mean symptom scores were within normal limits, there were also some therapists in this sample who experienced extreme and enduring distress related to secondary exposure to trauma. This was reflected in higher levels of symptomatology on trauma symptom measures and by narrative responses to open-ended queries included in the questionnaire. Several described extreme distress and debilitating anxiety reactions which necessitated treatment and in some cases resulted in career changes. While such extreme and long-lasting responses were few, they represent an extreme form of secondary stress response.

In seeking to minimize the impact of secondary exposure on therapists, this study supports suggestions for therapist self-care offered by this text and others (McCann & Pearlman, 1990; Dutton & Rubenstein, 1995; Figley 1995). Increased supervision and support for beginning trauma therapists seems particularly important. In this sample, less experienced therapists suffered the greatest distress. This is not surprising when they experience repetitious trauma, albeit secondary, during a critical period in their professional development. This, combined with data from many sources which suggest therapists report a higher percentage of childhood and other types of trauma than the general population, supports the notion that trauma, or the secondary experience of trauma, has the potential to alter the development of therapists in significant ways.

These data also suggest that certain periodic participation in training activities may perform an important mediating function for trauma therapists. While acquisition of skills and knowledge is the obvious benefit of participation, increased social/professional support and identification of a referral network may help to decrease feelings of isolation and overwhelming responsibility. These activities do not necessarily require a trauma focus. In this sample, the number of non-trauma specific CEU credits was associated with decreased anxiety symptoms.

Participating in a variety of activities rather than engaging in full-time clinical work with trauma survivors appears advisable. This can be accomplished by varying the caseload to include non-trauma cases. It may also involve including non-clinical activities in the professional repertoire. For example, participation in research activities may act as a mediator by necessitating a decrease in clinical contact and by possibly providing a means of thinking about clinical issues from a less interpersonal frame of reference.

Finally, it is important that other sources of life stress be minimized. In this study, income was a salient factor, but it is likely that other, more general sources of stress not assessed in this study may affect the resources of the trauma therapist. These include, but are not limited to, physical health of self and significant others, general job satisfaction, and satisfaction with family and interpersonal relationships. While these suggestions are based on data collected from therapists who work with trauma survivors, they do not represent a departure from what would be considered adequate self-care for any therapist, or indeed, any person.

A limitation of this study is the extent to which existing measures, designed to investigate symptomatology among survivors of trauma, are sensitive enough to detect differences among mental health professionals with secondary exposure. The differences that were detected do not reflect levels of symptomatology in the clinical range overall, although some subjects did received scores comparable to clinical samples. This suggests that differences, if they do exist, will be less extreme and will require more sensitive measurement techniques if they are to be detected. It is also possible that more extreme distress after secondary exposure to trauma may be an acute, rather than chronic, phenomena in therapists. The current approach may have failed to detect extreme distress because questions were too general, and because specific reactions and responses to specific incidents of secondary exposure were not queried. It will be important in future investigations to collect information about the temporal relationship between secondary exposure and therapists' distress.

R E F E R E N C E S

Blank, A. S. (1985). Irrational reactions to post-traumatic stress disorder and Vietnam veterans. In S. M. Sonnenberg, A. S. Blank, & J. A. Talbot (Eds.), *The trauma of war: Stress and recovery in Vietnam veterans*. Washington, D.C.: American Psychiatric Press.

Courtois, C. A. (1988). *Healing the incest wound: Adult survivors in therapy*. New York: W. W. Norton.

Crews, J. A., Polusny, M. M., Milstein, K., Arkowitz, L., & Follette, V. M. (1992). Professionals providing services to sexual abuse survivors: Stress and coping responses. Paper presented at the 26th Annual Meeting of the Association for the Advancement of Behavior Therapy, Boston, MA.

Danieli, Y. (1985). The treatment and prevention of long term effects and intergenerational transmission of victimization: A lesson from

Holocaust survivors and their children. In C. R. Figley (Ed.), *Trauma and its wake: The study and treatment of posttraumatic stress disorder*. New York: Brunner/Mazel.

Danieli, Y. (1988). Confronting the unimaginable: Psychotherapists' reactions to victims of the Nazi Holocaust. In J. P. Wilson, Z. Harel, & B. Kahana (Eds.), *Human adaptation to extreme stress: From the Holocaust to Vietnam*. New York: Plenum.

Dutton, M. A. & Rubenstein, F. L. (1995). Trauma workers. In C. R. Figley (Ed.), *Trauma and its wake: Secondary traumatic stress disorder* (v. 3). New York: Brunner/Mazel.

Elliott, D. M. & Briere, J. (1991). Studying the long-term effects of sexual abuse: The Trauma Symptom Checklist (TSC) scales. In A. W. Burgess (Ed.), *Rape and sexual assault: A research handbook* (v. 3). New York: Garland Publishing.

Figley, C. R. (Ed.). (1995). *Compassion fatigue: Coping with secondary stress disorder in those who treat the traumatized*. New York: Brunner/Mazel.

Haley, S. A. (1974). When the patient reports atrocities: Specific treatment considerations of the Vietnam veteran. *Archives of general psychiatry, 30* (2), 191–196.

Herman, J. L. (1992a). Complex PTSD: A syndrome in survivors of prolonged and repeated trauma. *Journal of traumatic stress, 5,* 377–391.

Herman, J. L. (1992b). *Trauma and recovery*. New York: Basic Books.

Horowitz, M. J., Wilner, N., & Alvarez, W. (1979). Impact of event scale: A measure of subjective stress. *Psychosomatic medicine, 41,* 209–218.

Janoff-Bulman, R. (1989). Assumptive worlds and the stress of traumatic events: Applications of the schema construct. *Social cognition, 7,* 113–136.

McCann, I. L. & Pearlman, L. A. (1990). Vicarious traumatization: A framework for understanding the psychological effects of working with victims. *Journal of traumatic stress, 3,* 131–149.

Mac Ian, P. & Pearlman, L. A. (1992). The behavior change checklist. Unpublished research instrument, Traumatic Stress Institute, South Windsor, CT.

Scurfield, R. M. (1985). Post-trauma stress assessment and treatment: Overview and formulations. In C. R. Figley (Ed.), *Trauma and its wake: The study and treatment of posttraumatic stress disorder*. New York: Brunner/Mazel.

3

The Risks of Treating Sexual Trauma: Stress and Secondary Trauma in Psychotherapists

Nancy Kassam-Adams

This chapter addresses the potential risks to a therapist when treating sexually traumatized clients. Like so many of the emerging empirical studies of STS, it provides evidence to encourage us to continue to study the issues and shows us how much we have to learn. A message from the 100 graduate level psychotherapists who were surveyed was that doing this work does have an effect. Interestingly, there was evidence that STS was not like general occupational stress. In fact, the trio of gender, personal trauma history, and exposure to sexually traumatized clients was predictive of reported intrusion and avoidance symptoms. As Nancy Kassam-Adams points out, this raises issues for future studies about self-selection into trauma work, the therapists' perceived vulnerability, and the therapists' experiences of working with their clients.

The concept of secondary traumatization in psychotherapists who treat traumatized clients has been receiving increased attention within the field of traumatic stress. The experiences of clinicians have provided much anecdotal evidence of this phenomenon, and several authors have put forward conceptualizations of the dynamics of indirect traumatization in psychotherapists, such as "compassion fatigue" (Figley, 1993) or "vicarious traumatization" (McCann & Pearlman, 1990). Descriptive reports of the reactions of psychotherapists to diverse populations of traumatized people (Wilson & Lindy, 1994) and to specific populations such as Holocaust survivors (Danieli, 1988), Viet Nam combat veterans (Blank, 1985; Haley, 1974), and survivors of torture (Bustos, 1990) emphasize the potency of the experience for the helper, and the probability that "trauma is contagious" (Herman, 1992, p. 140).

When a therapy client has experienced violence, and particularly when the client's traumatic experience and post-traumatic responses are the focus of therapy, then the therapist must come face-to-face with the reality of trauma and the existence of terrible and traumatic events in the world. Acknowledgement of this reality interferes with the therapist's adaptive assumptions of personal invulnerability, and of the world as meaningful and comprehensible (Janoff-Bulman, 1985), that allow the maintenance of a sense of safety and stability in daily living. Undoubtedly, many therapists find that working with survivors of trauma is meaningful and rewarding, and that they are truly privileged to witness clients' strength and resilience in the healing process. But the challenges of frequent exposure to human trauma are great. Steele (1991), in a moving essay about treating survivors of severe abuse, stated that "all the therapists I know who do this work have been blindsided at least once by the horror of it. Their own vulnerability, their helplessness in the face of such abuse is staggering" (p. 12).

Empirical evidence concerning secondary traumatization in therapists has lagged behind clinical and theoretical discussions of the phenomenon. This volume, like the ISTSS conference from which it arose, is especially timely and necessary since empirical studies which specifically address the effects on therapists of working with trauma survivors have only recently begun to be reported (Munroe, 1990; Pearlman & Mac Ian, 1993). This paper is intended as a brief report of a study which examined the relationship between therapists' level of exposure to sexually traumatized clients and the therapists' own report of PTSD symptoms or more general work stress symptoms.

The study was designed to sample the experiences of psychotherapists with a range of exposure to sexual trauma issues in their clinical work, in order to explore the relationship between level of exposure to these issues and the therapists' reported levels of stress or secondary trauma symptoms. In addition, therapists were asked about their exposure to other difficult client issues, in an attempt to test the potential alternative hypothesis that therapists could be adversely affected by many types of painful or difficult clinical work (i.e., that these effects are not specific to trauma clients).

Participants in the study were 100 masters' or doctoral level psychotherapists in outpatient agencies in central Virginia and central Maryland who completed and returned self-report questionnaires (273 questionnaires were distributed; response rate = 37%). Three-fourths of the participants were female and most were white. Participants ranged in age from 23 to 65, and in length of clinical experience from 1 to 32 years, with an average of 8.7 years of experience. All participants held at least a Masters' degree; 16% had a Ph.D. or other doctoral degree. Table 1 summarizes the work settings and professional disciplines represented in this sample of therapists.

In order to examine the potential contribution of situational or environmental factors to therapist stress, therapists were asked about their workload, their use of clinical supervision hours, and were asked to rate the emotional and technical support available to them at work. In addition, participants were asked whether they had ever personally experienced any of six types of trauma in childhood or in adulthood. Table 2 presents the percentages of therapist participants reporting each type of trauma.

In this study, exposure to sexual trauma issues in therapy was defined as the reported percentage of the therapists' caseload

TABLE 1. Characteristics of therapists in study.

Work setting	Percentage of therapists
Community mental health center	52
Sexual assault treatment center	16
University or college counseling center	15
Community counseling agency	10
Other out-patient setting	7

Professional discipline	Percentage of therapists
Social work	37
Counseling	25
Clinical psychology	16
Counseling psychology	10
Nursing	3
Other disciplines	9

(over the past year and over the course of their career as a therapist) that had presented these issues. Participants were asked to estimate the percentage of their caseload that had presented with any of six different categories of clinical problems or diagnoses in therapy. In order of the average amount of exposure reported (from most to least), these categories were: depression and other mood disorders, sexual assault or abuse issues, personality disorders, substance abuse, schizophrenia and other psychotic disorders, and post-trauma reactions (other than sexual assault/abuse trauma). Participants varied greatly in their reported exposure to sexually abused or assaulted clients, with both recent and career exposure ranging from 0% to 100% of their caseload (mean for the past year = 46.5% of the therapist's caseload with a standard deviation of 33.3; mean for career exposure = 41.9% of the therapist's caseload with a standard deviation of 28.4).

TABLE 2. Percentage of therapists reporting trauma history.

Type of trauma	Childhood	Adulthood
Physical abuse/maltreatment	10	5
Emotional abuse	30	22
Sexual abuse or assault	19	4
Death of an immediate family member	20	48
Home destroyed by fire or other natural disaster	0	4
Another traumatic experience	21	18
ANY TRAUMA	60	66

MAJOR FINDINGS

Two outcome measures were included in the study—a measure of general work-related stress and psychological distress (the Personal Strain Questionnaire [PSQ], Osipow & Spokane, 1981) and a measure of trauma symptoms commonly found in posttraumatic stress disorder (the Impact of Event Scale [IES], Horowitz, Wilner, & Alvarez, 1979). Looking first at the aggregate results for this sample of psychotherapists on the PSQ the group reported levels of symptoms similar to those of the PSQ's norm group of 900 workers in various professions. On the IES, however, nearly half of the participants scored in the "high" range—a level that in traumatized persons would suggest the need for clinical attention. In other words, therapists were reporting intrusive and avoidant symptoms related to their work with clients—such as "I had waves of strong feelings about it," "Pictures about it popped into my head," or "I tried not to think about it." This finding supports the idea that the work of psychotherapy does indeed have an impact on the therapist.

The only factor in this study that was found to be associated with general work stress symptoms (PSQ score) was the level of support that therapists reported in their workplace—higher support ratings were associated with lower levels of stress ($r = -.24$, $p < .05$). This general measure of work stress was *not* correlated with exposure to sexual trauma issues in therapy or with exposure to any of the other client problems or diagnoses. Nor were PSQ scores predicted by any of the other situational or individual therapist characteristics included in this study (for example, years of experience or current work load).

The central finding of the study was that therapists' level of PTSD symptoms, measured by the IES, was correlated with level of exposure to sexually traumatized clients. For cumulative (career) exposure, $r = .36$, $p < .001$. PTSD symptoms were also correlated with more recent exposure, reported as the percentage of the therapist's caseload over the past year that presented sexual trauma issues ($r = .26$, $p < .01$). As the two measures (career exposure and past year exposure) were highly correlated with each other ($r = .78$), only career exposure was used for subsequent analyses. In other words, those therapists who had a higher percentage of clients with sexual trauma issues in their caseload tended to report more PTSD symptoms themselves. The alternative hypothesis, that exposure to other difficult client diagnoses and problems would also account for therapists' trauma symptoms, was not supported by the data. PTSD symptoms were not related to exposure to any of the other client problems or diagnoses included in the study.

In an attempt to measure the potential importance of cognitive appraisal as a mediating variable in producing secondary trauma, therapists also were asked to rate the "personal impact" of each of the six types of client issues. The two issues receiving the highest average ratings were sexual assault or abuse and personality disorders. (In later analyses, which are not reported in detail in this paper, appraisal of impact, as measured in this study, did not turn out to be a mediator in the relationship between exposure and therapist trauma symptoms.)

Workplace characteristics, such as therapists' workload or the availability of supervision and other forms of support in the workplace, were not found to be related to the level of PTSD symptoms reported by therapists. Among the individual characteristics of therapists that were included in the study (age, gender, years of clinical experience, and personal history of trauma), only gender and personal trauma history were related to therapists' level of PTSD symptoms. Gender and overall trauma history were correlated ($r = .40$), with more female therapists reporting trauma. Interestingly, gender and *childhood* trauma history were not strongly correlated ($r = .14$).

Regression analyses were used to examine how therapist gender, personal trauma history, and exposure to sexual trauma clients might together contribute to therapists' PTSD symptoms. When entered simultaneously in the first step of a hierarchical regression model, gender and trauma history were statistically significant predictors of PTSD symptoms in therapists (Adjusted $R^2 = .12$; $F = 7.27$, $p < .001$). When exposure to sexually traumatized clients was entered in the second step of the regression model (i.e., with the effects of gender and trauma history partialled out), exposure to trauma therapy still added significantly to the predictive value of the model (increment in $R^2 = .05$; F [change] $= 6.58$, $p < .01$). The combined effects of gender, personal trauma history, and exposure to sexually traumatized clients were significant in predicting the level of PTSD symptoms reported by therapists (Adjusted $R^2 = .17$; $F = 7.33$, $p < .001$).

Closer examination of the correlations between PTSD symptoms and the different types of personal trauma history reported by therapists (childhood v. adult incidence, abuse v. non-abuse trauma, sexual abuse/assault v. all other types of trauma) revealed that only *childhood incidence of trauma* stood out as being strongly associated with PTSD symptoms in the therapist from his or her work with clients. When childhood trauma history is substituted for overall trauma history in the hierarchical regression model presented above, the model predicts as well or better, suggesting that trauma in childhood can account for the bulk of the contribution of the therapist's trauma history to later development of PTSD symptoms from psychotherapeutic work. When gender and childhood trauma history are entered simultaneously to predict IES score, the adjusted R^2 = .14 (F = 8.53; p < .001). When exposure to sexually traumatized clients is added in the next step of a hierarchical regression model, the overall adjusted R^2 = .18 (F [increment] = 6.08; p < .01).

DISCUSSION

The concept of secondary or vicarious traumatization of therapists implies a specific effect of trauma therapy on the therapist, akin to the intrusion and avoidance phenomena of post-traumatic responses in direct trauma survivors, and distinct from "burnout" or other forms of occupational stress. The results of this study provide empirical support for the notion of vicarious traumatization. In addition to the central finding that exposure to trauma clients is related to therapist PTSD symptoms, there are two aspects of these results which are particularly consistent with the concept of vicarious traumatization: (a) the measure of general occupational stress symptoms (the PSQ) was not related to the stressor of exposure to sexually traumatized clients and (b) exposure to other difficult types of client diagnoses was not related to the intrusion and avoidance phenomena of PTSD measured by the IES. These results strengthen the argument for a model of vicarious or secondary traumatization rather than generic occupational stress or burnout in accounting for therapists' responses to trauma clients.

The results of this study suggest the need for further examination of the role of gender and the therapist's personal history of trauma (particularly childhood trauma) as factors in the development of PTSD symptoms related to the work of psychotherapy with trauma clients. Although regression analyses allow us to see that each of these factors has some independent contribution to the therapist's reporting of trauma-like symptoms, it is also clear that the factors are interrelated. In this sample of therapists, women were more likely than men to report a personal history of trauma and generally reported higher percentages of their caseloads as presenting sexual trauma issues. (Interpretation of these results is limited by the relatively small number of men in the study [25, or one-fourth of the sample].) In addition, therapists with a personal history of trauma (particularly childhood trauma or sexual trauma) generally reported higher career-long exposure to sexual trauma clients. We need a better understanding of these linkages, as it seems likely that gender and trauma history might be related to (a) self-selection into trauma work, (b) the therapist's perceived vulnerability to the type of trauma material presented by clients, and (c) the ways in which the therapist experiences his or her working relationship with trauma clients.

Although female therapists reported greater PTSD symptoms than male therapists in the current study, we should not conclude that secondary trauma is primarily a risk for women. Munroe's (1990) study of male Veterans Administration therapists found similar results in that greater exposure to combat PTSD clients was related to secondary PTSD symptoms in the therapist.

The finding that therapists' personal history of trauma was a risk factor for PTSD symptoms is consistent with the work of Pearlman and Mac Ian (1993). In their brief report on a study of trauma therapists, Pearlman and Mac Ian noted that "therapists who reported a personal trauma history evidenced more disruptions across [outcome] measures" (p. 5). In the current study, trauma which had occurred in childhood appeared to be most closely associated with secondary trauma symptoms in the therapist. It might be that childhood trauma is more likely than adult trauma to produce personality dynamics or vulnerabilities that increase an individual's susceptibility to indirect trauma.

A commonly-held hypothesis about the relationship of personal trauma history to therapists' reactions to their work is that therapists who have experienced the same type of trauma as their clients may be more vulnerable to adverse effects or countertransference reactions (Wilson & Lindy, 1994). This hypothesis was not supported by the results of the current study—while therapists' sexual assault or abuse history correlated with higher exposure to sexual trauma clients, by itself it did not relate significantly to PTSD symptoms. Similarly, in Munroe's (1990) study of Veterans Adminstration therapists, those therapists with a personal history of combat experience differed in their level of exposure to combat PTSD clients (they saw more of them), but did not differ from the rest of the sample in level of PTSD symptoms nor in their level of general psychological distress symptoms. Future studies should look more closely at the possible connections between the specific types of trauma experienced by therapists and the therapists' responses to their clients with similar trauma histories.

This study and other recent studies are building a growing base of empirical support for the idea that therapists who treat trauma survivors are themselves vulnerable to secondary or vicarious trauma symptoms. To better understand this phenomenon, the mechanisms through which trauma may be transmitted from client to therapist deserve careful attention. We have an ethical duty as well to promote quality services to our clients by evaluating the effectiveness of specific coping and self-care efforts by therapists, and the value of institutional responses and structures that may lessen or ameliorate the effects of secondary trauma in therapists. Finally, the potential positive effects of doing trauma work that are reported by therapists—personal growth, spiritual connection, hope and respect for human resiliency—should also receive attention, as they are the factors most likely to retain talented and effective therapists in this important work.

REFERENCES

Blank, A. S. (1985). Irrational reactions to post-traumatic stress disorder and Viet Nam veterans. In S. M. Sonnenberg, A. S. Blank, Jr., & J. A. Talbott (Eds.), *The trauma of war: Stress and recovery in Viet Nam veterans.* Washington. D.C.: American Psychiatric Press.

Bustos, E. (1990). Dealing with the unbearable: Reactions of therapists and therapeutic institutions to survivors of torture. In P. Suedfeld (Ed.), *Psychology and torture.* New York: Hemisphere Publishing Corporation.

Danieli, Y. (1988). Confronting the unimaginable: Psychotherapists' reactions to victims of the Nazi Holocaust. In J. P. Wilson, Z. Harel, & B. Kahana (Eds.), *Human adaptation to extreme stress.* New York: Plenum.

Figley, C. R. (1993, February). Compassion stress: Toward its measurement and management. *Family therapy news, 3,* 16.

Haley, S. A. (1974). When the patient reports atrocities. *Archives of general psychiatry, 30,* 191–196.

Herman, J. L. (1992). *Trauma and recovery.* New York: Basic Books.

Horowitz, M. J., Wilner, N., & Alvarez, W. (1979). Impact of event scale: A measure of subjective stress. *Psychosomatic medicine, 41,* 209–218.

Janoff-Bulman, R. (1985). The aftermath of victimization: Rebuilding shattered assumptions. In C. Figley (Ed.), *Trauma and its wake: The study and treatment of post-traumatic stress disorder.* New York: Brunner/Mazel.

McCann, I. L. & Pearlman, L. A. (1990). Vicarious traumatization: A framework for understanding the psychological effects of working with victims. *Journal of traumatic stress, 3,* 131–149.

Munroe, J. F. (1990). Therapist traumatization from exposure to clients with combat related post traumatic stress disorder: Implications for administration and supervision. Unpublished doctoral dissertation, Boston: Northeastern University.

Osipow, S. H. & Spokane, A. R. (1981). *Occupational stress inventory.* Odessa, FL: Psychological Assessment Resources.

Pearlman, L. A. & Mac Ian, P. S. (1993). Vicarious traumatization among trauma therapists: Empirical findings on self-care. *Traumatic stress points: News for the international society of traumatic stress studies, 7,* 5.

Steele, K. (1991). Sitting with the shattered soul. *Treating abuse today*, *1*, 12–14.

Wilson, J. P. & Lindy, J. D. (Eds.). (1994). *Countertransference in the treatment of PTSD*. New York: Guilford Press.

PART TWO

THERAPIST
SELF-CARE MODELS

4

Self-Care for Trauma Therapists: Ameliorating Vicarious Traumatization

Laurie Anne Pearlman

Laurie Anne Pearlman's contribution to STS, or vicarious traumatization, is unquestionable. Her landmark paper, written with McCann in 1990, sparked heretofore unheard of interest in the transforming nature of doing trauma work. In Pearlman's words, vicarious traumatization "is a process of change resulting from empathic engagement with trauma survivors." While Pearlman is clear about the potential risks to the helper, one of the most refreshing aspects of her work is that she also provides a framework for positive transformation. Disruption—the word chosen to describe the process of this change—was carefully chosen to avoid assigning positive or negative value. In this paper, Pearlman continues her theoretical work on vicarious traumatization—supporting it with quantitative evidence.

Those who voluntarily engage empathically with survivors to help them resolve the aftermath of psychological trauma open themselves to a deep personal transformation. This transformation includes personal growth, a deeper connection with both individuals and the human experience, and a greater awareness of all aspects of life. The darker side of the transformation includes changes in the self that parallel those experienced by survivors themselves. We conceptualize these latter changes within Constructivist Self Development Theory (McCann & Pearlman, 1990a) as vicarious traumatization (McCann & Pearlman, 1990b).

Vicarious traumatization is a process of change resulting from empathic engagement with trauma survivors. It can have an impact on the helper's sense of self, world view, spirituality, affect tolerance, interpersonal relationships, and imagery system of memory. It is neither a reflection of inadequacy on the part of the therapist nor of toxicity or badness on the part of the client. It is best conceptualized as a sort of occupational hazard, an approach suggested by others as well (Munroe, Shay, Fisher, Makary, Rapperport, & Zimering, 1995). Anyone who engages empathically with trauma survivors is vulnerable to vicarious traumatization. While this chapter specifically addresses trauma therapists, these comments may apply equally to researchers, clergy, primary care providers, emergency room workers, shelter workers, prison workers, social services workers, attorneys, journalists, rescue workers, police, fire fighters, emergency medical technicians, and all who would understand and serve those who have endured psychological trauma.

Elsewhere we have elaborated both the factors that contribute to vicarious traumatization (aspects of the work, including organizational, social, and cultural contexts, and aspects of the therapist, including personal history and professional development) and its manifestations (Pearlman & Saakvitne, 1995a). We have also addressed in some detail approaches to dealing with vicarious traumatization (Pearlman & Saakvitne, 1995a, 1995b). This chapter outlines the areas impacted by vicarious traumatization and suggests self-care strategies that apply to each area of disruption.

These recommendations are based in part in research on vicarious traumatization. In one study (Pearlman & Mac Ian, submitted for publication), 135 female and 53 male self-identified trauma therapists completed a variety of questionnaires including one that asked them how they coped with the stresses of their work and how helpful they found these strategies. In another study (Gamble, Pearlman, Lucca, & Allen, work in progress), 45 female and 70 male psychologists completed a similar task. Two other studies have contributed useful and relevant data to this inquiry: Follette, Polusny, and Milbeck (1994) reported data on 119 female and 106 male mental health professionals, and Schauben and Frazier (in press) on 148 female sexual violence counselors and psychologists. These findings inform the recommendations that follow.

These self-care recommendations for therapists working with trauma survivors are based in theory, in the suggestions made by the many therapists who have attended our vicarious traumatization workshops, and in self-report data from a broad range of mental health professionals. These strategies fall within the personal, professional, and organizational realms. Some address the prevention or minimization of vicarious traumatization, others relate to self-care for the vicariously traumatized therapist. They are organized according to the area of the self that may be disrupted by doing trauma work.

As it is for our survivor clients, the right approach to self-care and healing for the therapist is that which feels right and works for the individual. These specific strategies are intended to stimulate the reader's own thinking. Understanding and responding to one's own needs is the essence of an effective self-care strategy for client and therapist alike.

FRAME OF REFERENCE

The hallmark of vicarious traumatization is disrupted frame of reference. One's identity, world view, and spirituality together constitute frame of reference. As a result of doing trauma work, therapists are likely to experience disruptions in their sense of identity (sense of oneself as man/woman, as helper, as mother/father or one's customary feeling states), world view (moral principles, ideas about causality, life philosophy), and spirituality (meaning and hope, sense of connection with something beyond oneself, awareness of all aspects of life, and sense of the non-material).

What antidotes can we create to these disruptions? Balancing work, play, and rest helps us to remain grounded in various aspects of our complex identities. Practices that renew a cherished sense of identity or that expand one's identity beyond that of trauma therapist are helpful in this realm. This might mean socializing with friends and family to reconnect with oneself as friend, parent, child, partner, or sibling (the activity that ranked second most helpful in Gamble et al.'s [work in progress] study of psychologists; see Table 1); engaging in activities that allow one to feel particularly like a man/woman or that allow one to be in a dependent or receiving role; engaging in creative endeavors such as writing, playing music, creating art, gardening, being physically active through exercise, dance, or hard physical work; reconnecting with one's body through massage, dance, yoga. Each of these activities in its own way balances some aspect of the helper/listener/nurturer roles we play in our work as trauma therapists.

In the trauma therapist sample, at least one-third of respondents found the following strategies helpful in coping with the demands of trauma therapy: socializing, exercising, spending time with family (Pearlman & Mac Ian, submitted for publication; see Table 2). Activities that ranked somewhat lower, although still endorsed by many as helpful, were engaging in social justice activities and having a massage. Over 35% of Schauben and Frazier's (in press) subjects reported engaging in activities that promoted physical health and well-being as a coping strategy.

Rest and leisure are extremely restorative to one's frame of reference as well as to one's self capacities. Taking a vacation and pleasure reading ranked first and fourth, respectively, as activi-

TABLE 1. Professional and personal self-care for 117 psychologists.

Mean ratings of how helpful 117 psychologists found those activities in which they engaged over the past six months (1 = not helpful, 6 = extremely helpful)

Activity	Mean
Took vacation	4.60
Social activities	4.34
Emotional support from colleagues	4.21
Pleasure reading	4.10
Sought consultation on difficult cases	4.06
Read relevant professional literature	3.91
Took breaks during workday	3.88
Emotional support from friends or family	3.83
Spent time with children	3.78
Listened to music	3.70
Spent time in nature	3.67
Attended workshop or conference	3.59
Aerobic exercise	3.00
Attempted to mitor or diversify case load	2.87
Community involvement	2.14
Relaxation exercises	2.04
Gardening	1.86
Artistic expression	1.51
Spiritual practice	1.29
Personal psychotherapy	1.17
Massage or bodywork	.95
Meditation	.88
Journal writing	.56
Yoga	.52

From Gamble, Pearlman, Lucca, & Allen (work in progress).

TABLE 2.   Activities balancing trauma work for 188 trauma therapists.

Activity	% performing on regular basis	% finding it helpful
Discussed cases with colleagues	87	85
Attended workshops	84	76
Spent time with family or friends	95	70
Travel, vacation, hobbies, movies	90	70
Talked with colleagues between sessions	74	69
Socialized	88	64
Exercised	73	62
Limited case load	62	56
Developed spiritual life	53	44
Received general supervision	56	44
Taught	48	43
Gave supervision	58	36
Performed community service	53	31
Had bodywork/massage	30	39
Wrote	44	28
Wrote in a journal	27	25
Engaged in social justice work	29	22
Conducted research	35	21
Referred out clients who might activate therapist's issues	23	20
Engaged in administration	40	16

From Pearlman & Mac Ian (submitted for publication).

ties psychologists found helpful in alleviating work-related stress (Gamble et al., work in progress). Over 35% of Schauben and Frazier's subjects reported engaging in leisure activities such as gardening, reading, listening to music, and going to movies as ways of coping with work-related stress.

World view, another aspect of frame of reference, is also very sensitive to both psychological trauma and to helping trauma survivors. We can attempt to rebuild these shattered assumptions (Janoff-Bulman, 1992) by spending time with happy, healthy children; working for social justice (activities engaged in by over 40% of Follette et al.'s [1994] subjects and that were found helpful by 22% of the trauma therapist sample [Pearlman & Mac Ian, work in progress]); and building or rebuilding a sense of community. Sixty-nine percent of our sample found travel helpful; in a very literal sense, travel expands our world view.

Finally, spirituality is highly sensitive to the effects of trauma and trauma recovery work. We use a broad definition of spirituality, an inherent human capacity for an awareness of an elusive aspect of experience (Neumann & Pearlman, manuscript in preparation). Approaches to addressing the spiritual damage that this work can incur include meditation, yoga, writing in a journal, engagement with art and beauty (poetry and nature). Forty-four percent of the trauma therapist sample found developing a spiritual life helpful in coping with the demands of trauma therapy (Pearlman & Mac Ian, submitted for publication). Although these activities were not rated as very helpful for most respondents in the psychologist sample (Gamble et al., work in progress), we note them here because some people do report using them and finding them helpful. Larger percentages of Follette et al.'s (1994) mental health professionals reported using some of these coping strategies (meditation/yoga, 44%; prayer, 38%), and over 35% of Schauben and Frazier's (in press) subjects reported engaging in spiritually-oriented activities, but we do not know how helpful they found them.

Finding forums in which to recall and name the rewards of doing trauma therapy is essential. It renews our sense of the meaning of this work, revitalizes our connections with others and with humanity itself, and reminds us of the importance of an awareness of all aspects of life (Pearlman & Saakvitne, 1995a).

SELF CAPACITIES

The inner abilities that allow us to maintain a sense of positive self-esteem are sensitive to the impact of trauma and of doing trauma work. Effective self-care strategies in this realm are those that reconnect us with our internalized images of loving others (perhaps letter writing, writing in a journal, meditation or prayer), reinforce a positive sense of self (through engaging in activities that we especially enjoy), or remind us of the value of our work. Activities that increase our affect tolerance or reconnect us with our feelings are particularly helpful in this realm. These might include obtaining emotional support from others, our own personal psychotherapy, meditation, yoga, and opportunities to experience and express the full range of human affect (sometimes most helpfully done in the presence of loving others) which might include writing or other creative pursuits. Forums for acknowledging the strong feelings elicited by trauma work in a supportive environment are extremely useful to the restoration of the therapist's self capacities. At the Traumatic Stress Institute, we devote the first hour of our two-hour case conference each week to "feelings time" for exactly this purpose. We have found that laughing and crying with colleagues normalizes our responses and renews us for the week ahead.

Our ways of working and being with clients have an impact upon our own self capacities. Engaging empathically with client after client can be draining, and one response is to shut down emotionally. Schauben and Frazier (in press) found that "behavioral disengagement" correlated positively with their measure of vicarious traumatization; that is, withdrawal was directly related to the negative impact of trauma work.

We have found that allowing oneself to enter into the emotional experience of the child who is being abused is particularly enervating. One approach to remaining connected with the client while protecting oneself emotionally is to purposefully remain aware of the broader context as the client is sharing his or her experience of abuse or victimization. That might mean keeping in mind that the person sitting before you has survived; that he or she now has access to helpful, caring others; that both are part of a network of people working on recovery; and so forth.

EGO RESOURCES

Those inner abilities that allow us to meet our psychological needs and to manage interpersonal relationships can also be impacted both by trauma and by doing trauma work. Resources such as self-examination, will power, sense of humor, empathy, the ability to set limits, and intelligence can all be impacted. Self-care strategies in this realm include both giving and receiving supervision, which reminds us of the importance of boundaries and self-protective judgments. Giving and receiving supervision were helpful for both the trauma therapists (Pearlman & Mac Ian, submitted for publication) and psychologists (Gamble et al., work in progress). Eighty-three percent of Follette et al.'s (1994) subjects reported using humor to cope with their work stress.

Introspection and an awareness of our own psychological needs can be enhanced through our own personal psychotherapy as well as through journal writing. While neither of these strategies ranked highly in the psychologist sample as a helpful strategy for alleviating work stress, some people clearly found them helpful. In Schauben and Frazier's (in press) study "active coping" and "planning," instrumental approaches to problem-solving, both correlated negatively with vicarious traumatization.

Education may also shore up ego resources. In the trauma therapist sample, those with more formal education showed fewer psychological disruptions (Pearlman & Mac Ian, submitted for publication). Very high percentages of the mental health professionals in Follette et al.'s (1994) study used education of self (96%), other professionals (62%), and the public (52%) about sexual abuse issues as a means of coping with the stresses of their trauma work. The psychologists studied by Gamble et al. (work in progress) found reading professional literature and attending workshops and conferences moderately helpful.

PSYCHOLOGICAL NEEDS AND COGNITIVE SCHEMAS

Five need areas have been identified as particularly susceptible to the effects of psychological trauma (McCann & Pearlman, 1990a; McCann, Sakheim, & Abrahamson, 1988; Pearlman & Saakvitne, 1995a). Safety, trust, esteem, intimacy, and control are areas of vulnerability for trauma therapists as well as for survivors. These needs, and our beliefs within each area, shape our relationships with others, so our own vulnerabilities here have a major impact upon both our personal and professional relationships. Self-care strategies aimed at restoring our sense of connection with others help to counter the isolation that can mark vicarious traumatization. Moreover, they provide a testing ground for schemas that have been disrupted through our work. The importance of professional and personal connection is illustrated by the trauma therapist sample: over two-thirds found it helpful to attend workshops, talk with colleagues between sessions, and discuss cases informally, and in the personal realm, to socialize and spend time with family.

Group supervision can also promote connection. Trusted colleagues can help us examine our distortions. In addition, reflecting upon one's cynicism, fears, mistrust of others, need for control, lack of intimacy with others, or misanthropy can illuminate and possibly reverse the disrupted cognitive schemas that can develop through trauma work and then become overgeneralized without awareness. Perhaps most important, as we learn from and support one another in this work, we remember that we are not alone, which can help mitigate the sense of isolation that can come from working under the highly demanding constraints of confidentiality.

IMAGERY

Certainly intrusive imagery is a hallmark of post-trauma adaptation (Brett & Ostroff, 1985; van der Kolk, 1989). Through their work with survivors, therapists may also experience intrusive imagery, often images of those scenes that survivor clients have described vividly which connect in some way with the therapist's own psychology. The self-care strategy that is most helpful here is for the therapist to identify his or her own salient theme in the material (which may differ from the client's). For example, the therapist may re-experience intrusive images of the moment at which the client became aware that an abusive stepfather was entering the client's bedroom. While for the client, this memory may represent primarily a disruption in her sense of safety, to the therapist what is salient may be the sense of betrayal, which is related to trust. Once the therapist has identified this theme (in a forum such as individual supervision or therapy), it can be connected to other issues related to trust disruptions in the therpist's life. This allows the therapist to begin to work with and over time to integrate the material; it can then cease to be intrusive for the therapist.

Another type of disruption reported by many trauma therapists is the intrusion of sexual trauma imagery into their awareness during their own sexual activity. Maltz (1992) has also noted this danger. This can be deeply distressing, because it represents an intrusion of the professional into one's personal life and because the demands of confidentiality prohibit the therapist from sharing the details with a partner. Here one effective approach is to acknowledge to one's partner the distraction and the need for reconnection. Educating partners generally about these hazards can be difficult but helpful; a supportive partner who experiences the return of a distracted lover will generally accept this as a fact of their partnership, and revealing confidential material is entirely unnecessary to the reconnection. It is the therapist's feelings, not the survivor client's material, that must be processed. Sexual withdrawal is not uncommon among vicariously traumatized therapists (Pearlman & Mac Ian, submitted for publication) and only serves to increase the sense of isolation that both creates and connotes vicarious traumatization.

GENERAL STRATEGIES

We have developed some approaches to self-care that span some of the areas elucidated above. Helpful strategies include balancing one's case load (trauma survivors and non-survivors; survivors of a variety of traumatic life events; genders; ages; individual, family, couple, and groups; chronic and acute trauma survivors); balancing one's day to intersperse therapy, supervision, meetings, and breaks; and balancing clinical and non-clinical (research, teaching, supervision) work. Creating time within each day for self-care (lunch, a phone call to a loved one, yoga breathing or stretching, a walk outdoors) can bring us back to our bodies and to our senses.

Overall, we recommend that therapists do for themselves the self-nurturing, self-building things they would have their clients do. Increasing our awareness of our needs and remaining connected with our bodies, our feelings, and other people will strengthen us as individuals and allow us to choose to continue to do this important work.

REFERENCES

Brett, E. A. & Ostroff, R. (1985). Imagery and posttraumatic stress disorder: An overview. *American journal of psychiatry, 142,* 417–424.
Follette V. M., Polusny, M. M., & Milbeck, K. (1994). Mental health and law enforcement professionals: Trauma history, psychological

symptoms, and impact of providing services to child sexual abuse survivors. *Professional psychology: Research and practice, 25* (3), 275–282.

Gamble, S. J., Pearlman, L. A., Lucca, A. M., & Allen, G. J. (work in progress). *Vicarious traumatization and burnout among Connecticut psychologists: Empirical findings.*

Janoff-Bulman, R. (1992). *Shattered assumptions: Towards a new psychology of trauma.* New York: Free Press.

Maltz, W. (1992). Caution: Treating sexual abuse can be hazardous to your love life. *Treating abuse today, 2* (2), 20–24.

McCann, I. L. & Pearlman, L. A. (1990a). *Psychological trauma and the adult survivor: Theory, therapy, and transformation.* New York: Brunner/Mazel.

McCann, I. L. & Pearlman, L. A. (1990b). Vicarious traumatization: A framework for understanding the psychological effects of working with victims. *Journal of traumatic stress, 3* (1), 131–149.

McCann, I. L., Sakheim, D. K., & Abrahamson, D. J. (1988). Trauma and victimization: A model of psychological adaptation. *The counseling psychologist, 16* (4), 531–594.

Munroe, J. F., Shay, J., Fisher, L., Makary, C., Rapperport, K., & Zimering, R. 1995. Team work prevention of STSD: A therapeutic alliance. In C. R. Figley (Ed.), *Compassion fatigue: Coping with secondary traumatic stress disorder in those who treat the traumatized.* New York: Brunner/Mazel.

Neumann, D. A. & Pearlman, L. A. (work in progress.) Toward the development of a psychological language for spirituality.

Pearlman, L. A. & Mac Ian, P. S. (submitted for publication). Vicarious traumatization: An empirical study of the effects of trauma work on trauma therapists.

Pearlman, L. A. & Saakvitne, K. W. (1995a). *Trauma and the therapist: Countertransference and vicarious traumatization in psychotherapy with incest survivors.* New York: W. W. Norton.

Pearlman, L. A. & Saakvitne, K. W. (1995b). Constructivist self development theory approach to treating therapists with vicarious traumatization and secondary traumatic stress disorders. In C. R. Figley (Ed.), *Compassion fatigue: Coping with secondary PTSD among those who treat the traumatized.* New York: Brunner/Mazel.

Schauben, L. J. & Frazier, P. A. (in press). Vicarious trauma: The effects on female counselors of working with sexual violence survivors. *Psychology of women quarterly.*

van der Kolk, B. A. (1989). The compulsion to repeat the trauma: Re-enactment, revictimization, and masochism. *Psychiatric clinics of North America, 12* (2), 389–411.

5

Helpers' Responses to Trauma Work: Understanding and Intervening in an Organization

Dena J. Rosenbloom, Anne C. Pratt, &
Laurie Anne Pearlman

A visit to the Traumatic Stress Institute leaves a professional aware that something is different here. Not only have the professionals at TSI—among them Dena J. Rosenbloom, Anne C. Pratt, and Laurie Anne Pearlman—written and studied Vicarious Traumatization, they have made its prevention an institutional issue. While a great deal of the atmosphere is undoubtedly attributable to the personalities of the members of the staff, the atmosphere has elements that can be identified. This paper outlines the experiences and processes of TSI from a theoretical perspective and offers suggestions for other groups that seek to build communities to protect helpers.

Today there is greater awareness than ever before of the tremendous, devastating, and often long-lasting impact of traumatic life events on those immediately involved. This increased awareness in recent years has been immensely helpful for victims of every type of traumatic life event, ranging from abuse at the hands of familiar as well as unknown others, combat veterans and others affected by war, and victims of natural disasters, to name a few. This chapter, however, will focus on issues pertaining to therapists and other individuals directly involved with providing services to clients and patients who are addressing difficult traumatic life events. Both professionals and paraprofessionals expend tremendous energy understanding how better to work with a range of presenting issues through supervision, workshops, consultation, and courses. They often take far less time examining aspects of the work which affect them. And yet, because of the highly personal nature of trauma work, helpers' emotional well-being has a significant impact on the work they do. Helpers' own reactions to the material they hear, if unexamined or unprocessed, may lead to a range of reactions; helpers may feel unable to hear additional trauma material, thereby discouraging clients from fully exploring feelings because the helper does not feel able to tolerate more affect. Helpers may also join with the client's anger, helplessness or other feelings, thereby losing contact with their own hope and helpful "third party" distance. Our ability to guide clients in examining other aspects of themselves, their lives, or their traumatic experience(s) may also be compromised.

An initial step toward self-care for the helper is to have a framework for understanding the impact of doing trauma work. One important issue is to recognize that exposure to traumatized clients can affect the helper. Too often training programs and work settings directly or inadvertently support a position which leaves helpers feeling weak, incompetent, or emotionally unstable if impacted by work with clients. It is a more realistic and, therefore, more helpful position to recognize the inevitability of being affected by the work. From here, one can understand the specific areas of impact, given the nature of the traumatic material to which one is exposed. The way helpers are affected is influenced and guided by the individual belief systems and emotional makeup stemming from their own history.

VICARIOUS TRAUMATIZATION

This chapter will present a theory-based structure to guide our understanding of how helpers are affected by their work at a given time. The concept of "vicarious traumatization" (VT) was created and initially described by McCann and Pearlman (1990a) and grew from Constructivist Self Development Theory (CSDT) (McCann & Pearlman, 1990b). CSDT assists the helper in understanding how trauma affects the development and personality of the survivor. Eventually, it was recognized that the impact of working with trauma survivors in many ways parallels the impact of traumatic life events on the survivor. The second part of this chapter will present an organizational model for self care, drawing from the experiences of the Traumatic Stress Institute.

Vicarious traumatization is a transformation in one's inner experience resulting from empathic engagement with clients' traumatic material (Pearlman & Saakvitne, 1995a). As previously noted, the changes experienced by the helper parallel those experienced by trauma survivors. These changes can result from direct exposure of working with trauma survivors, or indirectly through exposure to graphic descriptions of violence or victimization in supervision, readings, or professional presentations.

It is important to emphasize that such responses on the part of the helper are not viewed as pathological; just as Post Traumatic Stress Disorder (PTSD) is viewed as a normal reaction to an abnormal event, vicarious traumatization is a normal reaction to the stressful and sometimes traumatizing work with victims. And just as interventions may be very healing for individuals suffering from symptoms of PTSD, helpers may also find relief from symptoms related to vicarious traumatization. This is particularly true if they are able to identify the ways in which the work impacts them personally. In addition, it is important to note that this framework does not blame clients for traumatizing helpers, but rather, identifies an inevitable occupational hazard which may be mitigated. There are several common features of VT. First, its effects are cumulative; the impact of being repeatedly exposed to traumatic material may reinforce gradually changing beliefs about oneself and the world. Second, its effects are permanent, in that they may result in lasting changes in the way we think and feel about ourselves, the world, and others. Third, the effects may be emotionally intrusive and painful, in that certain residual images and feelings may remain with the helper, even after contact with specific material or a particular client has ended. We certainly would not write this chapter if the fourth characteristic were not also true, that is, that the effects of VT are modifiable. There are things helpers can do to minimize and ameliorate the negative impact of this work.

As mentioned, VT is conceptualized within our understanding of the impact of traumatic life experiences on the survivor. Just as the same, or similar, traumatic events affect people differently, exposure to traumatic material will impact individual helpers differently. The conceptualization of VT focuses on the numerous interactions between individuals and situations, taking into account variables about both the traumatic material and about the helper's personality. In addition, it helps define the specific areas in the helper which are affected by the work. This chapter will focus on the helper and the following aspects of the parts of the self that may be affected in working with trauma survivors: (a) frame of reference, which includes (1) world view, (2) spirituality, and (3) identity; and (b) psychological needs. Further discussion of other aspects of working with trauma survivors which contribute to VT are detailed elsewhere (McCann & Pearlman, 1990b; Pearlman & Saakvitne, 1995a; Pearlman & Saakvitne, 1995b; Pearlman, this volume).

FRAME OF REFERENCE

Helpers may experience shifts in their frame of reference as part of their experience of working with trauma survivors. World view, which is part of frame of reference, includes beliefs about other people and the world, as well as beliefs about causality. Helpers may begin to see other people and the world as dangerous and threatening, malevolent and evil, untrustworthy and unreliable, exploitative and controlling, and/or disconnected and alienating. Like their clients, helpers may find their basic assumptions shattered (Janoff-Bulman, 1992). Helpers experiencing VT may find themselves more often asking, "How can people be so cruel?"; "Are people not basically good?"; and "Is the world not a just place?" Where one may have believed that "the good guy wins" or that "hard work pays," helpers may come to find that their experiences no longer support these assumptions which previously helped make sense of the world. These can be very painful shifts, as helpers may feel themselves losing their sense of hope, optimism, and connection with others.

Helpers may also find their spiritual beliefs shifting, including their sense of meaning and purpose in life. One's sense of what is meaningful may come into question, and it may become more difficult to maintain a connection with a "higher power," be it God, nature, or being a part of humanity.

Sense of identity, one's sense of who he or she is, as a man, woman, spouse, therapist, doctor, human being, and so on, may also be impacted. Hearing traumatic material and experiencing the other's pain, eventually raises the question of how much one can do in the role of helper. When disciplining a child or arguing with a spouse, one may question his or her own behaviors in ways not previously questioned, asking "Am I being abusive?" If a helper accidentally hits an animal while driving, he or she may struggle with the question, "Am I a perpetrator?" In the past this might have been a regrettable albeit upsetting accident.

The other parts of the self impacted by VT are psychological need areas: (a) safety, (b) trust, (c) esteem, (d) intimacy, and (e) control. Everyone possesses all the five needs, but specific areas are more important or central for each individual. One's most important need areas are those most likely to be disrupted. For example, a trauma therapist with strong control needs will likely question the extent to which he or she can really control his or her own behavior and rewards; a therapist with stronger safety needs will likely experience the work-related strain in terms of an increased sense of personal vulnerability. It is useful in addressing VT to identify and listen for one's salient psychological need areas through self observation in interpersonal situations. This will set the stage for increased sensitivity to the areas where disruptions are more likely to occur. For example, a person with elevated control needs may begin to perceive a lack of control in day-to-day life, accompanied by thoughts like "I could leave anytime" or "you can't tell me what to do." Feelings of being trapped or angry may accompany this sense of being controlled.

Safety

For each of the psychological needs, there are two subcategories: the need as it relates both to oneself and to one's experience of others. Looking first at the need for safety, self-safety is the need to feel safe and invulnerable to harm, while other-safety is the need to feel that important others are safe from harm. For therapists with salient safety needs, sudden physical assaults such as the rape or mugging of a client can shatter the illusion of invulnerability. This can also happen with unexpected natural disasters in which people are subjected to massive physical harm. Disruptions in this area may be manifested by increased fearfulness, a heightened sense of personal vulnerability, excessive or paralyzing concern about keeping one's car or home locked, or concern about living on the ground floor. There may also be accompanying behavioral changes, such as installing a burglar alarm in one's home or taking a self-defense class. Cognitive changes, or schema shifts, may also occur. Where a helper may previously have believed, for example, "I am safe and secure in my home," one may lose this sense of security, replacing the former belief with "I'm not safe anywhere." Across the need areas, such disruptions inherently involve loss.

Disruptions in the area of other-safety may surface in the form of increased fears for our children, spouses, pets, or other loved ones, as we hear numerous stories about intentional as well as inadvertent harm done to children and others. Some helpers have found themselves becoming especially concerned about day-care, for example, and the safety of their children, where previously this may not have been a preoccupying or intrusive concern. For any of the need areas identified, there may or may not have been a previous awareness of its importance. In retrospect, one may recognize the importance of that need area previously; what shifts is the way one previously managed that need area or the ability which was formerly felt to meet that need. Exposure to traumatic material challenges previous strategies and identity, making conscious a need area about which one was quite unaware while it was effectively managed.

Trust

Trust or dependency is another psychological need area. Helpers for whom issues of trust and dependence are central can develop shattered schemas in response to traumatic events which involve betrayal of trust relationships, such as incest. Disasters that stem from errors in judgment, such as an airplane crash, can also lead to serious disruptions in the helper's ability to trust or depend upon others. Helpers may also feel betrayed by those they are trying to help, such as in the case of a woman who returns to a battering spouse. These are examples of clinical material which may precipitate disruptions in other-trust. Accompanying behavioral and schema shifts may also occur, such as disallowing trust or dependency to develop in relationships, or developing a belief that "you can't trust anyone." Again, individuals for whom this need was salient previously are especially vulnerable to such disruptions.

Self-trust may also be disrupted. One may experience diminished capacities for being independent or trusting one's own judgment. One may no longer feel able to accurately judge another's character, and may grow resentful with a sense of resulting inhibition in relationships. Painful questions may arise: "Do I know this person as well as I think I do?" or "Can I judge whether this person is trustworthy or not?" This type of questioning can leave one feeling increasingly uncertain with oneself, particularly when these doubts isolate one by preventing speaking about and challenging his or her concerns with others.

In fact, disruptions in any of the need areas may result in actual or perceived isolation from others, further increasing vulnerability to experiencing VT. One of the most powerful and effective antidotes to VT is a connection with others, a place to talk about one's internal experience, and an opportunity to experience interactions which challenge disrupted beliefs.

Esteem

Self-esteem is the need to feel valued by others. Helpers may experience difficulty maintaining a sense of self-esteem in light of perceived inadequacies in the helper role. Questions may arise: "Am I really competent, even when I don't even feel like I'm helping?" At times one may feel overwhelmed with the seemingly endless flow of stories of suffering and feel unable to address the roots of the problem to prevent further pain.

Other-esteem may also become disrupted, as helpers take in

people's capacity for cruelty and thereby develop a more pessimistic view of others and their motives. Those for whom high regard for others is central will likely find this disrupted by continued exposure to the cruel behavior of people toward one another. This could come about from exposure to situations of intentional injury, such as assault or murder. Experiences with strangers may shift, raising questions as to who is a victim and who is a perpetrator. The helper, upon seeing a parent and child, or a couple who looks happy at a social gathering, may wonder "What is really going on?" or "Are they what they seem to be?" Excitement and energy to meet new people and expose oneself to new ideas may be replaced by a sense of cynicism, doubt, and self-protectiveness.

Intimacy

Self-intimacy is the need to feel connected to oneself in a meaningful way. With disruptions in this area, one may experience difficulty enjoying time spent alone; at those times, painful feelings may emerge and it may be difficult to find ways of feeling soothed. In the face of this, one may avoid time spent alone, to avoid leaving oneself open to more feelings. One also may find it more difficult to be alone without being lonely or feeling a sense of emptiness. There may be a pressing need to fill time with distractions such as superficial relationships, self-medicating with food, alcohol, or other substances, or engaging in compulsive behaviors such as excessive work or exercise.

Other-intimacy—the need to feel connected with and close to others—may also be disrupted. Disruption in this area may lead a helper to pull back from others as a way of protecting oneself from more pain. A focus on the painful aspects of relationships or the inevitable breaks in connection rather than the possibilities for intimacy lead to distancing from others, further reinforcing a sense of estrangement and isolation. One may also pull away from colleagues who do different work or who view your work differently. For example, responses such as, "How can you do that work?" or "I couldn't stand to hear all those stories!" can lead to feeling misunderstood by and disconnected from others. People may seem to judge the clients with whom we work, questioning the validity of memories and atrocities which occur, or suggesting that victims should leave the past behind and move on.

Disruptions in other-intimacy can leave us less available to friends and family as well. Helpers may feel protective not only from hearing judgment, but also from hearing about more trauma. They may feel less available, interested in, or sympathetic to the difficulties encountered by people in day-to-day life. On the other hand, a disruption in this area may result in a complete preoccupation with work and related feelings, leaving one always wanting to "talk shop," and resulting in a sense of disconnection from other aspects of relationships.

Control

Control, or power, is another of the psychological needs. Self-control is the need to exert control over one's thoughts, feelings, and actions. Disruption in this area may leave a helper feeling less in control of various aspects of his or her life. Trauma work raises helpers' awareness of client exposure to a multitude of events which are largely outside of the individual's control. These may include victims of natural disasters, domestic violence, or other crimes. The helper's resulting feelings of helplessness or terror may parallel the victim's experience. In this form of VT, one's beliefs about personal power and ability to assert oneself or master a situation are undermined. Such a helper may feel increasingly unable to meet the challenges of day-to-day life. In the face of feeling overwhelmed by a perceived lack of control, one may seek situations less likely to present challenges, thereby restricting the types of activities and relationships in which one engages.

Other-control—the need to direct or exert control over the behaviors of others—may also be impacted by VT. Helpers may find themselves more controlling and directive in their work and personal lives in an effort to recapture some sense of control. Another manifestation of a disruption in this area may be a narrowing or constricting of one's world in an effort to exclude situations which are outside of one's control. Ambiguity and uncertainty may be increasingly difficult to tolerate, making relationships, including those with clients, increasingly frustrating. One may also feel stronger impulses to exert control over those in his or her personal life to compensate for a perceived lack of control in the work life.

VARIABLES THAT CONTRIBUTE TO VT

Any or all of these five psychological need areas may be effected to varying degrees depending upon one's individual psychological makeup, as well as the content of the material to which one is exposed through one's clinical work. While there are many variables which can contribute to VT, there are two which we will identify in this chapter.

First, the helper's own trauma history will influence the nature of response to clients' trauma material. Experiences which helpers share with clients may deepen their understanding and sensitivity to client reactions, thereby enhancing the client's feeling of being understood and not judged. If the helper's own trauma history remains unrecognized, unprocessed, or unresolved, however, helpers may be sensitized to their own disrupted need areas, and at greater risk for missing the client's more pressing themes. In addition, helpers may be more likely to experience the client's intrusive imagery or re-experience his or her own imagery which is reawakened by the client's material (Pearlman & Mac Ian, submitted for publication). Regardless of a helper's personal history, images (including reports of sounds, smells, and tactile experiences) that clients report in a vivid or highly distressed manner can stay with us. Those most likely to stick often connect with one's own central need areas. In order to be as self-aware and available to clients as possible helpers need to be aware of their own issues and seek the necessary support, for example, through their own therapy.

A second factor which influences the helper's experience of VT is the organizational context, that is, the ways the organization within which you work supports, undermines, understands, or otherwise responds to the work you do. The next part of this chapter describes the ways one organization has developed a comprehensive strategy to minimize the harmful effects of VT.

THE TSI ORGANIZATIONAL CONTEXT

Our organization, the Traumatic Stress Institute, has in place a strategy both to prevent the ill effects of VT and respond to helpers experiencing it. Prevention of potentially harmful effects from VT involves attention to both concrete issues, such as provision of supervision and adequate time off, as well as to less tangible sources of support, such as the organization's attitude toward the impact of trauma on helpers. Both tangible and intangible aspects can be seen to address the psychological need areas which CSDT identifies as affected by direct or vicarious traumatization. Most importantly, we practice within a theoretical framework (CSDT) which provides both a way to understand our clients' experiences as well as a path for healing, offering hope for the therapist (Saakvitne, 1994).

At the Traumatic Stress Institute, we place strong emphasis on the importance of adequate training and supervision for every individual doing clinical work. It is essential for every clinician to receive supervision, regardless of licensure status. This includes individual supervision, small group supervision, biweekly case conferences, biweekly seminars, and informal consultation whenever needed. Not only is it important to ensure that supervision is available, but, less tangibly, that supervision fosters an atmosphere of respect, safety, and control for the therapist who will be exploring the difficult issues evoked by trauma therapy. Respect can allow for maintenance of self-esteem and a sense of safety while a therapist examines mistakes or painful countertransference issues. Open examination of boundaries of the supervisory relationship can allow the therapist to maintain control of the situation and regulate the level of intimacy.

Supervision can mitigate the effects of vicarious traumatization by assisting the therapist in identifying painful transference/countertransference dynamics and recognizing traumatic reenactments. Supervision which is respectful of both the self of the therapist and the therapist's need to identify and express the powerful feelings elicited by this work can help to create an environment in which we can feel safe with the strong affects we are asked to hold in our clinical work.

In addition to multiple opportunities to discuss case material and countertransference responses in supervision, we set aside an hour each week for the entire clinical staff to express and process feelings raised by exposure to traumatic material and participation in traumatic reenactments. We work together to develop an atmosphere in which it is considered inevitable to be affected by the work. It is assumed that helpers will experience strong feelings and such reactions are not treated in any way that might shame or isolate the therapist. In this process, we maintain a high level of awareness of confidentiality and respect for clients.

In addition to thinking through ways to cope with the ongoing exposure to the traumatic material of clients who are survivors of trauma, the organization has addressed crises within our group with the same careful attention to employees' psychological needs. We provide ourselves the same type of interventions we use when called elsewhere to disaster sites. A critical incident stress debriefing, including early information, a formal debriefing session, and flexibility regarding scheduling and demands on each employee, is instituted when the organization faces a crisis. As with any similar situation, early intervention decreases the likelihood of long-lasting adverse effects.

Other methods utilized to protect therapists from the effects of VT are common to almost any organization, but are specifically designed for this purpose. The organization has been structured to encourage therapists to take adequate vacations, take time off for illness, continue their education, and vary the types of cases as well as the types of work (psychotherapy, evaluation, consultation, research, writing, training) undertaken. A health insurance plan was chosen with maximum latitude for employees to choose their own psychotherapists (that is, an indemnity plan as opposed to an HMO or PPO).

Thus the Traumatic Stress Institute has purposely developed policies and, less tangibly, an atmosphere designed to mitigate the inevitable effects of vicarious traumatization. It is our hope that in doing so, we have created a model in which it is possible to practice trauma psychotherapy without sustaining damage to the self, making it possible to continue this type of work. Skilled trauma therapists are much in demand, but must not become an endangered species through neglect of self care.

REFERENCES

Janoff-Bulman, R. (1992). *Shattered assumptions: Towards a new psychology of trauma.* New York: Free Press.

McCann, I. L. & Pearlman, L. A. (1990). Vicarious traumatization: A framework for understanding the psychological effects of working with victims. *Journal of traumatic stress, 3* (1), 131–149.

McCann, I. L. & Pearlman, L. A. (1990). *Psychological trauma and the adult survivor: Theory, therapy, and transformation.* New York: Brunner/Mazel.

Pearlman, L. A. & Mac Ian, P. Vicarious traumatization in trauma therapists: Empirical findings. (submitted for publication).

Pearlman, L. A. & Saakvitne, K. W. (1995a). *Trauma and the therapist: Countertransference and vicarious traumatization in psychotherapy with incest survivors.* New York: W. W. Norton.

Pearlman, L. A. & Saakvitne, K. W. (1995b). Treating traumatized therapists. In C. R. Figley (Ed.), *Compassion fatigue: Coping with secondary stress disorder in those who treat the traumatized* New York: Brunner/Mazel.

Saakvitne, K. W. (1994). The Traumatic Stress Institute: A model for psychoanalytic psychological practice. *Psychologist psychoanalyst, 14* (2), 1994.

6

Coping with Secondary Traumatic Stress: The Importance of the Therapist's Professional Peer Group

Don R. Catherall

Based on his experiences at the Phoenix Institute, Don R. Catherall suggests ways that trauma therapists can create safe environments in which to work. Catherall draws us into relationships not only with our clients, but with our peers. He believes that it is this carefully tended peer environment that affords us the necessary objectivity to do the highly subjective work with trauma clients. Peer groups of trauma therapists set norms, provide support, help correct distortions, and generally offer opportunities to reframe the traumas. These peer-rich environments can be ripe for facilitating the ongoing work of self-care of healing secondary trauma.

Therapists who work with trauma survivors are on the front-line of exposure to secondary traumatic stress. Though therapists may be able to see large numbers of traumatized clients without being significantly affected by the clients' traumas, inevitably some clients pierce therapists' ability to remain unaffected. At those times, therapists must have access to their own sources of support and psychological sustenance, or they will: (a) be unable to provide the proper connection for their disturbing clients and (b) be negatively affected themselves. One of the primary sources of support for therapists is the professional peer group. The therapist's professional peer group has the power to dilute the impact of secondary traumatic stress, to normalize the disturbing reactions, and to help the therapist maintain the therapeutic connection with clients despite his or her personal upheaval. On the other hand, the peer group also has the power to make the situation considerably worse.

THE INADVISABILITY OF OPERATING IN A VACUUM

Contact with peers is an important element in any profession but it is particularly important for psychotherapists. Because of the highly personal and intimate nature of our contacts with clients, we have a greater proportion of subjectivity in our work than do many professions. So, it is helpful for us to have access to the more objective viewpoints of our peers. Therapists have long understood this need and have pursued peer contact in the form of supervision and consultation with colleagues. Consulting with our colleagues can aid us in determining whether our perspective has become distorted by our proximity to the client. It also provides an outlet, a forum where we can share the reactions that we may deem inappropriate for sharing with the client.

Therapists who do not have the opportunity to consult with peers run the risk of losing their sense of perspective and responding inappropriately with their clients. The extremes of inappropriate therapist responses would include unethical or unprofessional behavior, but the more common, inappropriate response generally refers to behavior that is simply not in the client's best interest. The same process may underlie both ends of the continuum of inappropriate responses, i.e., that inappropriate therapist conduct can result when therapists do not have a forum for discussing their work and their personal reactions to their clients. Tansey (1994) has noted that the taboo against discussing erotic countertransference reactions probably contributes to therapist acting out in the form of sexual abuse of clients. Similarly, therapists who do not have a forum to discuss other kinds of countertransference reactions to clients are at greater risk for acting out those reactions.

The issue becomes pertinent to the therapist's personal functioning when the reactions fall in the realm of secondary traumatization. A therapist who is experiencing secondary traumatic stress (STS) as a result of working with a traumatized client is in danger of not only acting out—perhaps by distancing from the client or chasing the client out of treatment—but he or she also is in danger of developing a traumatic stress disorder. Thus both the client and the therapist are at risk when the therapist is experiencing STS. This risk is immediately lessened if the therapist has an appropriate forum where he or she can share reactions and receive support. It is for this reason that some trauma specialists have taken the position that it is unethical for therapists to work with traumatized clients if the therapist does not have a professional support system (Munroe, 1994).

A "SUPPORTIVE" SUPPORT SYSTEM

The importance of social support as a moderator of traumatic stress was examined by Flannery (1990), who found the components of social support to include: (a) emotional support, (b) information, (c) social companionship, and (d) instrumental support. The professional peer group of a psychotherapist generally provides all of these, particularly during times of stress. The social support provided by professional peers may be available in a limited degree through casual contacts but it is best obtained in the context of a professional group with some degree of explicit formal organization, such as a consultation group, treatment team, case conference, or clinical seminar. The opportunities for support which are available in such organized groups are explicit and amenable to organizational influence, i.e., support can be readily mobilized and distributed among group members in the most efficacious manner. Additionally a synergistic quality is generated that makes support from a group more than support from a collection of individuals. However it must also be recognized that obtaining support from a group means dealing with the particular dynamics of the group.

A group whose function is to provide support to someone affected by secondary traumatic stress can be modeled on the support obtained within a family by members affected by primary traumatic stress. The utility of family support in the management of general stress has been widely demonstrated (Cobb, 1976; Dean & Lin, 1977; Hirsch, 1980; Solomon et al., 1987) and includes emotional support, encouragement, advice, companionship, and tangible aid (Burge & Figley 1982; Figley, 1983). Figley has studied families affected by traumatic stress and has identified four skills common to those families that are most effective at supporting traumatized members (Figley, 1989). These include tangible assistance in the form of (a) providing resources, as well as specific social support skills, (b) clarifying insights, (c) correcting distortions, and (d) supporting reframes. To these, I would add (e) empathic attunement (Catherall, 1995). These skills can be stated in terms of the professional peer group.

1. Professional peers can be supportive by providing resources. Resources refer to tangible aid in the form of helping with paperwork, making phone calls, and providing backup during non-work hours.

2. Professional peers can help the (secondarily) traumatized therapist clarify his or her insights by listening carefully and non-

judgmentally, by getting the facts straight, and by accepting all the feelings which the traumatized therapist is experiencing.

3. Professional peers provide support by listening to the therapist who has been traumatized by STS and correcting distortions in the therapist's assessment of his or her behavior and responsibility in regard to the disturbing cases. This is particularly relevant when the therapist feels guilty. Informed listeners can help him or her assign blame and credit more objectively. Since other therapists have an intimate understanding of a therapist's role in dealing with traumatized clients, they can offer an invaluable perspective on the realities of the therapist's responsibilities and limitations.

4. The perspective that other therapists can offer the therapist traumatized by STS will often constitute a reframing of the trauma. They can offer and support more generous or accurate perspectives on the impairing stress reactions. This can lead the traumatized therapist to develop a different cognitive appraisal of his or her role in dealing with the original trauma survivor.

5. Professional peers provide support by being empathically attuned to the therapist traumatized by STS. They do this by recognizing and responding to the emotional experience of the therapist, and by maintaining the empathic link even when the affected therapist is experiencing strongly dysphoric emotions (Rowe & Isaac, 1989). A state of empathic attunement underlies the listening skills and creates the opportunity to offer a different perspective.

GROUP NORMS THAT FACILITATE HEALING

Groups vary along the same dimensions as families in regard to their ability to facilitate a healing experience for traumatized members. Figley (1989) has identified the importance of a number of variables in providing a healing environment for family members who have been affected by traumatic stress. All of those variables apply to the "family" environment of the therapist's professional peer group. The following describes the environment that is most facilitative for the recovery of traumatized group members.

1. The stressors are accepted as real and legitimate.

2. The problem is viewed as a problem for the entire group and not as a problem that is limited to the individual.

3. The general approach to the problem is to seek solutions, not to assign blame.

4. There is a high level of tolerance for individual disturbance.

5. Support is expressed clearly, directly, and abundantly in the form of praise, commitment, and affection.

6. Communication is open and effective; there are few sanctions against what can be said. The quality of communication is good and messages are clear and direct.

7. There is a high degree of cohesion.

8. There is considerable flexibility of roles and individuals are not rigidly restricted from assuming different roles.

9. Resources—material, social, and institutional—are utilized efficiently.

10. There is no subculture of violence (emotional outbursts are not a form of violence).

11. There is no substance abuse.

Ochberg (1991) has identified three principles that underlie effective Post-Traumatic Therapy. These principles—in concert with Figley's healthy family characteristics outlined above—form the foundation of a set of assumptions that characterizes a group that will most effectively process secondary traumatic stress among its members. Ochberg's principles refer to (a) individuality, (b) normalization, and (c) empowerment.

1. The individuality principle stresses that every individual has a unique pathway to recovery after traumatic stress. The members of the professional peer group must respect each individual member's unique needs and approach to recovery.

2. The normalization principle balances the emphasis on the uniqueness of the individual's recovery. It identifies a general pattern of post-traumatic adjustment and emphasizes the essential normality of the disturbing thoughts and feelings that comprise this pattern.

3. The empowering principle emphasizes the need for people affected by traumatic stress to be included as active agents in their own recovery so that they can recover their dignity and sense of power and control.

Issues Related to Group Dynamics

The intense primitive emotions precipitated by traumatization and experienced empathically in secondary traumatization can be very disruptive in groups. Such intense emotional states influence the group dynamics and can polarize group members (Gabbard, 1989). The common experience of the trauma survivor who feels alienated and misunderstood is easily enacted in the dynamics of the group.

When a therapist has been traumatized by his or her work with a trauma survivor client, it is inevitably a disturbing event for his or her professional peers. The simple occurence of this event is a reminder to all other therapists that they too are vulnerable. One way to defend against this experience of vulnerability is to view the event as something peculiar to the particular therapist involved, rather than to the work itself. This manner of defending against the experience of heightened vulnerability is usually manifested by a distancing reaction—for example, the traumatized therapist is viewed as not functioning well because of something being wrong *with* him or her rather than something having happened *to* him or her. Viewing the secondary traumatization as indicative of something wrong with the individual allows other therapists to disown their own vulnerability to traumatic stress and protects them from identifying with the traumatized therapist's disturbing affect, a mechanism that has long been recognized in group processes (Jaques, 1955).

Since relating to the reality of traumatization threatens everyone's fundamental assumptions and the consequent stability of their worldview and feelings of security (Janoff-Bulman, 1992), it is not uncommon—even among professional therapists—to acquire a viewpoint that denies the common link with the traumatized person. This experience occurs with both primary and secondary traumatization, and in both cases it is exacerbated in a group setting. Groups establish consensual perceptions of reality. Once several members of a group believe something to be so, that belief acquires considerable power.

When this defensive view—that the affected individual is only affected because he or she is different in the first place—gains prominence within a group, the traumatized individual is left feeling alienated, vulnerable, and personally damaged. This social cutoff then constitutes an additional trauma, a *relational trauma*, which exacerbates the original stress response (Catherall, 1989; Symonds, 1980).

From the perspective of group dynamics, the affected member is carrying the vulnerable feelings for the entire group when the other members disown their common link with him or her (Yalom, 1970). If the affected member can be pushed out of the group—either physically or psychologically—then the other members of the group are more able to maintain the illusion that they are free from the threat of traumatization.

THE PREVENTION OF VICTIM BLAMING WITHIN THE GROUP

When the professional peer group is formally organized in some manner, the possibility of a distancing and blaming reaction to a traumatized therapist can be discussed and anticipated. This possibility is best discussed within the group *before it occurs*. If the therapists in the group knowingly work with trauma survivors, then it is advisable that the group spend some time discussing the likelihood of secondary traumatization. An initial goal is to create a group norm in which countertransference disclosure is encouraged. Such disclosure generally occurs only in an atmosphere in which group members feel safe (i.e., free from fear of a judgmental response).

The group members need to recognize that it is inevitable that they will have an emotional reaction if one of the therapists in the group is affected by the work. The group's agenda should include regular opportunities for the group to meet and talk about their exposure to traumatic stress. A primary goal of such meetings is to normalize the experience of feeling affected by secondary exposure. These ongoing discussions are more likely to occur if someone in a position of leadership takes responsibility for seeing that they are part of the group's agenda.

When a therapist member of the group has been affected by traumatic stress, it must be discussed in the group and the other group members need to share their reactions. The group leaders can help discourage the process of ostracism by defining and approaching the issue as a group problem, not an individual problem.

The appearance of traumatization among one of the group's

therapists constitutes a crisis in the group's life. If the situation is accepted as a crisis for the entire group, then all the group's resources can be brought to bear upon the crisis. But if the magnitude of the crisis is denied, the likelihood of acting out and distancing reactions increases. Thus it is recommended that the group have rules in place that serve to protect groups during periods of crisis. The following rules are recommended in order to help to maintain an atmosphere of safety in the group setting:

1. There should be a general rule of confidentiality that restricts group members from discussing internal group events with non-members of the group.

2. There should also be a prohibition against sub-groups of two or more members discussing group events outside of the group meetings. Obviously, this rule can be carried to unrealistic extremes but the most important part is that sub-groups not make decisions or develop agendas for the larger group. It is much safer if all decisions concerning the structure of the group be made within the meetings of the whole group.

3. It is best that the group not go through changes in membership during crisis periods. This is not always possible but should be pursued whenever it is possible. If new members are brought into the group, they should be educated about STS and brought up to speed about the nature of the specific crisis state of the group. If members must leave the group, there should be an opportunity to discuss everyone's feelings about the loss, and the timing of the change, before the members are gone.

4. No member of the group should be exempt from sharing his or her personal reactions. In some settings, such as a seminar for students, the leader of the group may not be bound by the same standards as other group members. This should not be allowed to apply to the sharing of personal reactions to the crisis of a

traumatized group member. If some individuals are allowed not to participate in the sharing of personal reactions, it can impede the development of safety for all group members. The participation of all group members fosters the process of normalization and contributes to the cohesion of the overall group.

The development of within-group blaming and distancing is best prevented by employing psychoeducational activities before anyone is traumatized. The information should be presented to the group as a group so that the awareness does not reside within one individual but is instead carried within the group culture. Psychoeducational information should not be delivered to the group in a dry, lecture format. The group members need an opportunity to discuss and react to the material so that it comes alive and becomes part of the group's personal history and culture. When new members are brought into the group, the entire group should engage in the psychoeducation and ensuing discussion of the potential effects of secondary traumatic stress. New members should not be educated in some independent forum because that can allow the group awareness to fragment. In a sense, the group's appreciation of the potential effects of secondary traumatic stress must be developed over and over so that the awareness remains an important element in the ongoing identity of the group.

CONCLUSION

Although trained clinicians may have certain advantages in dealing with secondary traumatization, they also may have special needs for understanding and integration (Talbot et al., 1992). Experience and clinical sophistication do not necessarily safeguard individuals in a group from enacting defenses against acknowledging and effectively processing secondary traumatic stress. In order to make the best use of the therapist's professional peer group, it is imperative that the culture of the group itself be a primary focus. The ethos of the group can actually move in directions that would not be the choice of any particular members. When the powerful feelings of resistance to relating to traumatization are permitted to thrive in a group, therapists affected by their work with traumatized clients can be traumatized once more by the distancing response of the very colleagues they turn to for support.

ACKNOWLEDGEMENT

The insights in this chapter were gleaned from my experience as a member of an ongoing group of trauma therapists at The Phoenix Institute in Chicago. The rules to prevent victim blaming evolved within the group as we learned more about ourselves and our reactions to this challenging work. Being a member of this group has allowed me to stretch further as a trauma therapist, as well as taught me much about the everyday reality of the principles of normalization and individuality.

REFERENCES

Burge, S. & Figley, C. R. (1982). The social support scale. Unpublished manuscript, Purdue University, Lafayette, IN.

Catherall, D. R. (1989). Differentiating intervention strategies for primary and secondary trauma in post-traumatic stress disorder: The example of Vietnam veterans. *Journal of traumatic stress*, 2 (3), 289–304.

Catherall, D. R. (1995). Preventing institutional secondary traumatic stress disorder. In C. R. Figley (Ed.), *Compassion fatigue: Coping with secondary traumatic stress disorder in those who treat the traumatized*. New York: Brunner/Mazel.

Cobb, S. (1976). Social support as a moderator of life stress. *Psychosomatic medicine*, 38, 300–314.

Dean, A. & Lin, N. (1977). The stress-buffering role of social support. *Journal of nervous and mental disease*, 165, 403–417.

Figley, C. R. (1983). Catastrophes: An overview of family reactions. In C. R. Figley & H. I. McCubbin (Eds.), *Stress and the family, vol. II: Coping with catastrophe.* New York: Brunner/Mazel.

Figley, C. R. (1989). *Helping traumatized families.* San Francisco: Jossey-Bass.

Flannery, R. B. (1990). Social support and psychological trauma: A methodological review. *Journal of traumatic stress, 3* (4), 593–611.

Gabbard, G. O. (1989). Splitting in hospital treatment. *American journal of psychiatry, 146,* 444–451.

Hirsch, B. J. (1980). Natural support systems and coping with major life changes. *American journal of community psychology, 8,* 159–171.

Janoff-Bulman, R. (1992). *Shattered assumptions: Towards a new psychology of trauma.* New York: Free Press.

Jaques, E. (1955). Social systems as defence against persecutory and depressive anxiety. In M. Klein (Ed.), *New directions in psychoanalysis.* New York: Basic Books.

Munroe, J. F. (1994). Compassion fatigue: Secondary traumatic stress from treating the traumatized. Symposium presented with D. R. Catherall, M. A. Dutton, C. R. Figley, C. Harris, and J. Shay at the 10th Annual Meeting of the International Society for Traumatic Stress Studies, Chicago, IL.

Ochberg, F. M. (1991). Post-traumatic therapy. *Psychotherapy, 28* (1), 5–15.

Rowe, C. E., & Mac Isaac, D. S. (1989). *Empathic attunement: The "technique" of psychoanalytic self psychology.* Northvale, N.J.: Jason Aronson.

Solomon, Z., Mikulincer, M., & Hobfoll, S. E. (1987). Objective versus subjective measurement of stress and social support: Combat-related reactions. *Journal of consulting and clinical psychology, 55* (4), 577–583.

Symonds, M. (1980). The "second injury" to victims. *Evaluation and change,* special issue, 36–38.

Talbot, A., Manton, M., & Dunn, P. J. (1992). Debriefing the debriefers: An intervention strategy to assist psychologists after a crisis. *Journal of traumatic stress, 5* (1), 45–62.

Tansey, M. (1994). Sexual attraction invoking dread in the countertransference. *Psychoanalytic dialogues: A journal of relational perspectives, 4* (2).

Yalom, I. D. (1970). *The theory and practice of group psychotherapy.* New York: Basic Books.

PART THREE

BEYOND THE
THERAPY ROOM

7

Communication and Self Care:
Foundational Issues

Chrys J. Harris & Jon G. Linder

Chrys J. Harris and Jon G. Linder raise a beguilingly simple issue. The ability to understand others and to make ourselves understood is the very bedrock of our mental health. Moreover, under stress, our ability to communicate is challenged, thereby potentially raising the level of stress another notch. Harris and Linder invite us to examine our modes of communication and to think deeply about how we understand and are understood. They offer suggestions and exercises that can prepare us before a crisis or can help defuse an ongoing crisis. Understanding our own communication and how it is the same or different from another's has the potential to remove frustration and increase graciousness in our lives.

How many times have we wondered why we could not get someone to understand our actions, our feelings, how we think, or what we say? Why is it often so difficult to communicate even the most simple of impressions? How is our self-confidence affected when we cannot communicate our ideas to others? What are the barriers to understanding communication? How does communication change when one functions under stress?

Beginning with the last question, stress is a very personal and individual condition and can occur regardless of whether we are the actual victims/survivors of trauma and suffer from primary traumatic stress or if we are those who would assess and treat trauma victims and suffer from Secondary Traumatic Stress. It results when we perceive some pernicious stimulus acting upon ourselves. The degree of stress we discern and how we respond to it depends on a number of factors such as resources we can bring to bear, previous or existing levels of stress, and our coping skills (Patterson & McCubbin, 1983); and our personal perceptions and experiences. Whether we are stressed or not, it is our personal perceptions that dictate how we communicate anything. However, when we are stressed, we utilize our foundational and essential basic communication systems.

The present authors propose essential communication (like that we use when stressed) can be reduced to two fundamental issues: the human senses we use to integrate and account for our internal and external worlds and the personal sorting styles around which we assimilate sensory information. These two notions imply that our communication is sensory-based. In fact, the present authors suggest, and have suggested elsewhere (Simmerman & Linder, 1989; Harris, 1995), that this is exactly the case. The only way we have to understand our external environment or measure our environment's interaction with us is through our sensory experience.

The human senses, as we learned from our very early elementary school days, are visual (sight), auditory (hearing), olfactory (smell), gustatory (taste), and touch. For purposes which will become clear later we will add a proverbial sixth sense, that of feeling. This is not the same as touch (often labeled feeling). Our emotional feelings or *kinesthetic response* (Lewis & Pucelik, 1982) are the internal arousal which often accompanies our perception of the environment.

Even our internal-self is sensory-based. Our memories are recollections of circumstances linked to one or more of our senses.

When we recall memories we relate them in terms what we saw, heard, smelled, tasted, touched and/or the kinesthetics we felt. We relate our health, thoughts, wants, and needs in terms of senses. In fact, if there was a way to eliminate every bit of our sensory perception, we probably could not function, mentally or physically.

We all use the sum total of our available senses to some degree or another every day as we interact with our environment. However, we have our preferences. As a rule, we will use one of our core senses (visual, auditory, and kinesthetic) to search initially for information in our world. These are the senses we most frequently use for motivation, decision-making, and abstract thinking.

This does not mean that we do not use the rest of our senses, only that we use one of our core senses as a primary sensory channel. For example, one who discerns the world primarily from a visual perspective may originally describe a traumatic event by verbally painting a picture involving all that was seen—with little or no initial attention to other sensory data. However, one who comprehends the world primarily from an auditory perspective may characterize the same traumatic event by describing the sounds that were heard—equally with little or no initial attention to other sensory data. Finally, one who comprehends the world primarily from a kinesthetic perspective may depict the traumatic event by describing only the emotions and feelings of the moment, again, with little or no attention to other sensory data.

Our core senses are so basic in stressful situations that we often stay mired in the one we choose as a primary sensory channel to the exclusion of all other sensory data. In fact, during a stressful condition other sensory data may never register, consciously or otherwise.

It is not complicated to determine which of the core senses one primarily uses. Lewis & Pucelik (1982) suggest this can be done by identifying the indispensable verbs one uses in speech.

TABLE 1. Verb and core sense associations.

Visual Verbs	Auditory Verbs	Kinesthetic Verbs
see	listen	feel
saw	hear	touch
show me	tell me	grasp
picture	keep quiet	painful
discover	eavesdrop	soothe
imagine	speak of	excite
examine	button up	thrilling
inspect	keep a secret	shudder
look at	sounds like	irritate

Those who are primarily visual will tend to speak with visually-oriented verbs while auditory people employ auditory-oriented verbs. Predictably, kinesthetic individuals are inclined to use feeling-oriented verbs. Table 1 provides some examples of these verbs associated with the core senses.

Returning to our traumatic event descriptions, it is easy to recognize how the visual person could become confused by the kinesthetic's depiction of what was felt instead of what was seen. Concurrently, the auditory person would be baffled by the visual person's picturesque image instead of a depiction of the sounds of the event. Regardless of which core sensory description is used, none of the traumatic event characterizations can be considered wrong as they only depict different perceptions of the same event. It is the differences in perceptions that can cause many barriers to communication.

Here are some exercises to help minimize perceptual barriers to communication:

1. Find new verbs to add to the list in Table 1. This will increase your ability to identify primary core senses.

2. Pay attention to the verbs you and others predominantly use. As you do, try to establish primary core senses for yourself and others. This will help you know how you and others differ from a sensory perspective.

3. Try perceiving your environment from a core sense other than *your* primary one. Note how difficult it is to use verbs associated with the core sense you have chosen. What is the value of this exercise for you?

The meaning of communication does not come from the communicator, it comes from the receiver. In other words, the meaning of the communication is the response it elicits (Reese & Yancer, 1986). This is because our personal perspective is what we use to attribute meaning to any communication we receive. Staying with our traumatic event examples, we can recognize that regardless of the intent to describe the trauma from one's primary core sense, another's primary core sense will interpret (or try to interpret) the description. This is one of the reasons why we often cannot get someone to understand our actions, our feelings, how we think, or even what we say—our perceptions differ!

At the beginning of this chapter it was noted that effective communication requires a comprehension of two major issues: the human senses that we use to integrate and account for our internal and external worlds and the personal sorting styles we use to assimilate sensory information. We have accounted for the sensory basis of communication. Now we turn to our sorting styles.

Personal sorting styles refer to the mental mechanisms which help us to individually sort our world and integrate the information. Table 2 presents 12 different sorting styles (adapted from Densky & Reese, 1989) of which the previously discussed primary core sensory channel is usually our lead sorting mechanism.

TABLE 2.   Sorting styles.

Primary Core Sense	Positive/Negative
Global/Detailed	Time
Sameness/Difference	Switch Referential Index
Authority	Approach/Avoidance
Cause and Effect	Internal/External
Polarity Response	Random/Sequential

The *Positive/Negative Sort* is a personal sorting preference oriented towards focusing on circumstances that are either positive or negative. People unconsciously choose positive or negative experiences while rarely considering the opposite in their memories of the past and the orientation to the future. For reasons that remain unknown, some people seem to be only able to concentrate on things that are positive while others appear to focus on negative issues. Regardless of how we try to change this sorting style, it appears to be extremely resistant to modification.

The *Global/Detailed Sort* is a personal sorting preference oriented towards focusing on details that either involve large or small components. Some people are only able to see the "forest" while others can't see the "forest for the trees." However, many people seem to be quite flexible and sort for both comfortably.

The *Time Sort* is a personal sorting preference oriented towards focusing on details predominantly from the past, present, or future. Some people can't seem to get out of the past. They will base present and future decisions on successes or failures in the past. Others choose to ignore both the past and the future adopting a "live for today" attitude. Still others embrace a future-oriented life disregarding past and present requirements. Regardless of these specific time sorters who may be too singularly focused, many people are able to sort time through past, present, and future with a general ease.

The *Sameness/Difference Sort* is a personal sorting preference oriented towards identifying things which are similar or different. Some people choose to highlight those circumstances which they can account for as similar to other conditions in their lives. Contradictory to these folks are those who choose to identify situations and adjust so the resulting circumstances are dissimilar.

The *Switch Referential Index Sort* is a personal sorting preference which involves an ability to switch from one's own reference point to that of someone else. This sorting style can have a number of facets. One can switch from how "I" feel to how "he" "she" feels or how "they" feel. One can suppose what happened to another or others happened to oneself. The object of the referential index switch is to equate one's sensory perception to that of another or others. The ability to switch referential index is an important factor in achieving intimacy and understanding. It is also a valuable asset for those who would aid trauma victims.

The *Authority Sort* is an unconscious sorting preference oriented towards identifying one's personal source of authority. Such sources can include I, you, us, family, God (religion), culture, ethnicity, and others. Like the core sense verbs, one's sentence structure can identify one's source for authority. We give away our authority source when we say "I feel...," "Do you think...," "We should...," "His word...," etc.

The *Approach/Avoidance Sort* is an unconscious sorting preference oriented to move us towards a desirable outcome or away from an undesirable outcome. This sorting style determines our motivation strategies. Such strategies are based on the theory that our behavior is oriented to seeking pleasure and avoiding pain. This theory also suggests we will do more to avoid pain than to seek pleasure. Most of us use both strategies, however many use avoidance more than approach in their daily life.

The *Cause and Effect Sort* is a sorting preference which involves a personal need to account for why things happen *generally* in our lives as opposed to purposeful cause and effect thinking on the job or related to specific issues. This sorting mechanism is one we either have or we don't. People who have a cause and effect sort in their general lives are almost obsessive in their need to know why things are happening. These people often make good problem-solvers.

The *Internal/External Sort* is a personal sorting preference oriented towards the reference of one's experience, internal or external. Most of us reference internal experience using our sensory basis as a way to measure our perception of our environment. However there are those who measure the environment externally so they are dissociated from life, perceiving from a distance with little or no kinesthetic responses to life. Often an external sort is used to defend oneself against pain.

The *Polarity Response Sort* is a process that allows for an automatic contrary reaction to whatever is being said or done. The polarity responder typical takes the opposite position.

The *Random/Sequential Sort* is a personal sorting preference for managing information. One who sorts randomly will organize information in no apparent pattern while a sequential sorter uses a methodical approach.

When we experience someone who sorts as we do, we have a positive sense of commonality and security in communication. There is a connotation of understanding, connection, and being on the same "wave length." This state of rapport creates an awareness of harmony and unity. However, when rapport is either broken or not established (as in a conflict of sorting styles), we encounter a negative sense of detachment and discomfort in communication. This negative sense often leads us to consider the other person is wrong.

In the first set of exercises you established your principal core senses.

1. Now, try to determine your preferences in the remaining 11 sorting styles from Table 2.

2. Try to determine the sorting styles of those individuals in your life with whom you communicate on a regular basis.

3. Can you identify sorting strategies that are the same? Sorting strategies that are different?

4. Can you identify barriers to your communication with others in your life?

One of the major complications arising from a conflict in sorting styles is that of attaining understanding. In communication, understanding can only be achieved when sorting styles are similar. For example, when a positive sorter explains something to another positive sorter, ostensibly they can reach understanding because of the common positive perspective. However, when the sorting styles are dissimilar, conflict occurs.

When a positive sorter tries to explain something to one who sorts for the negative, contention usually ensues. The standard question, routinely denoting this contention is, "Why?" By asking why, one indicates an inability to understand how the other is sorting. Unfortunately understanding is often never realized between those of differing sorting styles. The lack of understanding between differing sorting styles may result in arguments or disagreements. So, how do we interact with others when sorting styles differ?

The answer to this question lies in the concepts of knowing and tolerance. Rather than trying to achieve understanding between differing sorting styles, we can be more successful in trying to achieve knowing. We need to know that there are sorting styles other than our own; and the method we use to sort our environment is appropriate for us yet may not be for others. Through knowing, one can concede an inability to understand disparate sorting styles and, at the same time, build in a tolerance for individual differences. Such a tolerance of individual differences allows for all sorting styles to endure concurrently and creates an atmosphere for respect and consideration of sorting divergence between individuals.

In summary, the stress response forces us to communicate in our most elemental ways, through our preferred sorting styles. When we have communicative rapport with another there is harmony and unity derived from common sensory awareness and sorting style(s). The barriers that arise in communication can be traced to conflicts in sorting styles. The easiest way to overcome these barriers is to (a) adopt a sense of knowing (about other sorting styles) rather than understanding and (b) to develop a tolerance for individual differences that result when others use sorting styles that differ from our own.

REFERENCES

Densky, A. B. & Reese, M. (1989). *Programmer's pocket summary*. Indian Rocks Beach, FL: Southern Institute Press.

Harris, C. J. (1995). Sensory-based therapy for crisis counselors. In C. R. Figley (Ed.), *Compassion fatigue: Coping with secondary traumatic stress disorder among those who treat the traumatized*. New York: Brunner/Mazel.

Lewis, B. A. & Pucelik, R. F. (1982). *Magic demystified*. Lake Oswego, OR: Metamorphous Press.

Patterson, J. M. & McCubbin, H. I. (1983). Chronic illness: Family stress and coping. In C. R. Figley & H. I. McCubbin (Eds.), *Coping with catastrophe*, vol. 2. New York: Brunner/Mazel.

Reese, M. & Yancer, C. (1986). *Practitioner manual for introductory patterns of neurolinguistic programming*. Indian Rocks Beach, FL: Southern Institute Press.

Simmerman, S. J. & Linder, J. (1989). *Mindworks*. Greenville, SC: Eagle Network.

8

Painful Pedagogy: Teaching About Trauma in Academic and Training Settings

Susan L. McCammon

The melodic title of "Painful Pedagogy" belies the potential struggle that lurks beneath the convoluted issues of teaching about trauma. Many of the people drawn to trauma training carry with them trauma histories. While supervision in psychotherapy training can be difficult, at least the supervisor is expected to work with the student. Imagine seeing a student flee the room in tears when you deliver a lecture to a large undergraduate class. Experiences like these can leave the professor with a sense of helplessness and without institutional guidelines. Susan L. McCammon's chapter offers succor to the teacher preparing difficult course material and suggests pedagogical strategies to lessen the negative impact of trauma material while preserving its integrity and the heart of the professor.

In their article on vicarious traumatization McCann and Pearlman (1990) noted that therapists are "not immune to the painful images, thoughts, and feelings associated with exposure to their clients' traumatic memories" (p. 132). That's true, I thought, when I read their article. And other professionals who work with traumatized people are susceptible as well. I recalled talking with an attorney who was prosecuting a child sexual abuse case. I asked him about the emotional effect of listening to children's accounts of abuse. It is part of his professionalism that these things do not cause emotional effect, he told me. But later in the conversation he recounted a dream he has had—he is standing by his boat dock and sees children's clothes washing up (a boat was involved in the abuse account) and is horrified when he recognizes his child's shoes among those floating in the water. I felt compassion for his experience of the grim nightmare, but was almost amused at his idea that his professionalism was protecting him from being emotionally affected. How unaware, I thought.

McCann and Pearlman (1990) observed that therapists experience alteration in their own "cognitive schemas, or beliefs, expectations, and assumptions about self and others" (p. 132). They reflected upon the irony of putting the finishing touches on their manuscript in a home office during the installation of a burglar alarm system in the house. The installation of the alarm system, they acknowledged, directly resulted from safety schema disruption from working with many crime survivors. Click! I am the one who has been unaware! It was not until reading that article that I began examining my new fitness interest—karate.

I had made a bargain with myself when I first began university teaching. If, or when, I became tenured, I would reward myself with piano lessons. However, by the time I was tenured, my interests were focused in a new direction. After taking a self-defense course several times at a local *dojo*, I enrolled in karate lessons. In retrospect, I realized that this interest coincided with my teaching of a new course I had developed, "Sexual Abuse: Incidence, Impact, and Prevention." In the course we reviewed a range of types of sexual abuse, their patterns of incidence, impact, treatments for survivors and perpetrators, theories about causes, and ideas and programs directed toward abuse prevention. Reading the material I had gathered and assigned, listening to the guest speakers, and hearing the confidences of my students who came to seek referral for addressing their abuse histories had certainly influenced my schemas. I began to recognize a parallel between the impact on the therapist of working with the traumatized and the impact of teaching about trauma on the teacher.

My thinking on teaching about trauma was further stimulated by an incident in another class. I was co-teaching an introductory women's studies course in which the topic of rape and sexual assault was covered. Some class members had expressed skepticism toward the concept of "acquaintance rape" and said its incidence is exaggerated. Other students rebutted this claim and the class continued without incident. However, during the last class of the semester a student put aside her scheduled report on volunteering at a local battered women's shelter and instead read a statement she had prepared recounting the rape she had recently experienced and the devastating reaction she encountered from the friend in whom she confided. This talk, the first public revelation she had made, appeared beneficial for her and for those in the class who had been insensitive about the issue. However, while she was speaking, first one woman, then another, and yet another, fled the room in tears. I slipped out after them, and discovered each crying in a separate stall in the women's room. Each had a personal history of rape or child sexual abuse. They were angry at the student who publicly revealed her rape, catching them by surprise. Caught off guard, they were unable to modulate their emotional response to the surprise disclosure. The other professor completed the class while I held a crisis counseling session with the three, first in the women's room, then moving to a faculty office.

Reflecting upon teaching about trauma, I am observing that sometimes this is a painful type of pedagogy, as it results in teacher and students becoming sadder but wiser. As Janoff-Bulman (1992) noted, experiencing a traumatic event shatters a victim's fundamental assumptions: "The world is benevolent[;] the world is meaningful[;] the self is worthy" (p. 6).

It seems to me that studying material about trauma and its impact also has the potential to make students and teachers recognize their own vulnerability and result in their fitting Janoff-Bulman's description of trauma victims as "less Pollyannaish in their perceptions of the world and themselves" (p. 90). Furthermore, some of the students or trainees in an educational setting are trauma survivors who may be in the process of reconstructing their assumptive world. Exposure to course material may cause them emotional distress.

This is not to say that such teaching should be avoided, but that as an educator I feel a responsibility to try to learn more about the impact of learning about trauma, and how my teaching and students' learning is affected. In my role as educator, rather than as a clinical-community psychologist, how can I be sensitive to the fact that many of my students have been exposed to the traumatic events and effects included in the curriculum, and still keep a focus on the educational goals of the course? What strategies can I use to set the tone of a class or workshop, manage classroom discussions of difficult topics, and respond to students in a teaching or training (not therapy) setting? The ideas that follow have been gathered through reading articles about teaching, as well as from my experience and that of colleagues who have shared their thoughts in symposia and discussion groups I have organized on this topic at professional meetings (McCammon, Bassman & Sorenson, 1991; Farr & Mc-Cammon, 1992; McCammon, Miller, Schmuckler & Violanti, 1994).

STUDENTS' TRAUMA HISTORIES

In academic and training settings, especially in educating human service, health care, and public safety employees, the curriculum is increasingly likely to include trauma-related material. These topics range from being a survivor, witness, or responder to rape or sexual abuse, other types of criminal victimization, natural or human-induced disasters, to war or political atrocities. While many of us in teaching roles have struggled at times to engage students in the material we teach, when the topic is trauma and its sequelae or responding to traumatic events, we encounter students who connect all too well to the material because of their personal histories. For example, in a stress management class one professor asked students to relate a stressful event they had encountered. He expected stories such as car trouble or oversleeping on an exam day, but students recounted sobering accounts of rape and exposure to death.

Recent studies document the prevalence of trauma histories in nonclinical samples. Vrana and Lauterbach (1994) found that 84% of undergraduate students in introductory psychology courses reported experiencing at least one event sufficiently enough intense to meet the stressor criterion for PTSD. Approximately one-third of the students reported four or more separate traumatic events, and 9% reported seven or more events.

Work by Stamm (1993, 1995) suggests something of the nature of trauma experiences in student populations. This survey of the most stressful life experiences reported by 1,012 college students found that 24.5% of the students experienced the death of family members (usually parents) or acquaintances. Of these students 4.3% were sexual assault victims; an additional 9.4% reported they had friends who had been assaulted. Accidents and disasters seriously touched the lives of another 15.2%. The most frequently reported stressful life experiences (46.5%) were general problems in living, such as unemployment, job-related forced relocations, and similar life stressors.

Follette, Polusny, and Milbeck (1994) surveyed childhood physical and sexual abuse histories of mental health and law enforcement professionals. They found that approximately 30% of therapists and 20% of law enforcement officers reported childhood abuse histories. These percentages are similar to those revealed in studies of the general population. As in the college student study, the male therapists and police officers were more likely to have encountered military combat service, and female therapists and police officers were more likely to have experienced adult sexual assault or an abusive relationship.

Based on these data, it seems likely that an educator or workshop leader can anticipate that a substantial number of students will be trauma survivors. Issues that the teacher may encounter include the possibility that students will disclose personal trauma experiences privately or to the class, and whether to discourage, encourage, or even model this.

CLASSROOM DISCLOSURE

Students may disclose trauma or abuse histories privately, such as in papers or journal entries or in conversations with the professor. They may also publicly reveal their experiences to the class. Other students may not reveal their histories, but may have emotional reactions to the material which may subsequently affect their learning. There are some benefits of self-disclosure. (a) It serves the role of providing *testimony,* which has been found to be of therapeutic value to trauma survivors (Agger & Jensen, 1990). Private pain can be put into a political and social context. The trauma can be reframed so that it has meaning. Those who hear or read the account become witnesses. (b) The act of speaking about one's trauma can help one turn from passivity to activity. Wolfenstein (in Janoff-Bulman) observed that "from being the helpless victim one becomes the effective storyteller, and it is the others, the audience, who are made to undergo the experience" (p. 109). (c) Disclosure breaks the secrecy conspiracy and voices the unmentionable. Those who have had similar experiences may discover they are not alone. Shame and guilt can be expressed and reframed. Herman (1992) stated that the central dialectic of psychological trauma is the conflict of wills between attempts to deny horrible, unspeakable events and attempts to proclaim them aloud. She conjured up the folk-tale image of ghosts who refused to rest in their graves until their stories were told. According to Herman, telling the truth about atrocities is necessary, not only for individual victims' healing, but also for restoring the social order. (d) Disclosure provides an opportunity for the student to obtain validation, support, and referral. Lee's (1989) article discusses the affirmation and validation violence survivors received in an introductory women's studies course (class size was 21; all were women). (e) Finally, public disclosures verify to other students the reality of these issues and the potential depth of their impact. For a classmate or professor to speak about their experience or tell stories of their families and friends can provide a personal link to the material. This may help prevent some students from dismissing or trivializing an event that seems unrelated to themselves. The teacher may arrange to have a guest speaker come to class with an agenda of providing testimony.

A colleague who teaches a course on literature of the Holocaust has speakers who are survivors or children of survivors. The professor sometimes tells stories about his aunt, who was a survivor, and his boyhood memories of her. In some classes I have talked about the gay-bashing attack which disabled a relative of mine. Some of my students tell me they do not know anyone who is gay, although (very) few seem indifferent to prejudice and persecution toward lesbians and gays. I hope that in hearing of my relative, and the impact on our family of his assault, that their compassion and empathy might be aroused.

However, there are also risks inherent in disclosure, especially public disclosure to the class. (a) There is risk of not receiving support. Other students may be disbelieving, non-supportive, or even angry with the disclosing student. As Janoff-Bulman (1992) warned, the responses of other people to one who was traumatized are not uniformly positive. Encountering someone who has been victimized or experienced misfortune may be threatening. Students may feel embarrassed or anxious about a disclosure and respond inappropriately. Thus there is potential for harm, as others' reactions are a significant influence on one's post-traumatic adjustment. (b) In a classroom there is no guarantee of confidentiality. In her instructor's manual for a sexuality text, Kolodny (1985) warned that after discussing a personal experience in class, students may find themselves the object of gossip or exploitation. (c) Sometimes after hearing another's account of victimization, abuse survivors discount their own abuse because theirs "wasn't as bad" as the other person's. At times this can be a helpful coping strategy, as Janoff-Bulman (1992) described, when we compare ourselves with another who is less fortunate to feel better about our own situation. But when social comparison results in survivors feeling ashamed of or not entitled to their emotional responses because their trauma was "less" than that of another, this may hinder their integration of the event. (d) A person's disclosure may be upsetting to other students (and to faculty) and they may become very emotionally aroused. Associations or memories of their experiences may be triggered. Students may feel unprepared to deal with the emotions, especially in a public setting.

SUGGESTIONS FOR FACULTY

Below are suggestions to stimulate faculty consideration and discussion regarding how to approach trauma-related topics and students' reactions. This involves examination of educational goals and motives for teaching this material.

1. Establish an accepting, but not confessional, tone for the class. In classes in which I discuss sexual abuse I begin by pointing our that "if this class follows patterns identified in studies of other college students, over 25% of the women will have experienced rape or attempted rape, and up to 16% of the men may have experienced a sexual assault. Therefore, this material is likely to touch some of you personally." In my undergraduate human sexuality course I point out that this course is not a therapy course (it doesn't teach you how to be a therapist and does

not provide psychotherapy), but observe that students may get ideas of treatment possibilities and resources. I offer that they may let me know if the material causes them problems so that I can help them find a therapist or other resources. I tell them I am *not* asking that they reveal their deepest, darkest secrets, and that they carefully evaluate making any personal disclosures to the class. I suggest they consider their readiness to discuss personal issues, as well as the readiness of their classmates to hear it, and the educational purpose that would be served by disclosing personal experiences.

2. Inform students regarding what topics will be covered each class period, and if audio-visual or other special materials will be used, so they can choose not to attend if they feel unable. After announcing a date-rape video scheduled for an upcoming class I received the following note from a student: "I do not think that I will be able to attend the next class. The subject matter is very personal to me and I don't feel as if I am prepared to discuss it openly. I have not yet reached that point. I hope to eventually come to deal with it. Thank you. I am very sorry. If you could give me a different assignment, I would be very appreciative. My dreams and nightmares still haunt me."

I've found that when students are caught by surprise on an issue, they are not able to emotionally steel themselves in preparation for a challenging topic. In a human sexuality class we finished two class sessions focused on rape with no incident. However, during the next class, prior to starting the new topic, a student asked a question related to the previous material. During that discussion a student fled the room in tears. She had emotionally prepared herself for the previous classes, but she was caught off guard when faced with the topic unexpectedly.

As Kolodny (1985) observed, even "innocuous" videos or films may be offensive or unpleasant to some students. One of my students was saddened as seeing the NOVA video "The Miracle of Life" with its pictures of fetal development. His girlfriend had recently had an abortion. Videos on HIV/AIDS are distressing to some students. I learned to sit by the classroom door while showing videos after an AIDs education video prompted a panic attack in one student.

3. Thoughtfully select lecture examples, teaching materials such as videos and case studies, and assignments. Consider the level of emotional intensity likely to be stimulated, as students who are too aroused may not be able to process or may be distracted from the intellectual point you want to make. In comparing therapists to teachers, Janoff-Bulman (1992) reminded that, "Excellent teachers recognize our special strengths and weaknesses and pace the learning task to coincide with our distinct needs and abilities" (p. 164).

Some faculty monitor students' reactions to the material through journal-writing. In a large class I require students to turn in a "thought card" every other week. On a 4" x 6" index card they write a few sentences or a paragraph with comments or reactions to course material. I do not grade them, but keep a record of the number turned in. If the student is on the borderline between two grades at the end of the semester, I round up the grade if the thought cards have been submitted. This is enough incentive that most students turn them in and I receive a great deal of feedback regarding students' responses to the lectures, discussions, and readings.

4. Inform yourself about counseling and support resources both off and one campus. Become informed about their intake and screening practices. I was distressed to find, after talking at length to a student and getting her to accept a referral to the university counseling center, that after she poured out her story the therapist refused to accept her as a client. She would have needed more than four therapy sessions and wouldn't fit with the short-term model of the center. (I was later able to link her with a therapist in private practice.) Find out who in your community has specific training and experience in various areas (adult survivors and trauma resolution, eating disorders, substance abuse, group facilitation, etc.). Be familiar with campus

policies regarding sexual assault, sexual harassment, and crime reporting, and in work settings, employee assistance programs.

5. Talk privately to the disclosing student, or write a response in the journal, at your earliest opportunity. Find out if the problem is current and ongoing. If so, help the student obtain crisis counseling, emergency shelter, medical and public safety (law enforcement) help if needed. Be prepared to listen, but do not interrogate. Be supportive of the student for talking with you.

Help to connect the student to a counselor or relevant service, if he or she is willing. To make a referral, give a name and phone number of an individual (not just an agency name) to contact, if possible. Explain why you think the referral is needed (e.g., "I'm not a counselor, and I think a counselor could help you sort out your feelings about...," "Therapists can often help rape survivors with fears such as the ones you mentioned," "Although I am a therapist, I am your professor and can't serve in both roles."). Ask the student to let you know if the referral is helpful (not to tell you the details of their therapy but to let you know if the person or agency is helpful). If I think a student is particularly in need of an appointment but may be reluctant to call, I ask permission to call the agency while the student is in my office, tell them what I will say, and then put them on the phone to schedule the appointment.

6. If the disclosure is made in class discussion, acknowledge the student's comment and relate it to the lesson. If other students are not appropriate in their response, model an empathic statement and guide the discussion in a constructive direction.

7. Students are often interested in self-help literature and recommended readings at the professional or lay level. I have sometimes loaned my own books and articles out—probably a result of my wishing I could do something to help. After losing several books, I am slower to allow my copies out of the building.

8. In organizing classes on topics such as rape and sexual assault, child sexual abuse, sexual harassment, and violence against gays and lesbians, I include discussion of treatment for

survivors and perpetrators, theories (including ideas about causes), and prevention. In this way, despite the depressing and alarming data, there can still be some upbeat focus. For example, in Katz's (1991) study of 87 rape survivors six-months to 15-years post-rape, about half of the women felt completely or nearly completely recovered at the time of the study, indicating that although rape may have long-term effects, it is also possible to recover from it. In one of my classes, a student wrote in a course evaluation, "This class has helped me in that my hope level of recovery has increased." Likewise, reviewing prevention strategies at the individual and societal level may help channel efforts to reduce victimization.

9. One team of educators has employed an adaptation of Critical Incident Stress Debriefing (CISD) for classroom use to ameliorate the potentially traumatic impact of discussing a deeply disturbing incest survivor's narrative (Zuk & Wetmore, 1993). Zuk, an English professor, determined from written student responses to their reading of Elly Danica's *Don't: A Woman's Word*, that a number of students had incest and abuse histories. She enlisted the help of Wetmore, a therapist, to help apply the CISD model to assist emotional processing and prevent the development of adverse reactions to the discussion. They presented a thoughtful account of their motives and process. Their argument is that "since ignoring the biographical fact of incest is pointless, while eliciting horrible stories about it is worse than meaningless, some version of a 'debriefing' session is necessary to clear the way for intellectual work on the incest narrative" (p. 25). While they acknowledge that most English professors do not have "a therapist sticking to her or his leg to teach this text," the use of an interdisciplinary team "seems a likely strategy for managing this pedagogical project" (p. 25).

10. Once you are identified as someone who is concerned about victimization issues, people confide in you and send students to you. Consider your potential for vicarious traumatiza-

tion and the impact of teaching about trauma on your assumptions and schemas. In sum, you should seek to engage in restorative activities.

CONCLUSIONS

Attempting to teach about trauma can be very challenging for the instructor, and for the student as well. A colleague lamented to me that he was angrily confronted by a student from an Abnormal Psychology class in which he lectured about Post Traumatic Stress Disorder and discussed rape sequelae as an example. The female student, a rape survivor, told him that as a man he had no right to talk about rape, that he could not truly understand its impact. The professor told me that he had decided the topic of rape was too emotionally charged and that he has dropped it from his PTSD lecture. While I do not agree with the student that one must have experienced an event to be able to feel empathy for survivors, I understand the professor's concern that to raise provocative topics in class the professor should be willing to take the time and have the skill in managing class discussion to adequately process the material. To start his PTSD lecture he now uses a trigger film of a local apartment building explosion to open a discussion of rescue workers' responses to their work, but discovered this topic wasn't neutral or completely safe, as one of his students lived in the apartment complex at which the disaster occurred!

In teaching about trauma it is important to acknowledge that in such teaching, students "don't merely discover the traumatic experience of the Other," they "confront and formulate narratives of their own experience" (Zuk & Wetmore, 1993, p. 21). But the goal in tackling these topics is not to "privilege the victimized," or encourage them "to wallow in scandal or melancholy" (p. 25), but to increase students' knowledge and capacity for empathy.

In 1985, Figley noted a growing concern for the welfare of the trauma victim and an increasing recognition of societal responsibility to victims of catastrophe. He suggested that in our own way, each of us can bolster this sense of societal responsibility by making sure that the emotional impact of trauma is neither minimized nor forgotten, and by promoting the transition of victims and their families to productive and happy survivors. As educators, teachers, and trainers we work toward this goal from many directions. In training of public safety and medical professionals we address not only their technical skills but also their knowledge of the potential impact of their work, how to engage in self-care, and how to establish supportive interventions and systems. As educators of mental health professionals we teach about trauma sequelae and interventions to promote positive coping and adjustment. And in college teaching of students who do not enter public safety or mental health occupations, we are also performing an important educational service in teaching about trauma to develop informed citizens, voters, jurors, attorneys, judges, parents, and social support agents.

Many of the positive effects McCann and Pearlman (1990) identified for trauma therapists are also applicable to educators. By teaching about trauma, coping, and resiliency we can promote

> a heightened sensitivity and enhanced empathy for the suffering of victims, resulting in a deeper sense of connection with others...a deep sense of hopefulness about the capacity of human beings to endure, overcome, and even transform their traumatic experiences; and a more realistic view of the world, through the integration of the dark sides of humanity with healing images (McCann & Pearlman, 1990, p. 147).

Although teaching trauma topics is difficult, there is much to be gained by working through the challenges.

REFERENCES

Agger, I. & Jensen, S. B. (1990). Testimony as ritual and evidence in psychotherapy for political refugees. *Journal of traumatic stress, 3,* 131–149.

Farr, M. & McCammon, S. (1992). What do we do when teachers' theory meets students' experience? Trauma survivors in the introductory women's studies course. Paper presented at the Southeastern Women's Studies Association, Tampa, FL.

Figley, C. R. (1985). From victim to survivor: Social responsibility in the wake of catastrophe. In C. R. Figley (Ed.), *Trauma and its wake: The study and treatment of PTSD.* New York: Brunner/Mazel.

Follette, V., Polusny, M., & Milbeck, K. (1994). Mental health and law enforcement professionals: Trauma history, psychological symptoms, and impact of providing services to child sexual abuse survivors. *Professional psychology: Research and practice, 25,* 275–282.

Herman, J. L. (1992). *Trauma and recovery.* New York: Basic Books.

Janoff-Bulman, R. (1992). *Shattered assumptions: Towards a new psychology of trauma.* New York: Free Press.

Katz, B. L. (1991). The psychological impact of stranger versus nonstranger rape on victims' recovery. In A. Parrot & L. Bechhofer (Eds.), *Acquaintance rape: The hidden crime.* New York: John Wiley & Sons.

Kolodny, N. J. (1985). *Instructor's manual for Masters, Johnson, and Kolodny's human sexuality* (2nd. ed.). Boston: Little, Brown and Company.

Lee, J. (1989). "Our hearts are collectively breaking": Teaching survivors of violence. *Gender and society, 3* (4), 541–548.

McCammon, S., Bassman, M. & Sorenson, S. (1992). Teaching college courses about trauma. Paper presented at the International Society for Traumatic Stress Studies, Beverly Hills, CA.

McCammon, S., Miller, M., Violanti, J., & Schmuckler, E. (1994). Painful pedagogy: Trauma survivors in academic or training classes. Paper presented at the International Society for Traumatic Stress Studies, Chicago, IL.

McCann, I. L. & Pearlman, L. A. (1990). Vicarious traumatization: A framework for understanding the psychological effects of working with victims. *Journal of traumatic stress, 3,* 131–149.

Stamm, B. H. (1995). Contextualizing death and trauma: A preliminary endeavor. In C. R. Figley (Ed.), *Death and trauma*. New York: Brunner/Mazel (manuscript under review).

Stamm, B. H. (1993). Conceptualizing traumatic stress: A metatheoretical structural approximation. Ph.D. dissertation, Laramie, WY: University of Wyoming.

Vrana, S. & Lauterbach, D. (1994). Prevalence of traumatic events and post-traumatic psychological symptoms in a nonclinical sample of college students. *Journal of traumatic stress*, 7, 289–302.

Zuk, R. J. & Wetmore, A. A. (1993). Teaching the incest narrative: Problems and possibilities. *Feminist teacher*, 7 (3), 21–26.

9

Trauma-Based Psychiatry for Primary Care

Lyndra Bills

Primary care providers see many trauma cases pass through the health care system. However, current health care pedagogy provides little training in traumatic stress. Consequently, primary care providers may find themselves faced with frustrating patients—patients they may even avoid out of the providers' frustration. Stories of how these patients are shuffled from provider to provider with little or no truly helpful treatment abound. It is easy to side with the patient against the provider, but in doing so, we may miss the provider's genuine distress. Lyndra Bills, trained both as an internist and a psychiatrist, offers a systematic approach with which the primary care provider can treat the unique health problems of the traumatized patient. This approach affords the primary care provider better options in treating the trauma patient while simultaneously supporting the provider's need to be helpful.

Thanks to amazing technological advances in modern medicine, primary care practitioners can now more easily diagnose symptomatic coronary artery disease, hypertension, cerebrovascular accidents, meningitis, and many other physical illnesses that have plagued humankind. Modern technology has also improved psychiatric care thanks to some very effective psychotropic medications like clozapine for schizophrenia, valproic acid, carbamazepine and lithium for bipolar affective disorder, and the serotonin-specific reuptake inhibitors like fluoxetine which are very effective for most major depressive disorders and many types of anxiety disorders. However, there are still numerous patients presenting to the primary care provider and to the mental health provider with complaints which are far more difficult to diagnose adequately.

Because primary care providers are trained to provide rapid and efficient relief of the patient's symptoms, an inability to diagnose correctly and relieve the patient's symptoms can be a major work-related stressor for a primary care provider. Most caregivers have identified patients that they consider problem patients. These patients continue symptomatic, regardless seemingly, of the caregiver's best efforts. These difficult patients may engender several different responses in the caregiver. For example, the caregiver may begin to reject the patient and assume the patient does not want to get well. Or the caregiver may refer the patient to a series of specialists who seem to do no better. Finally, the caregiver may begin to doubt his or her own competency, which may leave the caregiver vulnerable for secondary traumatic stress (See Stamm & Pearce, in this volume).

Interestingly, many of the complaints of the problem patient are stress related. Although providers know about the negative impact of chronic stress on the physical and emotional well-being of the patient, a coherent framework for understanding the effects of stress has not always been clearly articulated in medical training. As a preventive measure for the caregiver, this paper presents a trauma-based approach to psychiatry in a primary care setting.

Many patients will present to their primary care provider with somatic complaints like chest pain, chronic pain, chronic headaches, and gastrointestinal complaints, as well as anxiety, depression, sleep problems, nightmares, suicidal ideation, and memory disturbances. This complex array of symptoms does not necessarily meet criteria for a specific medical or psychiatric diagnosis. These *in-between* patients have physical and/or psychological complaints which are neither easily pegged into a diagnostic category nor felt clinically to be a condition which will present itself after proper testing and evaluation. And yet the suffering of the patients and their families is unmistakable. In cases such as these, a trauma-based approach may be helpful and the most important thing you can do for these patients is to ask them questions about has happened to them recently or in the past.

Post-traumatic stress disorder (PTSD) describes the mind and body changes which occur after a traumatic event. Specifically, PTSD refers to someone who reacts with intense fear, helplessness, or horror to a major (or minor) trauma by developing (a) intrusive reexperiencing symptoms; (b) avoidance responses to evidence of the trauma and generalized psychological numbing and isolation; and (c) widespread physiologic arousal (Tomb, 1994). In other words, PTSD often causes biopsychosocial changes in patients. Thus, when care providers see someone in a clinic or an office with difficult and/or confusing constellations of complaints, they should consider the possibility of the PTSD diagnosis.

PTSD can be acute, chronic, or delayed. Furthermore, it is often co-morbid with many psychiatric and medical conditions. How and why some people develop a post-trauma reaction to a stressor is dependent upon the nature, intensity, and duration of the stressor; the person's history and vulnerability to previous trauma; and the treatment received following a traumatic event.

Roberts (1994) estimates that up to 75% of all visits to primary care providers involve presentation of psychosocial problems through physical complaints. In one survey of a primary care clinic, the rate of childhood sexual abuse was 37% and the rate for adult sexual assault was 29% (Walker, 1993). The same survey revealed that only 4% of the patients had been asked by their primary care provider about a history of victimization. Another survey in a primary care setting correlated the number of unexplainable physical complaints with increasing prevalence of a potentially treatable anxiety or mood disorder—up to 60% for an anxiety disorder and 48% for a mood disorder (Kroenke, 1994).

The *in-between* patient's presentation may be explained through a trauma-based approach. Trauma can refer to physical, sexual, or emotional abuse, as well as events such as motor vehicle accidents, natural disasters, combat experiences, rape, witnessing assaults and violence, kidnapping, torture and/or terrorist attacks, and/or trauma from medical procedures (Stuber et al., 1991).

Consider the following case of a 21-year-old female college student who presented to the primary care office with recurrent complaints of vaginal infection, as well as pelvic and lower abdominal pain. She had a history of sexually transmitted disease, recurrent upper respiratory infections, and irritable bowel syndrome. She presented vaginal and pelvic complaints on three consecutive visits, but had normal physical and gynecological exams, negative pregnancy tests, and no evidence of urinary or gynecological infection. She nevertheless insisted on both a pelvic exam and the fact that she must have an infection. When asked about a history of victimization, she gave a history of childhood sexual abuse and adult sexual assault. The frequent gynecological symptoms without medical etiology turned out to be the somatic representation of her traumatic memories. These decreased in frequency once the abuse issues were recognized.

Another example is a 45-year-old male who presented to his primary care doctor for chronic pain in his right leg following a severe coal-mining accident. During the next 10 years he continued with frequent primary care visits and subsequent psychiatric hospitalizations for chronic pain and depression. No one, however, asked him about his accident during that 10-year period. When that vital information finally came out, he began to tell the story of his accident, which then reduced his pain, depression, and PTSD symptoms.

Research supports a definite connection for trauma as the etiology in many cases of somatization (Blank, 1994), dissociation, and mood disturbances. Two-thirds of patients diagnosed with a dissociative disorder also met criteria for a somatization disorder (Saxe, 1994). In a survey of general medical outpatients, the hypochondriac patients recalled more childhood trauma before age 17 (Barsky, 1994). In a population of adult psychiatric patients, 40% to 70% were survivors of abuse (Briere & Runtz, 1987). Prisoners of war consistently show increased mortality from suicide, homicide, and accidents (Segal et al., 1976). In a study of battered women, 42% had attempted suicide (Gayford, 1975). Dissociation and the disturbance of time sense, memory, and concentration are common to survivors of prolonged and repeated trauma and victimization (Putnam, 1989). There are many more statistics which all point to the same thing: the need for more health care providers to ask questions about traumatic experiences and be open-minded when routine treatment strategies fail to fix the problem.

A trauma-based approach, therefore, can assist primary care providers to understand some possibilities for the somatic complaints. This has at least two benefits. First, primary care providers can guide their patients to gain insights which may end the somatization. Secondly, and just as important, primary care providers themselves can gain a measure of competency and thus relieve some of the uncertainties of dealing with *in-between* patients. Usually, patients who have a normal stress response to traumatic events do not suffer persistent or untreatable symptoms, the kind which baffle, confuse, or otherwise challenge the competence of the provider. Knowledge of the trauma-based approach, however, alerts the primary care provider to the possibility that difficult or *in-between* patients often manifest a post-trauma stress response which causes some type of functional impairments. Thus the primary care provider is uniquely positioned to view the importance of the mind/body connection, which is an advantage for managing psychiatric problems generally and *in-between* patients particularly.

All patients presenting for help with a physical or psychological problem need a thorough history and physical. This should include gaining some type of trauma history. The following questions should be included as a minimum for a routine trauma history in a primary care setting.

1. What is the most traumatic incident that has ever happened to you?

2. What is the most traumatic incident that has ever happened to someone in your family?

3. Have you ever been the victim of a crime?

4. Have you ever been in an accident serious enough so that you had be examined medically?

5. Have you ever had excess fear concerning medical procedures or surgery?

6. Have you ever served in the armed forces? If yes, were you involved in combat? Explain.

7. Have you ever been sexually or physically assaulted as a child or as an adult?

8. At any point during this (these) experiences(s) did you think you were in danger of serious personal harm or losing your life? (Peterson et al., 1991).

As part of the history and physical, the mental status exam should include elements of orientation, appearance and behavior, mood and affect, thought content, cognitive function, judgment, and insight. Appropriate assessment should also include some fundamental laboratory tests such as a sensitive TSH (thyroid stimulating hormone), drug screens, chest X-ray, and an EKG when indicated. If the history and examination indicate the appropriateness of trauma-based intervention, several avenues of action should be considered.

SELF-HELP PROTOCOLS

Self-help and support are two treatment modalities available to the primary care provider in taking care of the *in-between* patient. They can be used for psychiatric problems generally, but are particularly good for patients recovering from post-trauma conditions. People who have been traumatized generally feel a sense of loss of control, isolation, and a tendency to become immobilized by a sense of victimization. Therefore, it is often therapeutic to allow them to do things for themselves and to lend them solid support.

Primary care providers can have an advantage in managing psychiatric problems because of their practical problem-oriented approach. The primary care provider can guide patients to do many things for themselves which will promote overall health. Also, patients who present to primary care providers generally have an understanding that they will be expected to contribute to improving their own health and will accept homework assignments or some of the responsibility to help themselves. One example of this is the behavioral contract—patients sign agreements and promise to make certain behavioral changes within a specified time (Neale, 1991). This has been successful in improving weight and cholesterol, but is also applicable to problems with decreased sleep, self-harm, and safety.

Health and safety are essential to everyone's overall well-being. The following protocols are guides which recognize the fact that there often is no place for patients to be referred or that the primary care provider and the patient must manage a crisis in a physically remote location. Thus, they are checklists for the health provider to engage patients in helping themselves.

1. *The Healthy Protocol* includes aspects of diet, exercise, stress management, sleep, hygiene, physical health, fun/relaxation, and preventive health. The stress management component can include meditation, self-hypnosis, controlled breathing, anger management, education, and exercise.

2. *The Safety Protocol* is meant primarily for patients who are suicidal and includes identification of risk factors, a contract for safety, and a phone contact/support list. Identification of risk includes items such as guns, alcohol, pills, gender, age, medical problems, and relative isolation (Beaumont, 1992). The contract for safety should have the patient agree to 24 hours of safety and contact; have the patient make phone or personal contact within 24 hours; be written in the patient's chart (with the patient's signature) and whenever possible, witnessed by a supportive family member. Patients should agree to have a friend or family member stay with them for a specified period of time. Finally, the phone/contact list should include five people or resources to whom the patient can turn for help when he or she feels overwhelmed or unsafe. This list also could include a list of places or homes to visit in the absence of phone resources.

3. *The Self Harm Protocol* includes behavioral monitoring, self-evaluation, and practical suggestions to increase patient safety. The patient should contract to remove all sharp or otherwise potentially harmful objects. Patients should be asked to focus on what may have precipitated the episode of self-harm by writing about how they were feeling, what preceded the self-harm, what they could do to prevent it next time, etc. Ask patients to monitor their time and activities by writing them on a time-sheet, with updates every 30 minutes. After 24 hours, intervals can

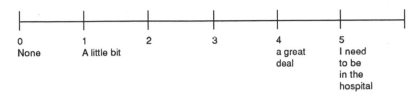

Sample Self Abuse Scale

| 0 | 1 | 2 | 3 | 4 | 5 |
| None | A little bit | | | a great deal | I need to be in the hospital |

gradually increase as patients exhibit safer behavior and decrease self-harming attempts. Patients should ask for help from family and friends until patients can keep themselves safe; the family and friends should be informed of their importance in this task. The primary provider should acknowledge that the main etiology for self-harming behavior is trauma, but the continuation of violence is the basis of the self-harming behavior. Patients need to learn to manage their anger and stress, but they also need to understand that their own self-harming behavior is violence to themselves. Provide support groups, therapy, journaling opportunities, etc., in order to help patients address their trauma issues. Finally, use a self-abuse scale to enable patients to monitor their own severity of self-harm.

The Self-Abuse Scale is simple—the meaning of severity by number should be agreed upon by the patient and provider. For example, a 5 on the scale might indicate the need for medical attention which may require inpatient treatment or more intense means of intervention, such as a mental health referral.

4. *The Anti-Regressive Protocol* is used to reduce regression, a common and serious manifestation of several psychiatric conditions. It refers to a loss of ego boundaries (Peterson, 1991). Regression occurs in severe depression, psychosis, delirium, dementia, and dissociation. Practically speaking, it refers to patients who are suffering with an inability to have a clear sense of their body and mind, who often are disoriented, and who have problems with routine sleeping and eating schedules. The

anti-regressive protocol (Tinnin, 1990) is a guideline for the primary care provider and the patient to decrease and hopefully stop the regression. It includes attempts to restore ego boundary-orientation by regulating sleeping and eating schedules; by maximizing physical safety, including closer observations by close friends or family members (who have well-defined ego boundaries of their own and who can provide positive social support); by removing dangerous items; and by resorting to grounding techniques to help restore the patient's sense of reality, orientation, eye-to-eye contact, physical grounding (feet on the ground), and object awareness (touching objects), etc.

5. *Self-Help Books.* Patient education is a valuable tool for the primary care provider in helping patients understand their problems more clearly. Below is a sample list of books that the provider may wish to consider suggesting to his or her patients; however, there are many patient education options available and providers should to seek out books that he or she considers particularly good.

The Authoritative Guide to Self-Help Books, John W. Stantrock
Mind Body Medicine, Daniel Goleman, Ph.D. and Joel Gurin, eds.
Ten Days to Self-Esteem, David D. Burns, M.D.
Feeling Good Handbook, David D. Burns, M.D.
Mastery of Anxiety and Panic, David H. Barlow, Ph.D. and Michelle G. Craske, Ph.D.
Courage to Heal, Ellen Bass and Laura Davis
Courage to Heal Workbook, Ellen Bass and Laura Davis
Victim No Longer, Michael Lew
The Castle of the Pear, Christophe Biffle
Workbook for Survivors of War, Joel Osler-Brende, M.D.
I Can't Get Over It: Trauma Survivors Handbook, Aphrodite Matsakis, Ph.D.
Adult Survivors of Childhood Abuse Workbook, Christine Courtois, Ph.D.

6. *Support and Self-Help Groups.* In addition to these self-help protocols, there are other useful self-help resources available for the primary care provider and the patient. A primary care provider can even facilitate the beginning of a patient-directed support group. Although the primary care provider may be too busy to lead many support groups, primary care practice can bring together patients with similar problems who could benefit from such groups. Primary care practitioners can play an important role in directing their patients towards each other, encouraging and supporting them sufficiently to engage their self-help skills. These self-help groups can serve all kinds of functions, but primarily serve as a means for mutual solace, education, and personal change (Self-Help Groups, "Harvard Mental Health Letter," March 1993). Such groups include Alcoholics Anonymous, Adult Children of Alcoholics, Veterans Centers, incest survivors and battered women support groups, local churches and/or religious centers, and provider supported/guided groups.

GENERAL LIVING PROBLEMS

General living problems include common issues faced by nearly everyone at one time or another. Although they may be common, that does not necessarily mean that everyone is capable of handling the particular problem or that the problem does not cause significant stress. It is estimated that general living problems may explain up to 90% of psychiatry seen in the primary care setting (Kathol, 1988). In a study of 1,081 college students, nearly 50% of the participants reported stress-related problems in living (Stamm, 1993). These problems include marital stress, occupational problems, academic problems, uncomplicated bereavement, parent-child conflicts, financial stress, noncompliance with treatment, and religious or spiritual issues.

In a primary care setting, it is possible to provide brief but effective therapy for many of these general problems in living. The most important thing you can do as the primary care clinician is to ask questions about the patient's problems and direct them to help or encourage their efforts to help themselves. It is very important to recognize that even though your health care resources may be limited, your community resources probably are not. Take advantage of local religious leaders like ministers, priests, rabbis, as well as friends of patients, local support groups, and local counselors. Also, as previously suggested, you could consider advising some of your patients with similar problems to get together and support each other.

In addition, stress management techniques can easily be taught and encouraged in a primary care setting. Antoni (1993) suggests four basic coping strategies for handling stress: (a) recognizing irrational thinking patterns or cognitive distortions; (b) receiving assertiveness training, which helps people to express wishes concretely but still respect the needs and desires of others; (c) providing information about the causes and signs of stress and aspects of specific illnesses; and (d) acquiring social support by recognizing the support available and augmenting the weak spots of a support network.

In the primary care setting, office visits are usually very brief and focused. For most patients, goal directed, brief therapy will be very effective. Just because you have only 15 or 20 minutes with a patient, do not assume that you will be ineffective. Primary care providers do a lot of bedside therapy—usually with very little training. There are several simple steps you can follow which will help you focus your brief therapy for general living problems. These are: (a) listen to and observe patients as they explain the problem; (b) ask patients how they are handling the specific problem; (c) educate patients about resources or ways to handle their specific problem; (d) explore alternatives with patients and help them to think about how to handle their problem; and (e) in some cases, give specific recommendations about what he or she should do. Remember, in terms of your qualities as a therapist, you need empathic ears, a willingness to be honest with the patient, a general positive regard for the patient as a human being, and a realization that medications are generally not necessary (Kathol, 1988). If these steps do not seem to be useful, you should consider referring the patient for psychiatric evaluation.

PRACTICAL APPROACH ALGORITHMS

Algorithms are certainly no substitute for the art of clinical practice, but they can serve as useful guides to decisionmaking in patient care. What follows is a series of algorithms based on how the patient presents his or her primary complaint. It should be noted that they are not necessarily dependent on the primary psychiatric diagnosis. Within the algorithms, there are references to the self-help protocols which have already been suggested.

In terms of the actual psychiatric symptomatology, references will be made for more detail. Remember, the approach here is simplified and geared for a busy primary care setting without access to many resources. The most important aspect of these guides is the ability to determine the etiology of the psychiatric symptoms and not just to treat them with psychotropic medication and stabilize. Of course, psychotropic medication can be helpful and may be an important part of the overall patient care. The primary care practitioner has an advantage in deciding on a course of treatment since he or she usually is already focused on overall mind/body health and getting the patient and patient's family involved in taking care of themselves.

Many primary care clinicians are incredibly busy and overburdened with a large volume of patients who have all kinds of health problems. If you can ask the questions and provide direction for your patients to be able to take responsibility for their own cases, both you and your patient will benefit. Shared responsibility can reduce the stress related to patient care for both the clinician and for the patient.

This shared responsibility may be particularly important for trauma-based patients. Asking the questions about trauma exposure can decrease the number of clinic/hospital visits which are confusing and reduce the number of misfires when the patient does not respond well to a standard medical treatment. Moreover, patients really appreciate that you want to know why they are having so many problems, which is a refreshing change from the "Take this pill" approach for both the patient and the caregiver.

The algorithms that follow include General, Depressed Patient, Anxious Patient, Substance Abusing Patient, Traumatized Patient, Somatizing Patient, Psychotic Patient, Suicidal Patient, and Self-Harming Patient.

CONCLUSION

The patients that many primary care practitioners have considered as problem patients or the patients "I just can't help" may in fact be the part of our population who have suffered from a trauma or significant stressors. These traumas could be dysfunctional family systems, childhood physical and sexual abuse, emotional and physical neglect, combat experience, earthquakes, floods, and other natural disasters, a random shooting in a subway, or any other of the major or minor traumas that we read about every day in the newspaper. One of the ways these patients try to correct the social, physiological, and psychological deficits they have experienced is by engaging the health care system.

Primary care providers are often on the front line and have a unique opportunity to recognize and treat many trauma-based problems for their patients. This opens many possibilities for education, prevention, and motivating patients to become involved in their own healing. Educational and preventive think-

GENERAL ALGORITHM:
Unclear Psychiatric/Medical Problem
History & Physical Exam/Trauma History/Mental Status Exam

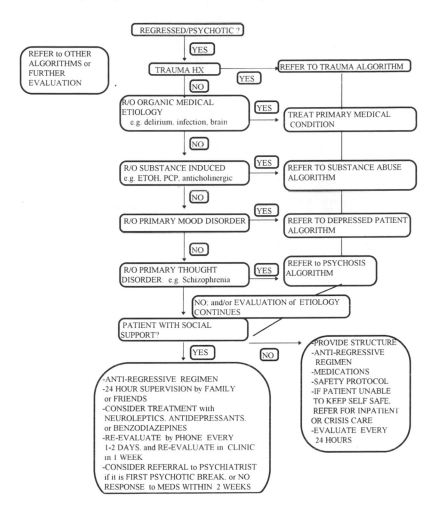

REGRESSED/PSYCHOTIC ?

YES

REFER to OTHER ALGORITHMS or FURTHER EVALUATION

TRAUMA HX → REFER TO TRAUMA ALGORITHM

YES

NO

R/O ORGANIC MEDICAL ETIOLOGY
e.g. delirium, infection, brain

YES → TREAT PRIMARY MEDICAL CONDITION

NO

R/O SUBSTANCE INDUCED
e.g. ETOH, PCP, anticholinergic

YES → REFER TO SUBSTANCE ABUSE ALGORITHM

NO

R/O PRIMARY MOOD DISORDER

YES → REFER TO DEPRESSED PATIENT ALGORITHM

NO

R/O PRIMARY THOUGHT DISORDER: e.g. Schizophrenia

YES → REFER to PSYCHOSIS ALGORITHM

NO, and/or EVALUATION of ETIOLOGY CONTINUES

PATIENT WITH SOCIAL SUPPORT?

YES

NO

-PROVIDE STRUCTURE
-ANTI-REGRESSIVE REGIMEN
-MEDICATIONS
-SAFETY PROTOCOL
-IF PATIENT UNABLE TO KEEP SELF SAFE, REFER FOR INPATIENT OR CRISIS CARE
-EVALUATE EVERY 24 HOURS

-ANTI-REGRESSIVE REGIMEN
-24 HOUR SUPERVISION by FAMILY or FRIENDS
-CONSIDER TREATMENT with NEUROLEPTICS, ANTIDEPRESSANTS, or BENZODIAZEPINES
-RE-EVALUATE by PHONE EVERY 1-2 DAYS, and RE-EVALUATE in CLINIC in 1 WEEK
-CONSIDER REFERRAL to PSYCHIATRIST if it is FIRST PSYCHOTIC BREAK, or NO RESPONSE to MEDS WITHIN 2 WEEKS

DEPRESSED PATIENT ALGORITHM

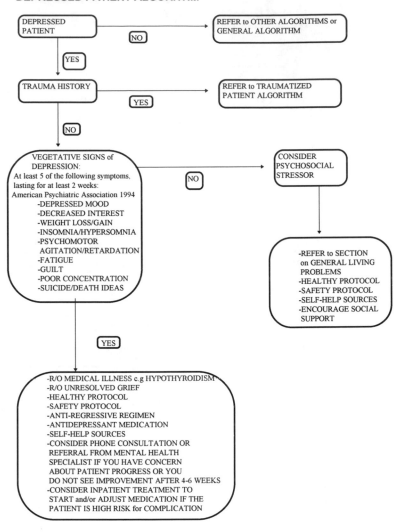

ANXIOUS PATIENT ALGORITHM

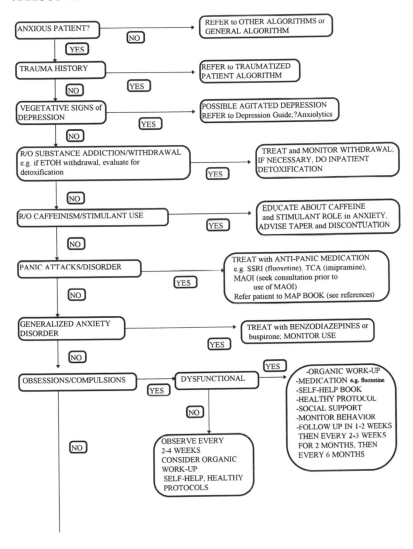

ANXIETY ALGORITHM CONTINUED :

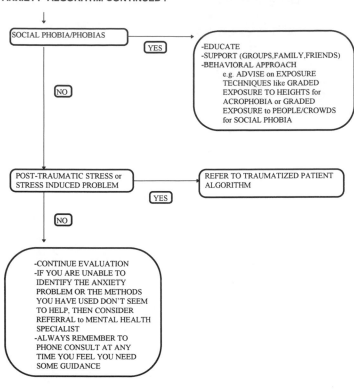

SOCIAL PHOBIA/PHOBIAS

YES

NO

-EDUCATE
-SUPPORT (GROUPS,FAMILY,FRIENDS)
-BEHAVIORAL APPROACH
    e.g. ADVISE on EXPOSURE
    TECHNIQUES like GRADED
    EXPOSURE TO HEIGHTS for
    ACROPHOBIA or GRADED
    EXPOSURE to PEOPLE/CROWDS
    for SOCIAL PHOBIA

POST-TRAUMATIC STRESS or
STRESS INDUCED PROBLEM

YES

NO

REFER TO TRAUMATIZED PATIENT
ALGORITHM

-CONTINUE EVALUATION
-IF YOU ARE UNABLE TO
IDENTIFY THE ANXIETY
PROBLEM OR THE METHODS
YOU HAVE USED DON'T SEEM
TO HELP, THEN CONSIDER
REFERRAL to MENTAL HEALTH
SPECIALIST
-ALWAYS REMEMBER TO
PHONE CONSULT AT ANY
TIME YOU FEEL YOU NEED
SOME GUIDANCE

SUBSTANCE ABUSE ALGORITHM

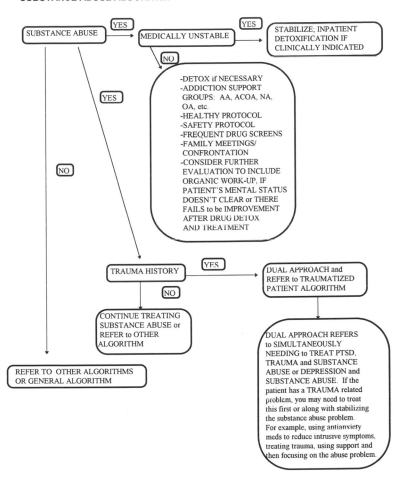

SUBSTANCE ABUSE — YES → MEDICALLY UNSTABLE — YES → STABILIZE; INPATIENT DETOXIFICATION IF CLINICALLY INDICATED

NO

-DETOX if NECESSARY
-ADDICTION SUPPORT GROUPS: AA, ACOA, NA, OA, etc.
-HEALTHY PROTOCOL
-SAFETY PROTOCOL
-FREQUENT DRUG SCREENS
-FAMILY MEETINGS/CONFRONTATION
-CONSIDER FURTHER EVALUATION TO INCLUDE ORGANIC WORK-UP, IF PATIENT'S MENTAL STATUS DOESN'T CLEAR or THERE FAILS to be IMPROVEMENT AFTER DRUG DETOX AND TREATMENT

YES

NO

TRAUMA HISTORY — YES → DUAL APPROACH and REFER to TRAUMATIZED PATIENT ALGORITHM

NO

CONTINUE TREATING SUBSTANCE ABUSE or REFER to OTHER ALGORITHM

DUAL APPROACH REFERS to SIMULTANEOUSLY NEEDING to TREAT PTSD, TRAUMA and SUBSTANCE ABUSE or DEPRESSION and SUBSTANCE ABUSE. If the patient has a TRAUMA related problem, you may need to treat this first or along with stabilizing the substance abuse problem. For example, using antianxiety meds to reduce intrusive symptoms, treating trauma, using support and then focusing on the abuse problem.

REFER TO OTHER ALGORITHMS OR GENERAL ALGORITHM

SOMATIZING PATIENT ALGORITHM

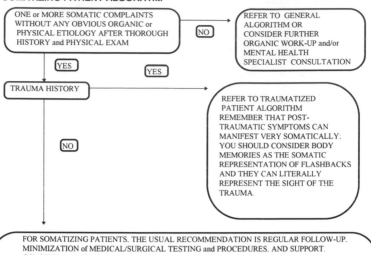

ONE or MORE SOMATIC COMPLAINTS WITHOUT ANY OBVIOUS ORGANIC or PHYSICAL ETIOLOGY AFTER THOROUGH HISTORY and PHYSICAL EXAM

[NO]

REFER TO GENERAL ALGORITHM OR CONSIDER FURTHER ORGANIC WORK-UP and/or MENTAL HEALTH SPECIALIST CONSULTATION

[YES]   [YES]

TRAUMA HISTORY

[NO]

REFER TO TRAUMATIZED PATIENT ALGORITHM REMEMBER THAT POST-TRAUMATIC SYMPTOMS CAN MANIFEST VERY SOMATICALLY: YOU SHOULD CONSIDER BODY MEMORIES AS THE SOMATIC REPRESENTATION OF FLASHBACKS AND THEY CAN LITERALLY REPRESENT THE SIGHT OF THE TRAUMA.

FOR SOMATIZING PATIENTS, THE USUAL RECOMMENDATION IS REGULAR FOLLOW-UP. MINIMIZATION of MEDICAL/SURGICAL TESTING and PROCEDURES. AND SUPPORT. CONSIDER ADVISING THE PATIENT to DRAW or WRITE ABOUT the AREA or BODY PART CAUSING the PROBLEM. ASK THEM TO FOCUS ON HOW THIS IS DECREASING OR INCREASING THEIR DAILY FUNCTIONING. ONCE THEY COMPLETE THIS TASK (remember to give them a specific time by which they should have completed the task). THEN ASK THEM TO WRITE OR DRAW ABOUT HOW THEY WANT TO CHANGE THINGS OR HOW THEY WANT THEIR BODY TO CHANGE AND WHAT THEY SHOULD DO IN ORDER TO GET THERE. THESE TASKS SHOULD BE ACCOMPLISHED ALONG WITH THE USUAL REGULAR SUPPORT.

TRAUMATIZED PATIENT ALGORITHM

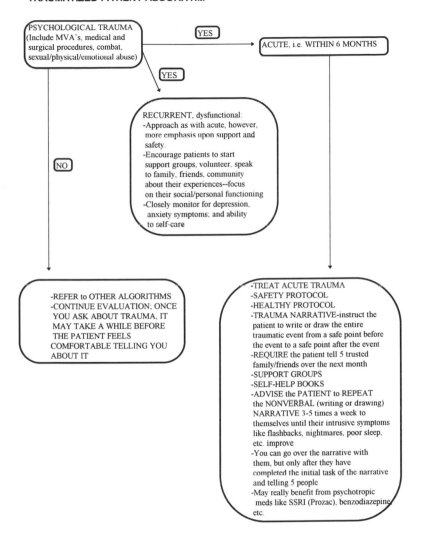

PSYCHOLOGICAL TRAUMA (Include MVA's, medical and surgical procedures, combat, sexual/physical/emotional abuse)

YES → ACUTE, i.e. WITHIN 6 MONTHS

YES

RECURRENT, dysfunctional:
-Approach as with acute, however, more emphasis upon support and safety.
-Encourage patients to start support groups, volunteer, speak to family, friends, community about their experiences--focus on their social/personal functioning
-Closely monitor for depression, anxiety symptoms; and ability to self-care

NO

-REFER to OTHER ALGORITHMS
-CONTINUE EVALUATION; ONCE YOU ASK ABOUT TRAUMA, IT MAY TAKE A WHILE BEFORE THE PATIENT FEELS COMFORTABLE TELLING YOU ABOUT IT

-TREAT ACUTE TRAUMA
-SAFETY PROTOCOL
-HEALTHY PROTOCOL
-TRAUMA NARRATIVE-instruct the patient to write or draw the entire traumatic event from a safe point before the event to a safe point after the event
-REQUIRE the patient tell 5 trusted family/friends over the next month
-SUPPORT GROUPS
-SELF-HELP BOOKS
-ADVISE the PATIENT to REPEAT the NONVERBAL (writing or drawing) NARRATIVE 3-5 times a week to themselves until their intrusive symptoms like flashbacks, nightmares, poor sleep, etc. improve
-You can go over the narrative with them, but only after they have completed the initial task of the narrative and telling 5 people
-May really benefit from psychotropic meds like SSRI (Prozac), benzodiazepine etc.

PSYCHOTIC PATIENT ALGORITHM

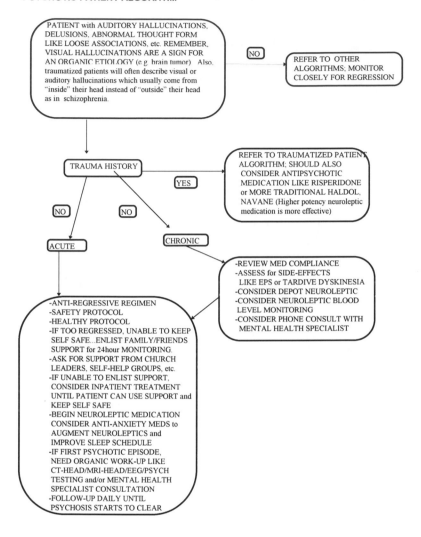

PATIENT with AUDITORY HALLUCINATIONS, DELUSIONS, ABNORMAL THOUGHT FORM LIKE LOOSE ASSOCIATIONS, etc. REMEMBER, VISUAL HALLUCINATIONS ARE A SIGN FOR AN ORGANIC ETIOLOGY (e.g. brain tumor) Also, traumatized patients will often describe visual or auditory hallucinations which usually come from "inside" their head instead of "outside" their head as in schizophrenia.

NO

REFER TO OTHER ALGORITHMS; MONITOR CLOSELY FOR REGRESSION

TRAUMA HISTORY

YES

REFER TO TRAUMATIZED PATIENT ALGORITHM; SHOULD ALSO CONSIDER ANTIPSYCHOTIC MEDICATION LIKE RISPERIDONE or MORE TRADITIONAL HALDOL, NAVANE (Higher potency neuroleptic medication is more effective)

NO

NO

ACUTE

CHRONIC

-REVIEW MED COMPLIANCE
-ASSESS for SIDE-EFFECTS
 LIKE EPS or TARDIVE DYSKINESIA
-CONSIDER DEPOT NEUROLEPTIC
-CONSIDER NEUROLEPTIC BLOOD
 LEVEL MONITORING
-CONSIDER PHONE CONSULT WITH
 MENTAL HEALTH SPECIALIST

-ANTI-REGRESSIVE REGIMEN
-SAFETY PROTOCOL
-HEALTHY PROTOCOL
-IF TOO REGRESSED, UNABLE TO KEEP
 SELF SAFE...ENLIST FAMILY/FRIENDS
 SUPPORT for 24hour MONITORING.
-ASK FOR SUPPORT FROM CHURCH
 LEADERS, SELF-HELP GROUPS, etc.
-IF UNABLE TO ENLIST SUPPORT,
 CONSIDER INPATIENT TREATMENT
 UNTIL PATIENT CAN USE SUPPORT and
 KEEP SELF SAFE
-BEGIN NEUROLEPTIC MEDICATION
 CONSIDER ANTI-ANXIETY MEDS to
 AUGMENT NEUROLEPTICS and
 IMPROVE SLEEP SCHEDULE
-IF FIRST PSYCHOTIC EPISODE,
 NEED ORGANIC WORK-UP LIKE
 CT-HEAD/MRI-HEAD/EEG/PSYCH
 TESTING and/or MENTAL HEALTH
 SPECIALIST CONSULTATION
-FOLLOW-UP DAILY UNTIL
 PSYCHOSIS STARTS TO CLEAR

SUICIDAL PATIENT

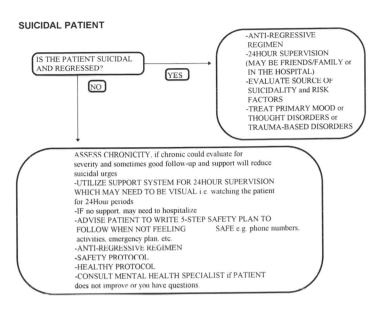

IS THE PATIENT SUICIDAL AND REGRESSED?

YES

NO

-ANTI-REGRESSIVE REGIMEN
-24HOUR SUPERVISION (MAY BE FRIENDS/FAMILY or IN THE HOSPITAL)
-EVALUATE SOURCE OF SUICIDALITY and RISK FACTORS
-TREAT PRIMARY MOOD or THOUGHT DISORDERS or TRAUMA-BASED DISORDERS

ASSESS CHRONICITY, if chronic could evaluate for severity and sometimes good follow-up and support will reduce suicidal urges
-UTILIZE SUPPORT SYSTEM FOR 24HOUR SUPERVISION WHICH MAY NEED TO BE VISUAL i.e. watching the patient for 24Hour periods
-IF no support. may need to hospitalize
-ADVISE PATIENT TO WRITE 5-STEP SAFETY PLAN TO FOLLOW WHEN NOT FEELING   SAFE e.g. phone numbers. activities. emergency plan. etc.
-ANTI-REGRESSIVE REGIMEN
-SAFETY PROTOCOL
-HEALTHY PROTOCOL
-CONSULT MENTAL HEALTH SPECIALIST if PATIENT does not improve or you have questions.

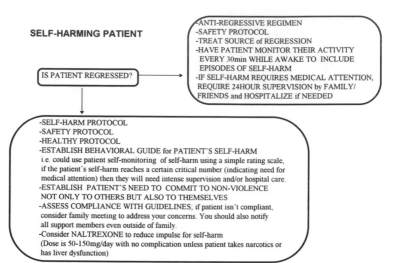

SELF-HARMING PATIENT

IS PATIENT REGRESSED?

-ANTI-REGRESSIVE REGIMEN
-SAFETY PROTOCOL
-TREAT SOURCE of REGRESSION
-HAVE PATIENT MONITOR THEIR ACTIVITY
  EVERY 30min WHILE AWAKE TO INCLUDE
  EPISODES OF SELF-HARM
-IF SELF-HARM REQUIRES MEDICAL ATTENTION,
  REQUIRE 24HOUR SUPERVISION by FAMILY/
  FRIENDS and HOSPITALIZE if NEEDED

-SELF-HARM PROTOCOL
-SAFETY PROTOCOL
-HEALTHY PROTOCOL
-ESTABLISH BEHAVIORAL GUIDE for PATIENT'S SELF-HARM
  i.e. could use patient self-monitoring of self-harm using a simple rating scale,
  if the patient's self-harm reaches a certain critical number (indicating need for
  medical attention) then they will need intense supervision and/or hospital care.
-ESTABLISH PATIENT'S NEED TO COMMIT TO NON-VIOLENCE
  NOT ONLY TO OTHERS BUT ALSO TO THEMSELVES
-ASSESS COMPLIANCE WITH GUIDELINES; if patient isn't compliant,
  consider family meeting to address your concerns. You should also notify
  all support members even outside of family.
-Consider NALTREXONE to reduce impulse for self-harm
  (Dose is 50-150mg/day with no complication unless patient takes narcotics or
  has liver dysfunction)

ing is needed for medical and surgical procedures, stress management, preventive health care, social support, and a self-help viewpoint.

Patients do better when they take an active role in a medical or surgical procedure (Bennett, 1993) Thus, to help reduce the stress of caregiving for the provider and the stress of healing for the patient, you should encourage your patients to design their own pre-surgical or pre-medical procedure program. For example, they should be involved in gaining information and education about the procedure and why they are having it done. They should have an opportunity to learn ways that they could decrease pain, decrease heart rate and be able to influence bodily function like their immune system, bowel activity, as well as other autonomic functions (Bennett, 1993).

Primary care providers usually excel in the areas of preventive health care and patient education. This aspect of the primary care setting is advantageous for trauma-based problems. The primary care provider will expect the patient to have basic health care needs met and patients will expect their primary health care providers to know and understand the latest and best treatments. So, this too can be expanded to reflect the latest information about violence prevention, the dangers and consequences of childhood physical and sexual abuse, the effectiveness of rapid debriefing after a traumatic event, etc.

The nature of primary care offices or clinics involves an interaction between someone who has a lot of skill and information (the caregiver) with someone who has a need or problem (the patient) and the desire for it to get better or go away. People can be encouraged to begin to take responsibility for their own care and healthier lifestyles, but they must be given that responsibility. There is an enormous opportunity to take advantage of limited clinical resources and encourage the development of patient organized self-help or support projects. The primary care provider in the best-case scenario can become a guide, shaman, and mentor about how to become healthy.

Spiegel's studies at Stanford on social support show that people who are the least connected socially have twice the death rate of a connected group, even after smoking, alcohol, physical activity, and obesity are considered (Spiegel, 1993). A decrease in immune function is noted for single, separated individuals, but an unhappy marriage is also a health hazard. Primate studies suggest that positive relationships may possibly decrease the flow of stress hormones, such as cortisol (Spiegel, 1993).

The more technically advanced health care becomes the more primary care providers will need to pay attention to the potential healing value of the human-to-human interaction. The most important point about trauma-based psychiatry and primary care is the willingness to listen and hear about reasons for why "My chest hurts" when there is no cardiac problem or why "My head hurts" when there is no migraine. The reasons are obvious. It is a matter of listening to what the patient tells you and being willing to believe that their traumatic experiences really can cause somatic pain and symptoms. Just as you routinely try to isolate which bacteria is causing Mrs. Smith's urinary tract infection, so too must you pursue what events or traumas preceded the onset of Mr. Jones's persistent atypical chest pain. Instead of giving in to frustration when patients do not fit into the usual constellation of symptoms for a particular diagnosis, your challenge is to keep an open mind and be willing to ask the question "What happened to you?", not just "What is wrong with you?" (Bloom, 1992).

References

Antoni, M. H. (1993). Stress management: Strategies that work. In D. Goleman & J. Gurin (Eds.), *Mind body medicine: How to use your mind for better health.* New York: Consumer Reports.

Barsky, A. J., Woll, C., Barnett, M. C., & Cleary, P.D. (1994). Histories of childhood trauma in adult hypochondriacal patients. *American journal of psychiatry,* 151, 397–401.

Beaumont, G. (1992). Patients at risk of suicide and overdose. *Psychopharmacology,* 106 (Supplement), S123–S126.

Bennett, H. L. & Disbrow, E. A. (1993). Preparing for surgery and medical procedures. In D. Goleman and J. Gurin (Eds.), *Mind body medicine: How to use your mind for better health.* New York: Consumer Reports.

Blank, A. S., Jr. (1994). Clinical detection, diagnosis, and differential diagnosis of post-traumatic stress disorder. *Psychiatric clinics of North America, 17* (2), 351–383.

Bloom, S. (1994). The Sanctuary model: Developing generic inpatient programs for the treatment of psychological trauma. In M. B. Williams and J. F. Sommer (Eds.), *Handbook of post-traumatic therapy* Westport, CT: Greenwood Press.

Briere J. & Runtz, M. (1987). Post sexual abuse trauma: Data and implications for clinical practice. *Journal of interpersonal violence, 2,* 367–379.

Gaylord J. J. (1975). Wife-battering: A preliminary survey of 100 cases. *British medical journal, 1,* 194–197.

Harvard Mental Health Letter. (1993). *Self-help groups,* 9 (9, 10). Boston, MA: Harvard Mental Health Newsletter.

Herman, B. (1991). Naltrexone shown to decrease frequency of self-injurious behavior. *Psychiatric times, (August),* 32.

Kathol, R. (1988). Psychiatry in the medically ill. Course curriculum in med/psych residency. Training at University of Iowa, Iowa City.

Kroenke, K. (1994). Physical symptoms in primary care: Predictors of psychiatric disorders and functional impairment. *Archives of family medicine, 3* (9), 774–779.

Mehlman, Kanoti, & Orlowski. (in press). Informed Consent to Amnestics.

Neale, A. V. (1991). Behavioural contracting as a tool to help patients achieve better health. *Family practice, 8* (4), 336–342.

Peterson, K. C. Prout, M. F., & Schwartz, R. A. (1991). Post-traumatic stress disorder: A clinician's guide. New York: Plenum Press.

Putnam, F. W., Guroff, J. J., Silberman, E. K., Barban, L. & Post R. M. (1986). The clinical phenomenology of multiple personality

disorder: Review of 100 recent cases. *Journal of clinical psychiatry,*
47, 285–293.

Roberts, S. J. (1994). Somatization in primary care: The common presentation of psychosocial problems through physical complaints. *Nurse practitioner,* 19 (5):47, 50–56.

Saxe, G. N. (1994). Somatization in patients with dissociative disorders. *American journal of psychiatry,* 151, 1329–1334.

Segal, J., Hunter, E. J., & Segal, Z. (1976). Universal consequences of captivity: Stress reactions among divergent populations of prisoners of war and their families. *International journal of social science,* *28,* 593–609.

Spiegel, D. (1993). Social support: How friends, family, and groups can help. In D. Goleman & J. Gurin (Eds.), *Mind body medicine: How to use your mind for better health.* New York: Consumer Reports.

Stuber, M. L., Nader, K., Yasuda, P., Pynoos, R. S., & Cohen, S. (1991). Stress responses after pediatric bone marrow transplantation: Preliminary results of a prospective longitudinal study. *Journal of the American academy of child and adolescent psychiatry,* 30 (6), 952–957.

Tinnin, L. (1990). Personal correspondence of anti-regressive measures.

Tomb, David A. (1994). The phenomenology of post-traumatic stress disorder. *Psychiatric clinics of North America,* 17, (2), 237–250.

Walker, E. A. (1993). The prevalence rate of sexual trauma in a primary care clinic. *Journal of the American board of family practice,* 6 (5), 465–471.

1 0

Kelengakutelleghpat: An Arctic Community-Based Approach to Trauma

Michael J. Terry

At some time in our lives, most of us have dreamed of running away to a place at the far end of the world to create a new stress free life. Here we can see what awaits us in the real version of this fantasy. This unique paper, which details the story of an Arctic Alaska Native community, reframes the traditional white western perception of treatment— both physical and mental. In "Kelengakutelleghpat," Michael J. Terry offers us a window into a world where entire communities can come together to address issues of trauma. This paper saddens us because it brings the reality of trauma to our fantasy, but it heartens us because it offers hope for a cooperative, community approach in which everyone in the community is part of the healing.

Many people imagine Alaska to be a vast, barren, and frozen landscape dotted with peaceful remote Eskimo villages; each one isolated from the stresses and traumas common to crowded city environments. In truth, however, Alaska offers a diversity of climates and landscapes, as well as a plethora of the contemporary consequences of traumatic stress. While it is true that village life moves at a slower pace, a hidden epidemic of trauma and its effects frequently goes unnoticed, particularly as trauma impacts the indigenous paraprofessionals who form the backbone of the Alaska's health care delivery system to those villages.

This paper describes the lessons learned while developing a program of support for these village-based clinicians. In the face of overwhelming primary and secondary traumatic stress, a critical incident stress management program was revised to emphasize collaboration and traditional Native values.

BUSH ALASKA

The "Bush" is the Alaskan version of Australia's "Outback." Most tourists get about as far into Alaska as the city of Anchorage. But then most residents of Anchorage never get into the Bush either. You cannot access most of the Bush by car because much of it is off the road system, yet most of Alaska's 570,374 square miles of land and 86,051 square miles of water lies within the Bush. It is as diverse as it is huge, comprising at least five distinct geoclimatalogical zones that vary from rainforest to treeless tundra.

The Bush is also home to most of Alaska's Native residents, who have lived here continuously for several thousand years, yet by 1990 accounted for less than 16% of the population. Approximately 45,000 Alaska Natives (Eskimos, Athabascans, Aleuts, and American Indians) live in the 171 small, remote villages without roads, hospitals, or physicians (Alaska Population Overview, 1991 Estimates).

Although this introduction may sound like the beginning of a piece from the travel channel, my intent is really to emphasize that this is a different world. Practical and researched approaches that worked "outside" (in the lower 48 states) may not transplant here easily. The stunted development of a critical incident stress management program for Native para-professional health-care workers illustrates this problem.

THE COMMUNITY HEALTH AIDE PROGRAM

This paper is an outgrowth of an Alaska Native health-care program that has now become a model for health care delivery systems from rural and inner-city America to the frontiers of developing nations. In fact, when Senator David Pryor queried the Congress' General Accounting Office for innovative ways to improve access to health care, the GAO responded with a report lauding Alaska's unique Community Health Aide Program (U.S. General Accounting Office, 1993).

The Community Health Aide (CHA) is a Native para-professional trained at a regional center to provide primary health care to her village under the remote supervision of a physician. The average CHA is 34 years old, female (94%) with four children, was raised in the village where she works, and has been providing primary care for about seven years. She was selected by her people for this role and then employed by the local Native regional health corporation. Most CHAs have completed high school or have a GED (Alaska Area Native Health Services, 1991).

Basic CHA training consists of 4 four-week sessions of classroom instruction, skills practice, and clinical experience with at least 200 hours of village clinical experience between each session. Instruction is provided by physician assistants (PA) and nurse practitioners at four training centers located in Nome, Bethel, Sitka, and Anchorage. The CHA is also required to complete Emergency Trauma Technician (ETT) and/or Emergency Medical Technician (EMT) classes as part of her basic training. At the end of the two to four years it typically takes to complete this training, the CHA enters a formal preceptorship with a physician, physician's assistant, or nurse practitioner (NP), who reviews the skills and evaluates the CHA's actual patient assessments and interventions. The CHA is then eligible to sit for a comprehensive exam. Upon passing, the CHA is certified as a

Community Health Practitioner (CHP). Thereafter, each CHP must re-certify every six years. Re-certification requires 24 hours of annual, continuing medical education and successful completion of a re-certification exam.

CHA/P's function under a tiered set of medical standing orders which are based on their level of training (I-IV) and are authorized by a physician in a regional hospital. These standing orders list conditions that the CHA/P may treat without routinely contacting a physician. The interview, exam, and treatment for each of these approved conditions is found in the Community Health Aide Manual (CHAM), sometimes referred to as the "Health Aide Bible." The physician routinely contacts each clinic daily to discuss patient care. Health Aides present cases that are problematic or that fall outside their standing orders. In addition, a physician is available for emergency calls at all times. A Health Aide's typical workload at the village clinic might include prenatal exams, laceration repair, immunizations, treating ear or upper respiratory infections, arranging patient travel to see a specialist, assisting a visiting dentist, drawing blood for lab tests, or dispensing chronic medications ordered by the physician.

Daily clinic management and personnel supervision of the Health Aides are handled by a team of Coordinator/Instructors (C/Is) who are CHPs, RNs, PAs, or NPs. C/Is routinely fly out to the village clinics to evaluate, coordinate, and support the CHA/Ps. But the C/I is much more than a remote supervisor and frequently offers emotional support, counseling, and problem-solving guidance to the Health Aide in the course of her work.

The Community Health Aide Program actually began in the 1950s as a means of dispensing TB medication in the villages of Alaska and evolved into the current formal program in 1968. Now celebrating its 27th year, the program is a key component of the Indian Health Service (IHS) system and is supported as well by funding through the state of Alaska.

The Norton Sound Health Corporation's Program

Fifty-six Norton Sound Health Corporation Health Aides provide services to 15 villages along the coasts of Norton Sound and the Bering Straits in Northwest Alaska and logged over 40,000 patient care visits in 1994. A survey has shown that patients are about as satisfied with Health Aides as they are with physicians. Patients were either satisfied (53%) or very satisfied (14%) with the care rendered by the Health Aide, compared to satisfied (51%) and very satisfied (19%) after a visit to a physician (Norton Sound Health Corporation, 1990).

These CHAs are employees of the Norton Sound Health Corporation (NSHC), a regional Native health corporation located in Nome, a town of 3,500 people and the local regional center. NSHC operates a 21-bed regional hospital, a 15-bed nursing home, and an eight-bed alcohol/drug treatment center, as well as an outpatient medical/dental program and public health nursing department.

An On-Going Problem

The Health Aide is a vital link in the Alaskan health care system. Thus the recruitment, retention, and training of these key personnel is a primary concern. A state task force estimated that the training costs alone equal $17,000 per Health Aide, a figure that omits expenses involved in the on-going field training, medical supervision, advanced education, and recruitment efforts. However, Health Aide attrition rates chronically run between 20% to 30%.

By 1988 the statewide attrition rate had already compromised the quality of care in the villages all over the state, prompting the U.S. Congress to appropriate an additional $10 million for the program. Job stress and low pay were seen as the primary causes of turnover. The increased funding allowed for improved salaries and for the hiring of additional Health Aides in impacted areas. Unfortunately, much of the stress in the Health Aides' lives was unmitigated by these improvements (Caldera, 1988, Williams, 1990).

THE NEED FOR A CRITICAL INCIDENT STRESS MANAGEMENT PROGRAM

Many of the situations ordinarily faced by Health Aides on a regular basis would necessitate Critical Incident Stress Debriefings (CISD) had they occurred in other areas of the country where Critical Incident Management Programs are more common than they are in Bush Alaska. Debriefings are routinely held when the incident-related stressors increase the risk for the development of traumatic stress (Mitchell & Bray, 1990; Mitchell & Everly, 1993).

For example, in the small remote villages in Alaska, the Health Aide is related by blood or marriage to most, if not all of the residents, and is often a close friend to many others. Also, many rescues require evacuation to regional hospital by airplane, usually with lengthy response and/or transport times. Sometimes these flights are accomplished under dangerous conditions with adverse and extreme weather situations.

Although press coverage and lawsuits about village rescues are rare, the Health Aide is often in the public eye of the entire village during an emergency. Blame and misunderstanding are not uncommon. If a resident experiences a poor outcome at a receiving hospital, the Health Aide is often the first to be blamed, in spite of a flawless performance by the Health Aide. In some villages, the Health Aides have an adversarial relationship with the most influential families or village leadership. Poor communication, perceived slights, and the lack of emotional support all add to the stress.

Even spousal support is not guaranteed. The husband of the

Health Aide might deny emotional support because of the difficulties provoked by the cultural role reversal. The Health Aide is usually the breadwinner, and is dependent on husband or family to care for the children while she runs the clinic, is on call, or leaves suddenly on an emergency. Because of increased family duties, the husband may find it difficult to engage in even occasional subsistence hunting and fishing activities.

The Health Aide often wears a counselor's hat as well. Because of the unavailability of mental health personnel in the village, the Health Aide must support the victim's family and other community members in distress as a result of the incident. One hat Health Aides truly dislike wearing is the undertaker's; imagine the distasteful responsibility of cleaning up a relative or friend's body before an autopsy or village funeral.

THE DEVELOPMENT OF A LOCAL PROGRAM IN CISM

In an attempt to address these needs, a plan for the development of a Critical Incident Stress Management (CISM) program was drawn up. It would include services not only for Health Aides, but also hospital staff, Nome police and fire services, the volunteer ambulance service, pilots, state troopers, and Department of Corrections officers. In the fall of 1993, the Norton Sound Health Corporation Board of Directors approved the budget for a Trauma Support Services Program (TSSP).

Twenty-eight peers and counselors representing all services were trained in basic CISD. Since that time debriefings have been provided for a wide variety of traumatic events. Several pilot deaths, village homicides, cluster suicides, an employee suicide, intense, unsuccessful rescues, and the drowning of a Health Aide's infant daughter are among those incidents debriefed.

Advanced training seminars were held dealing with a variety of subjects, such as multiple trauma families, grief, stress management, care for the caregiver, and Depression: Awareness, Recognition and Treatment (D/ART). The mental health and the self-care components of the basic CHA training were beefed up statewide as recognition grew over the effects of traumatic stress. Several Health Aides went through an intensive mental health and substance abuse instruction and then continued their training through special telephone audio-conferences with college credit. Presentations and seminars about CISM, traumatic stress, and the TSSP were provided in state and circumpolar forums.

Although resources were insufficient to develop a full-fledged employee assistance program, several components were initiated. EAR, a 24-hour, telephone-access counseling and referral service, was contracted to provide anonymous services for village- and Nome-based employees. Alcohol intervention and recovery services were provided for health aides with demonstrated problems, and, as a result, 20% of all the health aides in the region received treatment over a two-year period. Numerous referrals to the Community Mental Health Center and the Bering Sea Women's Shelter were initiated for Health Aides and their families for various issues, including depression, domestic violence, child abuse, panic attacks, and PTSD.

WHY THE PROGRAM DID NOT WORK

After listing all the accomplishments of the Trauma Support Services Program, how can I say that it didn't work? This is not to say that all the debriefings, trainings, treatments, and referrals did not help anyone. More people were informed about traumatic stress, CISD, and mental health issues in general. Many people expressed heartfelt thanks and relief after a debriefing. Some Health Aides became interested in professional mental health careers. The persistence and support has helped build trust. Several Health Aides have celebrated sobriety anniversaries.

I suppose that in the spirit of self-edification, I should just elaborate more fully on the first two years or simply stop now while I'm ahead. But this paper and this book have been adduced in the spirit of inquiry rather than commendation.

From this reflective vantage point, I can see that the program was superficial; its roots did not reach deep enough and were insufficiently extensive to bring about real change for the Health Aides. The program was unable to deal with one of the real consequences of trauma—the victimization of the rescuers. But before we take on that issue, I want to briefly evaluate some of the standard interventions used by this program, and by other programs as well, that have questionable efficacy and appropriateness in this setting or in other Native communities.

CISD is often a preventative mainstay of a Critical Incident Stress Management program. We continue to provide debriefings in our program, but with some modifications, because in our experience the individuals who seemed to benefit most from the debriefings were those whose roles or responsibilities in the rescue were clear and those who lived in Nome rather than a village.

Because Health Aides have frequently overlapping roles as village residents, family members, and rescue workers, their responsibilities in village situations can be multiple and confusing. A similar problem occurred among paramedics and firefighters in Southern California. When some aspect of the rescue brought about the connection to another vital role, such as a spouse or parent, added distress often ensued. Referrals and follow-ups were more frequent after the debriefing. It seemed that the experience of wearing multiple hats brought up meanings that were not sufficiently processed in a debriefing setting designed to help accommodate occupational roles and meanings. Stuhlmiller addresses similar concerns debriefing rescue workers following the San Francisco Bay Area earthquake in 1989 (Stuhlmiller, 1994).

The teaching phase of the debriefings had mixed reviews. Bio-behavioral explanations of the stress response were used during debriefings to assist in understanding symptoms and behaviors that, in themselves, were disconcerting. This approach appealed to village teachers and Health Aides possibly because of their previous training. However, this model is somewhat at odds with a Native worldview, which may explain why village public safety officers, village national guardsmen, council members, and leaders rarely seemed to find this explanation helpful (Swinomish Tribal Mental Health Project, 1991, Mander, 1992).

Most of our debriefings were conducted with participants seated in a circle with only one person speaking at a time, and this format was familiar and easy for most village CISD participants. Periods of silence and attention to one speaker are traditionally accepted. The circle has been increasingly familiar in Alaska since Talking Circles were introduced to the state by Native Americans from elsewhere.

On the other hand, the CISD emphasis on personal self-care and individual responsibility for the practice of basic stress management routines generally failed to find much support. More stress is placed on social identification and behaviors in the village. Group exercise, like basketball and even aerobics, has been more favorably received. Moreover, any dietary recommendations must be translated into available Native subsistence foods (Jensen & Nobmann, 1994).

A family/significant other support program has proven difficult to ignite for a number of reasons. The Health Aide's role is sometimes already resented by the spouse and family for reasons mentioned earlier. A significant investment by a counselor of time within the village is required if work with the family is to be undertaken at all. The limited number of Health Aides in each village often precludes getting enough families together to form a stable support group or auxiliary. Handouts taken home are rarely read by the family members or spouse. We are still considering a Peer Counselor Program. However, as I will explain later, we are directing more efforts toward group programs.

Referrals for counseling and substance abuse met with uneven success. Maintaining sobriety in the absence of a local village support group is difficult at best, and a village-based aftercare program is not yet available. While sponsors are available through a toll-free number into Nome, they were only sporadically used. Alaska Natives with alcohol problems are typically binge drinkers who often go weeks or months between binges; because of this, the standard addictions treatment models have been criticized as inappropriate by counselors in Nome and elsewhere in Alaska.

The Health Aides rarely followed up mental health referrals. Because of funding limitations, counseling is available in the village only for two to four days every second or third month with caring, but inadequately-trained, paraprofessionals (Graf, 1992). Regular counseling for the Health Aide or her family would require moving to Nome and resigning her position.

"WE'RE GONNA NEED A BIGGER BOAT"

About a year ago, as it was becoming clear that the program as originally planned was just not enough to do the job that was needed, I was reminded of a scene from the movie *Jaws*. Roy Scheider and Richard Dreyfus are heading out on open seas looking for the Great White Shark. Suddenly they see him, and he is *enormous*. Roy Scheider, suddenly looking pale and becoming weak in the knees, swallows hard and murmurs, "We're gonna need a bigger boat." I had that same feeling of being in over my head and unprepared.

A CISM program, even when implemented and run appropriately, is intended primarily as a preventative approach to traumatic stress. It was never intended to offer treatment (Mitchell & Everly, 1993). I realized early on that more was needed, but I had no idea of the magnitude of what we were up against. The Health Aides not only treat victims, they are themselves victimized in numerous ways. Directly and indirectly, Health Aides are traumatized; from the sequelae of historical events that occurred before they were born, to psychological, physical, and kinship proximity to victims, and even by personal violence within their own homes and communities. The consequences of these traumas are only just beginning to be understood.

CULTURAL AND HISTORICAL TRAUMA

More and more each year, the devastating effects of the cultural traumas endured by Alaska Natives and American Indians becomes public. A genocide of Holocaust proportions threatened the very survival of the indigenous peoples of this continent (Stannard, 1992).

In Alaska, it began with raging epidemics from the early 19th Century through the middle of the 20th. Alaskan physician and historian Robert Fortuine chronicles these plagues in his book, *Chills and Fever*. Smallpox, influenza, measles, and the Spanish influenza came in lethal waves, devastating whole villages and regions in the space of a few months to a few years and leaving in their wakes crippled and starving survivors in social disintegration. The tuberculosis epidemics that brought about the Community Health Aide Program were widespread by 1930 and remain endemic today throughout the state (Fortuine, 1989). The tragedy can be measured, not by the quantitative numbers of the dead, but by the qualitative loss of the great repository of culture that was buried with those who perished (Napoleon, 1991).

The physical deaths were only the beginning. Capricious and incongruent government economic policies, religious intolerance of Native beliefs, cultural suppression through schooling, forced relocation, and boarding schools continued the assault (Stamm et al., 1994; Stannard, 1992). These events secured an enduring dependency and moved the leadership of the Alaska Natives Commission to remark, "the shift in emphasis from self-control to a control imposed by powerful others encompassed all realms of Alaska Natives' lives, from governance to health. The insidious effects of this imposition have grown to enormous proportions" (Alaska Natives Commission, 1993, p. 7).

In addition to this widespread loss of control, the chronic effects of historical traumas have multiple intergenerational consequences. Alcohol and drug abuse, suicides, and family violence have roots in previous traumatic experiences. Families may be perceived as multi-generational emotional systems and the consequences of previous trauma are thus passed down to subsequent generations, affecting their ability to mourn, create support systems, and cope with subsequent traumatic stress (Bowen, 1988; Danieli, 1985; Figley, 1978; Paul, 1967). Some of the problems of Health Aides today may derive from their traumagenic heritage.

CONTEMPORARY TRAUMAS

Another source of both direct and indirect traumatization for Health Aides arises from another more contemporary epidemic—escalating episodes of both intentional and accidental violence in villages throughout Alaska. Deaths of Alaska Natives due to injuries were nearly 10 times that of the United States as a whole. Homicide rates were two to three times the U.S. average, while suicide rates were nearly double. Suicides outnumbered homicides by a two-to-one margin (Brenneman et al., 1992; Kettl, 1993). Mortality has now become more of a social than a medical problem.

The Health Aide is often the only medically-trained person in a village when these episodes of violence and death occur. Not only does the Health Aide treat the victim, but she must then turn around and assist the family in its distress. In addition, the Health Aide may be connected to the victim by blood, marriage, or friendship. Thus the Health Aide is repeatedly exposed to multiple primary and secondary traumatic stressors (Figley, 1994). Anecdotal data from this region and around the state shows that the range of these maladies is extensive, and includes psychopathology and addictive disorders, developmental disability, as well as physical illness and disability.

The information presented earlier in this section shows a clear risk for a Health Aide developing a post-trauma disorder. Health Aides are exposed to an overwhelming diversity of traumatic stressors, from direct victimization and exposure to primary traumatic stressors to indirect intergenerational effects and multiple secondary traumatic stressors. We have no way of knowing the true extent of the problem, but the signs are all too obvious: anniversary distress, sleep problems, intrusive symptoms, enduring startle reactions, avoidance behaviors, and frequent complaints of somatic problems, among others.

The legacy of loss brought about by the epidemics is rarely discussed and less frequently mourned (Napoleon, 1991). Add to this the escalating losses from intentional and unintentional trauma in the villages, a pervasive sense of loss of control, and you have a recipe for depression. When Beck's Depression Inventory was administered to Health Aides during a D/ART seminar, six of the 10 respondents scored 10 or higher. During the past two years, one CHA was hospitalized for a suicide attempt and three were referred for suicidal ideation.

Alcohol abuse is the source of another Bush epidemic: Fetal Alcohol Syndrome and Fetal Alcohol Effect (FAS/FAE). The more obvious FAS runs at rates two to four times the national average (Brenneman, et al., 1992). But the more insidious FAE is of more concern for the Health Aide Program, since it is a hidden handicap, as much as 10 to 15 times more prevalent than FAS, and can be a source of problems in training and job performance. The at-risk population, as measured by frequency of binge drinking in pregnant mothers, varied from 14% to 71% around the state (Hild, 1992).

Like other village residents, Health Aides risk physical illness and disability. Health Aides live in areas that are often endemic for tuberculosis and hepatitis. Consequently, treatment and absenteeism issues related to these diseases are not uncommon. Alcohol-related accidents, as mentioned earlier, are extremely common, and Health Aides are among the victims of a variety of traumas including head injuries, ankle fractures, and back strains. Other alcohol-related problems also show up, like frostbite and hypothermia from exposure while intoxicated, or alcoholic hepatitis and gastritis.

Physical injuries from domestic violence are another cause of missed work days for Health Aides. The Health Aide is all too often victimized by physical and emotional abuse within her own home. Anecdotal information from program directors, coordinator/instructors, and trainers from around the state as well as from the Health Aides themselves, testifies to a chronic history of childhood molestation, rape, and domestic violence. Thus, our health care providers also become our patients.

THE RISK OF TRAUMATIC-IMPAIRMENT

Van der Kolk's 1994 article on the evolving psychobiology of post traumatic stress prompts some interesting questions regarding Health Aides' performance under stress and resources for coping with other significant life events off the job. His review of the literature showed that under normal conditions traumatized individuals functioned normally, but in stressful situations they respond as they would to a traumatic stressor. Their actions can be exaggerated, illogical, and self-defeating (van der Kolk, 1994). Even innocuous events are then misperceived and a crisis response initiated.

As described repeatedly in this paper, a Health Aide works under anything but normal conditions. In addition to the traumatic stressors, the Health Aide is exposed to many significant work-related stressors, such as isolation from peers, extensive on-call periods, overwhelming job responsibilities, and unrealistic community expectations. Off-work stressors may consist of domestic responsibilities and environmental problems. Many of our Health Aides tell us that they still do all the meal preparation and cleaning even though working full-time. In addition, they take over childcare as soon as they get off work. Other stressors of village life might include inadequate housing, overcrowding, poverty, and a lack of electricity and running water, and sewage disposal (Alaska Dept. of Labor, 1991; Marshall & Soule, 1994).

Van der Kolk's theories could account in part for some of the problems that Health Aides and their supervisors find most frustrating. In a crisis mindset, there is a tendency to see every event as a crisis and to respond in like manner. Minor changes may be met with alarm. Rather than seek clarification from a perceived slight, a grudge may be nursed for years. Health Aides often report feeling attacked by another Health Aide or village resident. The response many times is to withdraw, blame, or take the offensive. Altered psychobiological mechanisms might partly explain the prevalence of shame, blame, and abuse, or lateral violence, that is associated with the unresolved grief and loss from the historical traumas of Native peoples (DeBruy et al., 1993).

Life-in-crisis mode can mean failure to plan ahead, to organize effectively, or to take routine preventive measure on a regular basis. The provision of preventive care services, such as scheduling visits for routine pap exams or immunizations, seems trivial when compared to rescue work. Equipment maintenance and the pre-planned ordering of supplies can get displaced when everything that happens seems like a priority. Concomitant problems, such as the limitations inherent in FAE and impoverished or rigid coping styles imported from dysfunctional relationships, could additionally influence one's ability to cope. Co-morbidity, such as addictive disorders, depression, or physical illnesses, also factors into the equation.

It is important to see this situation from a contextual perspective that considers stressors, coping, and consequences in an interactive format (Stamm, 1994; Green, 1985). Of principal concern here is whether crisis mode responses, concomitant problems and/or co-morbidity might seriously deplete, undermine, or shun resources potentially available for use in coping with traumatic stressors, stressful life events, and work-related stressors faced by the Community Health Aide.

This problem raises a number of interesting ethical, legal, and research issues. Some of these issues are not new for chemically-impaired workers, law enforcement personnel, and high-risk occupations exposed to trauma. From the discussions in this book and elsewhere about the extensiveness of secondary traumatic stress and STSD, as well as the hard-wired dysfunctional responses of a traumatically-altered neurological system, new questions must now be addressed.

From the perspective of occupational health, should a traumatically-impaired worker be subjected to additional stressors? What kind of work limitations would apply in this situation? From the human resource perspective, what criteria would managers use to detect and refer a traumatically-impaired primary care provider? The Americans with Disabilities Act precludes screening or inquiring about disabilities in the course of hiring a new worker, but can an employer realistically modify the workplace to accommodate hidden needs? Should clinical assessment tools be employed in a preventive mental health attempt to screen for disabilities or obtain early interventions? From a risk management perspective, is patient safety compromised by the continued use of a traumatically-impaired employee? What advice can we give to the employers of indigenous paraprofessionals in these high-risk environments?

But even if the resources were available to provide therapeutic interventions, there would still be additional concerns about treatment efficacy, cost, and cultural appropriateness; not to mention that if all chemically and traumatically-impaired Health Aides were referred for treatment, adequate clinic coverage would be difficult to ensure. If treatment implications are overwhelming, and CISM and preventive measures underwhelming, what can be done to protect and support the frontline providers of Alaska's health care delivery system? A new approach was proposed as a result of an enlightening incident that moved the program in a different direction. The following story formed a pivotal base, guiding us towards a strategy that embraced traditional values and collaboration as a means of support and healing.

KELENGAKUTELLEGHPAT

In February 1993, a debriefing was requested by the Health Aides in Savoonga following the suicide of a 14-year-old girl with a gun. The CISD team flew out to St. Lawrence Island in the frozen Bering Sea. It was a clear day and the coastline of Siberia could be seen off in the distance. Savoonga is a Siberian Yup' ik village that grew from a reindeer camp to a chartered city with over 500 inhabitants, and is one of the few places in Alaska where everyone is fluent in their native language as well as English.

We planned to provide three debriefings to several groups who had been involved in the search and the cleaning of the body. But following these debriefings, I was asked to meet with the City Council, whose members were very concerned about the safety of other children who they had learned were talking about suicide. My one-semester course in conversational Siberian left me mostly in the dark while the Council members talked, so I called the team to tell them what I had learned about the potential for copycat or cluster suicides. The team called to Nome for additional help. The meeting was breaking up when I came back and I was told that I should meet with the Traditional Council.

When I called the president of the Traditional Council, I asked if I could meet with both Councils together. He explained how difficult that would be. The Councils had not met jointly for years and there was a lingering distrust of each other's motives. But under the circumstances, he said he would be willing to give it a try. The City Council also agreed. Although awkward at first, relationships were quickly mended and some hard issues confronted openly in a spirit of cooperative dialogue. When these village leaders met the assembled community the next day, they stood side by side in a unified demonstration of their commitment to their people and their determination to make their village a safe place for their children.

During their joint meeting the day before the community gathering, they discussed the traditional values that had worked for so long and cast about for some way to apply them now. After an interpreter told me what was being discussed, I asked if there were a word of phrase that people used that conveyed these values of community stewardship and protection. After much discussion, an elder murmured something which was quickly taken up by the group with much excitement. I asked my interpreter what was going on.

"Kelengakutelleghpat," he told me with a smile. "It's a whaling term. It means 'watching out for each other'!"

The next day the community responded to that watchword and to a vision. They formed a team of representatives from most of the village organizations, created a logo, published a newsletter, and substituted family activities for two nights a week of gambling.

COLLABORATION AND TRADITIONAL NATIVE VALUE

The community leaders in Savoonga demonstrated, in a very natural way, the power and potential of collaboration and traditional values. The impetus for their collaboration was the need to protect a precious resource—their own children. They illustrated the core values that I believe must be woven through a program if it is to provide the protection and support for Health Aides or any similar group of providers. With respect to these leaders, I offer here my understanding of these values and the means by which our program seeks to embody them.

Collaboration is itself a key virtue in a traditional values system. These leaders drew from their traditional values of collective rather than individual action to guide not only their actions that day, but to empower the phrase that had become the metaphor for their vision. They also held discussions that respected the views of the individual while accessing the wisdom of the group.

Traditional values also honor the connectedness of each member of the group to each other and to the environment. This is crucial because trauma is more than an event or a psychobiological process. It is a way of thinking that sees things only in parts, without the perspective of the whole. Carving up a village into opposing agencies, each with an allegiance to a different institution, is a product of this kind of thinking. Trauma is a force that severs our connections; that cuts us off from that which has meaning. In a sense, all healing is some form of reconnecting to that which has meaning and value in our lives. Traditional values underscore the serviceability of these connections.

Collaboration and traditional values both emphasize social

support as a means to create opportunities for collective sharing of ideas, stories, aid, and resources. Hobfall and Vaux maintain that creating social support is a basic human need. Groups, like the village leaders in Savoonga, endeavor to protect that which has value for them and may even sacrifice that which is less valuable in order to accomplish this goal (Hobfall & Vaux, 1993). Activities consistent with this value would emphasize collective efforts over individual ones and could be achieved through face-to-face interactions or through innovations in telecommunications.

A collective learning format would also embody this value. Collective learning is a kind of teamwork where the organization or group learns how to improve a situation or solve a problem better than individuals working in isolation or at odds with each other. Direction for the group or organization occurs from within rather from the top down. According to Senge many Fortune 500 companies are realizing that their ability to adapt to rapid change depends upon their ability to engage the collective minds of everyone in the company as a "learning organization" (Senge, 1990).

The collective learning approach by groups employs a special form of dialogue as a means of collaboratively sharing ideas. This kind of dialogue is quite different from a regular discussion, and generates a spirit of inquiry and the freedom to risk. It is grounded to a commitment to participation, to the group process, and to a belief that the group can access meaning that cannot be accessed individually (Bohm, 1994; Senge, 1990).

A New Approach

Based on these values, our Community Health Aide and Trauma Support Services Programs are making substantive changes in both the content and direction of their services. All of our changes are still early efforts and we welcome correspondence and feedback from individuals and organizations involved in similar ventures. The modifications in our approach to CISD were presented earlier in this paper. The revised debriefing format, as well as the approaches that follow, seek to create forms of participation, connection, social support, and collective learning that embrace the values learned from our experiences.

One caveat, however, is necessary. Providing support services is an undertaking that will never succeed if done piecemeal; there seems to be an under-investment phenomena that dooms efforts that fall short of a critical mass. Furthermore, services that are carried out piecemeal risk creating additional trauma because of their gaps, inconsistency, and conflicting intentions. Programs that were intended to help may thus become the inadvertent source of further distress.

Public relations and education campaign: Having identified lack of social support and unrealistic community expectations as major work stressors for the Health Aides, public relations and education campaigns were undertaken. These included radio spots from Board Members, corporate leaders, physicians, village leaders, and the Health Aides themselves. Pamphlets detailing the educational preparation and professionalism of the Health Aide Program were designed and distributed region-wide. Poster boards with pictures and descriptions were placed in the hospital and outpatient department. Hundreds of "Hug a Health Aide" buttons were produced and handed out. A radio interview, aired frequently, portrayed the CHA Program as a model used worldwide. To date, this program has improved awareness of the Health Aide as a limited and valuable resource within the corporation. We are still evaluating whether village residents will see the Health Aide as more valuable and will act in ways to collectively protect that resource.

Self-governance and new services: NSHC became one of the first groups nationwide to operate under a self-governance compact for health care delivery. Villages are empowered to re-engineer the system to meet their needs rather than conform to the directives and regulations of the Indian Health Service. Village-based counselors, physician assistants, and nurse practitioners could substantially improve the situation for Health Aides by creating collaborative teams in the village. The addition of counselors to the village team should decrease Health Aide exposure to secondary traumatic stressors, since the counselors would more often provide support and counseling to families and victims. The Trauma Support Services Program could then also assist the new counselors as they are exposed to these stressors. Health Aide turnover statewide seems to be decreased when the CHAs work together with mid-level practitioners who reduce the professional isolation, share the workload, and ameliorate the unrealistic expectations of the village patients toward the Health Aide.

Monthly clinic audio-conferences: Every month the Alascom teleconference operator calls each clinic on a speakerphone and links them all up with the administrative team here in Nome. Any other department that is requested by a clinic can also be linked to participate. Sessions typically last one to two hours and are very informal. Most of the agenda is set at the onset of the session by suggestions from the clinics. After the agenda is finished, the Health Aides remain on the line under the direction of a selected leader to conduct a Health Aide Association audio-conference. In this telephonic experiment in collective learning, many positive and useful ideas have been generated.

The CHAIN: Each clinic was set up with a computer and linked to a server in Nome. The Community Health Aide Information Network currently offers e-mail, medical record management, patient education information, and medical reference sources for the Health Aide. Future plans include diagnostic interactive programs, distance delivery education, a CD-ROM server, and Internet access.

Health Aides can contact each other more frequently through the e-mail system that connects to the CHAIN server through an 800 number. Previously, contacts were infrequent and brief, because these long-distance calls between villages were paid for by the village councils. Following a stressful event, a Health Aide can seek support from selected individuals or collectively from the group. Relationships forged by pairs and small groups during the Peer Support Colloquium can be maintained or strengthened.

Peer Support Colloquium: Quarterly meetings are planned with groups of 10 to 15 Health Aides from various clinics. Most of the three-day retreat will be spent in dialogue and collective learning activities. In a facilitated, supportive environment, Health Aides will share with each other stressful situations and creative approaches based on methods used by the National Health Service Corps. Traditional healing methods and massage therapy may be available.

INNOVATIVE APPROACHES ELSEWHERE

In Alaska and elsewhere around the globe, unique programs are being launched to provide support to front-line primary care and mental health providers, and to render assistance to those suffering from traumatic stress and its sequelae. The programs described here represent attempts to provide support services that benefit remote areas, that incorporate traditional Native practices and values, or that perform both of these. It is hoped that these examples will serve to stimulate productive modifications with appropriate local alterations.

Village Response Teams: It is common for one or more village CHAs to provide interventions in mental health emergencies. In the past several years, a new approach to collaborative teamwork has emerged. The Village Response Teams (VRT) concept began in Kodiak and has now been used successfully in several areas of Alaska. The VRT consists typically of one or more CHAs, CHRs (Community Health Representatives), Village Public Safety Officers (VPSO), teachers, school counselors or administrators, students, ministers, elders, and other community leaders. Agencies in the regional centers, such as the state troopers, Department of Family and Youth Services (DFYS), legal services, and the community mental health center staff communicate regularly with the teams and provide assistance as needed. The VRT initiates a coordinated response using local resources early in a crisis and then calls for appropriate additional backup from agencies in the area regional center as necessary.

The VRT eliminates blame on one individual, improves agency and community communication, and more effectively manages critical situations. In a case of suspected child abuse, for example, the mandated report is filed by the entire team rather than a single person. Once the report is turned in, the team does not simply sit by and wait for the DFYS or the state troopers to send someone to the village. Instead, the team meets to offer suggestions and resources that could be deployed from within the village.

The VRT may also employ a watchdog approach to prevent the escalation of on-going or potential problems, such as patients with chronic mental illnesses or families with limited resources and histories of abuse. Using a problem-solving approach, the VRT meets regularly and surveys problems and resources for the village. Services may be as simple as locating an elder to assist with childcare or collecting food for families whose demand overstresses their resources.

Rural Human Services Program: The College of Rural Alaska at the University of Alaska-Fairbanks offers a certificate and Associate of Arts degree in a program that trains Native counselors to provide services back in their remote villages. The program, which emphasizes Alaska Native traditional values, takes about two years to complete, and the total cost, which includes tuition, room and board, and books, but not travel, is $10,280. Several villages are now supporting counselors that they have sent through this program.

Alaska Native Family Systems' "In the Spirit of the Family": This program, originally developed through a contract with the National Native Association of Treatment Directors of Canada, is offered throughout Alaska. Three- and five-day workshops are provided upon request in a village for group or community-wide training. Regularly scheduled five-day classes for individuals are held at specified locations. The approach focuses on cultural strengths and resiliency rather than on problems. The teaching is based on historical experiences common to indigenous peoples and presents family and community development skills which are then practiced in supportive environments.

Alaskan Peer Helper Programs: Recognizing that young people seek out peers for help with their problems, this school-based program provides a structured format for creating peer helper programs with partnerships of local schools, villages, towns, and community mental health centers. The peer helper initially attends a three-day training, and then receives on-going training through additional seminars or classes, such as those listed above, become available in each village.

Swinomish Tribal Mental Health Project: Provides comprehensive, culturally-appropriate mental health programs to the Swinomish and the Upper Skagit communities in the state of Washington. The project has developed its own college-accredited training program, as well as innovative approaches for a wide variety of problems. The project offers numerous examples of ways to incorporate contemporary mental health services and traditional Native values and practices. A book describing these efforts is used as a text in several mental health training programs in Alaska (Swinomish Tribal Mental Health Project, 1991).

Prairie and Northern Critical Incident Group: This program offers both CISD and community debriefings in the Canadian Provinces of Manitoba and Saskatchewan. The group combines professional intervention and follow-up, peer support, and community empowerment as part of its services and programs presented in the remote areas of Canada (Ramsey, 1993).

CONCLUSION

The Community Health Aide is often the sole health care provider in the remote villages of Bush Alaska. She is frequently confronted with numerous lifestyle, environmental, and work-related stressors. As a consequence of her job, she also knows the concomitant effects of both primary and secondary traumatic stress. Recent research and discussions, including those in this volume, raise concerns about potential traumatic impairment and about the adequacy of our interventions in situations such as those facing the Community Health Aide.

Some programs and approaches that produced excellent results elsewhere seem wholly inadequate in the face of these interacting influences. However, a trend towards autonomy and self-governance is spreading, not only among the villages of Alaska but among tribes in other states as well. This new mood emphasizes collaboration and traditional Native values, which promote meaningful re-connections, participation, collective wisdom, and social support. Since the effects of trauma seem to disrupt these same elements, it seemed reasonable and prudent to take advantage of this paradigm shift and incorporate these values into our support programs.

The insights and experiences presented in this paper are held out to the reader in the theme of collaboration and support that animates the spirit of Kelengakutelleghpat. It is sincerely hoped that, through our collective wisdom and sharing, we may continue "watching out for each other."

REFERENCES

Alaska Area Native Health Service. (1991). *Alaska CHA program description*. Anchorage, AK: Alaska Area Native Health Service.

Alaska Department of Labor. (1993). *Alaska population overview, 1991 estimates*. Juneau, AK: Alaska Department of Labor.

Alaska Natives Commission. (1993). *Report of the task force of the Alaska natives commission*. Anchorage, AK: Alaska Natives Commission.

Barnett-Queen, T. & Bergmann, L. H. (1991). Posttrauma response programs. Presentation at the 7th Annual International Society for Traumatic Stress Studies, Washington, D.C.

Bohm, D. (1994). The shared power of dialogue. *Metanoia*, *1* (1), 94.

Bowen, M. (1988). *On the differentiation of self: Family therapy in clinical practice*. New York: Jason Aronson.

Brenneman, G., Middaugh, J., Wainwright, R., McMahon, B. & Templin, D. (1992). Human health trends in the Arctic. *Arctic research of the United States*, *6*, 17–22.

Caldera, D. (1988). *Alaska community health aide program in crisis*. Anchorage, AK: Alaska Area Native Health Board.

Danieli, Y. (1985). The treatment and prevention of long-term effects and intergenerational transmission of victimization: A lesson from Holocaust survivors and their children. In C. R. Figley (Ed.), *Trauma and its wake: The study and treatment of post-traumatic stress disorder.* (Vol. 1) New York: Brunner/Mazel.

DeBruyn, L., Eagle Chasing, L. K., Jordan, M. B. & Obago, L. (1993). Reclaiming our sexuality: Healing from historical trauma and child sexual abuse. Presented at the 5th Annual National Association for Native American Children of Alcoholics Conference, Albuquerque, NM.

Figley, C. R. (1995). Compassion fatigue: Toward a new understanding of the costs of caring. This volume.

Figley, C. R. & Sprenkle, D. H. (1978). Delayed stress response syndrome: Family therapy implications. *Journal of marriage and family counseling*, *4*, 53–59.

Fortuine, R. (1992). *Chills and fever*. Fairbanks, AK: University of Alaska Press.

Graf, M. (1992). *Why village counselors fail.* (unpublished manuscript).

Green, B. L., Wilson, J. P. & Lindy, J. D. (1985). Conceptualizing post-traumatic stress disorder: A psychosocial framework. In C. R. Figley, (Ed.), *Trauma and its wake: The study and treatment of post-traumatic stress disorder*. (Vol. 1) New York: Brunner/Mazel.

Hild, V. (1992). Fetal alcohol syndrome in Alaska: Has our time bomb already exploded? Presented at the Northwest Alaskan FAS/FAE Conference, Nome, AK.

Hobfoll, S. E. & Vaux, A. (1993). Social support: Social resources and social context. In L. Goldberger & S. Breznitz (Eds.), *Handbook of stress: Theoretical and clinical aspects*. New York: Free Press.

Jensen, P. G. & Nobmann, E. D. (1994). *What's in Alaskan foods*. Anchorage, AK: Alaska Area Native Health Service.

Kettl, P. (1993). Homicide in Alaska Natives. *Alaska medicine, 35* (2): 168–171.

Mander, J. (1992). *In the absence of the sacred*. San Francisco, CA: Sierra Club Books.

Marshall, D. L. & Soule, S. (1994). Proceedings of the Alaskan and Russian natives' health and social issues conference. *Alaska medicine, 36* (3):151–158.

Mitchell, J. T. & Bray, G. (1990). *Emergency services stress*. Englewood Cliffs, NJ: Prentice Hall.

Mitchell, J. T. & Everly, Jr., G. S. (1993). *Critical incident stress debriefing*. Ellicott City, MD: Chevron Publishing Corporation.

Napoleon, H. (1991). *Yuuyaraq: The way of the human being*. Fairbanks, AK: University of Alaska, Fairbanks College of Rural Alaska.

Norton Sound Health Corporation. (1990). *Health survey 1990*. Nome, AK: Norton Sound Health Corporation.

Paul, N. L. (1967). The role of mourning and empathy in conjoint marital therapy. In G. H. Zuk & L. Boxzormenyi-Nagy, (Eds.), *Family therapy and disturbed families*. Palo Alto: Science and Behavior Books.

Ramsey, B. (1993). Community crisis intervention in Canada. Presented at the IX Annual International Congress on Circumpolar Health, Reykjavik, Iceland.

Senge, P. M. (1990). *The fifth discipline*. New York: Doubleday.

Stamm, B. H. & Stamm, H. E. (1995). Creating healing community: An historical native American approach. Trauma, Loss, and Dissociation Conference, Washington, D.C.

Stamm, B. H., Stamm, H. E., & Weine, S. (1994). Genocide and communal identity: Shoshone Indians and Bosnian Muslims. Presented at the 10th Annual Conference of International Society for Traumatic Stress Studies, Chicago, IL.

Stamm, B. H. (1995). Contextualizing death and trauma: A preliminary endeavor. In C. R. Figley (Ed.), *Death and trauma*. (Manuscript under review).

Stannard, D. E. (1992). *American holocaust*. New York: Oxford University Press.

Stuhlmiller, C. M. (1994). Occupational meanings and coping practices of rescue workers in an earthquake disaster. *Western journal of nursing research, 16*, (3), 268–287.

Swinomish Tribal Mental Health Project (1991). *A gathering of wisdoms*. LaConner, WA: Swinomish Tribal Community.

U.S. General Accounting Office. (1993). *Health care access: Innovative programs using nonphysicians*. Gettysburg, PA: U.S. General Accounting Office.

van der Kolk, B. A. (1994). The body keeps the score: Memory and the evolving psychobiology of posttraumatic stress. *Harvard review of psychiatry, 1*, 253–65.

Williams, F. (1990). *Fiscal year 1990 community health aide status report*. Anchorage, AK: Alaska Area Native Health Service.

Creating Virtual Community:
Telehealth and Self Care Updated

B. Hudnall Stamm

This chapter offers another new way of addressing community. What is our place in this shrinking globe? Our traumatic material seems more than ever to be shared thanks to changes in the transmission of information in the news media. Lives are lived at an ever increasing pace. What options can exist for development of community? This paper examines options for creation of virtual community using emerging technologies that are distance insensitive. The rapidly changing information and telecommunications environment can also be used to create friendships and to empower our caregiving, both to our clients and patients as wells as to ourselves and our professional peers.

Over half of the chapters in this book direct one toward community for effective Self-Care. For many, however, connecting with community can be quite difficult, particularly for professionals who work in remote areas. Less ob-

---

AUTHOR'S NOTE: The principles of virtual community as a protective factor for secondary traumatic stress have in large part remained the same since this chapter was first written in 1995. However, the number of and degree of access to technology-based resources have grown exponentially. When this paper was first written, probably less than 25% of the readers had access to the Internet. Now, it is likely that more than 75% of you use the Internet (Stamm, 1998). More importantly, technology is less expensive and easier to use, making it a realistic tool for increasing our ability to do our work well. Accordingly, I have kept intact the core of this chapter but updated the technological information to reflect current resources.

vious are those professionals whose isolation comes from their schedules or from working with colleagues who cannot or will not form a supportive community. Therefore, what kinds of community-based resources are available to these isolated professionals?

One expanding resource area is telehealth. Broadly defined, telehealth is any medical (or more correctly, health care) activity that uses telecommunications (see Nickelson, 1998 for a discussion of terminology). Stereotypically, telecommunications conjures up images of fancy video transmissions, fiber optics or the use of other high-tech equipment, and/or savvy, sophisticated computer programmers. Yet the most common telehealth/telemedicine techniques involve common garden-variety tools such as telephones, fax machines, and basic computer skills. Telehealth applications encompass a broad range of activities, including direct patient services, supervision, education, and research (Stamm, 1998). This paper introduces some of these basic applications, particularly the use of e-mail, as a means of developing professional community for supporting the isolated professional.

CONTROL, COMPETENCY, AND SECONDARY TRAUMATIC STRESS

Susceptibility to Secondary Traumatic Stress stems from two basic, and related, areas: (a) lack of control and (b) questions of competency. Questions of competency, at least in part, arise from the professional's feelings of lack of control of traumatic material. Therefore, controlling the trauma is a necessary component of competency. When people feel as if they are prepared, or at least have the ability to act positively during an event (that is, to exert some control during the event), there is a better outcome (Hartsough & Myers, 1985; Janoff-Bulman, 1992; Stamm, 1993, 1995; Stamm, Varra & Sandberg, 1994). When people feel as if they have no control the prognosis is quite poor (e.g., Herman, 1992).

Direct control, however, is not always possible when dealing with traumatic stress. In these situations, monitoring or limiting the professional's exposure and/or validating his or her distress over lack of control may be the keys to regaining authority over the traumatic material, and thus a renewed sense of competency. Positive peer social support and supervision—perhaps the best method to deal with the consequences of exposure to other's traumas—are crucial elements in preventing or at least blunting Secondary Traumatic Stress (e.g. Hartsough & Myers, 1985; McCann & Pearlman, 1990; Pearlman, in this volume; Pearlman & Saakvitne, 1995; Rosenbloom, Pratt & Pearlman, in this volume; Catherall, in this volume; Terry, in this volume; Saranson, Levine, Basham, & Saranson, 1983).

Consulting with colleagues yields other benefits—namely, access to information, whether through direct links to the colleague or indirectly through databases containing colleagues' work. This contact can increase competency, offer opportunities for direct control, or enhance the professional's ability to understand and interpret feelings about the situation. Difficult situations become easier to manage when one is well-informed; informed decision-making strengthens control and sustains competency. Therefore, issues of competency, as well as control, hinge to some degree on direct and indirect access to collegial information.

MEDICAL INFORMATICS: INDIRECT ACCESS TO COLLEAGUES

Because of advances in technology, access to collections of collegial information is becoming easier and, in many cases, cheaper. This emerging field of information science, or *informatics*, is often housed in the academic departments of *Decision Science* or *Li-*

brary Science. Most professionals are accustomed to searching professional electronic databases. With the advent of the Internet and the ability for computers to be linked to each other, it is possible to have a Virtual Library which has global online access. These resources can be text based or they may be multimedia—what is called the World Wide Web (WWW). One of the great advantages of this technology is *hypertexting*, or electronic links to other topics and papers. In a hypertexted journal article it is possible to link a citation in a paper to the actual paper. For example, if this book were online and hypertexted, when we said "(Stamm, in this volume)" with the click of a mouse you would find yourself in the introduction written by Stamm. This is such a powerful medium, if you have used hypertexted materials once, you will probably notice when it is not there. While creating documents in Hypertext Markup Language (HTML) used to be difficult, automatic hypertexting is standard in many word processing programs.

Websites, or multimedia resource locations, can be accessed in a number of ways including from the home or office computer through the use of a modem or through one of the other direct communication links that are becoming available. Increasingly, public areas such as airports and malls have kiosks and jacks for computing-on-the-go. Various web sites are available through commercial online services but the most powerful professional level ones are generally maintained by libraries or institutions. Through United States federal funding, the National Library of Medicine has made Medline available free online at http://www.nlm.nih.gov/databases/freemedl.html. Other search engines, such as PsycInfo (http://www.apa.org/psycinfo), provide subscription or a mix of free and subscription services. Most databases link to the growing number of full text journals. Some institutions provide databases which even facilitate printing an article on your own printer.

In addition to online databases, many professional resources are available on compact disk to facilitate rapid and accurate access to information. These products can supplement or even replace the multitudes of diagnostic guides, medical texts, and informational texts that have traditionally been used.

Using a portable version of the electronic database, The Brigham & Women's Hospital at Harvard Medical School has replaced traditional texts with handheld pocket computers called Personal Digital Assistants (PDAs). These PDAs, used by the residents, contain nearly all of the prescription and diagnostic information that a person could use—the equivalent of 10 to 15 large medical reference texts (Labkoff, 1995). Similar technology is being used to develop medical language translators—computers programmed to translate standard medical phrases into a multitude of languages. The caregiver simply chooses the appropriate term from the side written in the caregiver's native language and the computer speaks the equivalent phrase in the language of the patient. These translators are constructed to give meaningfully equivalent phrases rather than literal translations (Brooks, 1995). Many home health agencies use handheld computers to facilitate patient care. Rather than having to transfer information into a patient's chart after each visit, the health care worker simply synchronizes (downloads) the information on the handheld computer with the patient's chart.

All of these tools can be used effectively and easily by the caregiver to improve patient care and improve his or her real and imagined competency. None of these tools can replace good clinical judgment, nor were they intended to do this. What they can do, and do well, is to provide rapid easy access to information so that the practitioner can make informed decisions.

E-MAIL AND DISCUSSION LISTS: DIRECT ACCESS TO COLLEAGUES

Beyond the telephone, e-mail is perhaps the most commonly used type of telehealth. This technology is computer-based and uses a worldwide network of computers to relay messages to people who have access to the network. While most academics have network access through their institutional affiliations, rapidly proliferating commercial services like America Online, Prodigy, and Delphi provide widely available access to e-mail options. Freenets—community-based free access organizations —offer yet other sources of connectivity.

Two basic types of messaging take place: mail is sent by one person to another person (or private e-mail) and mail sent to a central distribution point for redistribution to anyone who subscribes to that distribution list. The latter type of e-mail comes in several forms commonly known as bulletin boards (bbs), listservs, chat lines, Usenet discussion lists, or electronic conferences. Moreover, these interactions can take place in delayed time (receiver picks up message after the sender has sent it) or real-time (receiver gets message at the same time the sender sends it). Regardless of the form, the basic technology is the same.

This type of communication can be used for the development of friendships, for sharing data, for transferring papers and other files, for teaching, for consultation, and for supervision. Many people, who normally avoid writing letters because of time constraints, find excitement in this easy-to-use and expeditious form of information transfer. Moreover, the standards of good manners that have developed for e-mail are much less formal than letter writing and thus, e-mail communications take less time and effort to compose. Also, depending on the location of the sender or recipient, the widespread networks of computers result in negligible cost differences compared to other types of communication.

All of the features mentioned above work together to create one of the most interesting aspects of the Internet—most communications are world-wide. For example, one listserv conversation might have contributors from many countries. This results in providing global perspectives to solving practical problems. The net result has been to enlarge the scope of conceptual and/or theoretical discussions enhancing the opportunities for multicultural thinking and tolerance.

VIRTUAL COMMUNITY DEVELOPMENTS

A practitioner can seek direct consultation on difficult problems, ask for supervision, or simply discuss his or her experiences with other colleagues. In these ways, the professional can begin to create a peer-group network of support without leaving the office. The community is real in the sense that real relationships can develop, but since the participants in this community may never meet face to face, it has a virtual aspect to it. These communities are developing worldwide as a reflection of the changes in the workplace and in technology.

These "Fingertip Communities" can improve the caregiver's access to opportunities for self-care, which in turn improves the probability of mentally healthier caregivers, ultimately leading to better care-giving. In the scope of education, virtual community offers distinct advantages in that the virtual community takes the information to the person rather than taking the person to the information (Stamm & Rudolph, in press). Moreover, this type of continuing education is situation specific and has a regular flow that is directly connected to the caregiver's life. Much remains to be learned about the extent to which virtual community can (or should) replace face to face education; however, it is possible to obtain all of one's continuing education or even a complete degree online.

One of the most common forms of virtual community is the online professional forum. These groups are sometimes called a "chat group" although in the strictest sense of the word, a chat group is real time and a professional forum may be delayed or real time. These forums can be used to disseminate new research and treatments or to discuss "hot topics." Requests for information can be posted; answers usually are returned quickly and apply directly to the problem at hand. However, professional forums are not the only type of professional resource available. Supervision and mentoring and professional forums are also options for most people.

Training, Supervision & Consulting

One of the promising aspects of telehealth is an improved ability to provide training, supervision, and consultation. A number of training programs around the world are working toward incorporating e-mail into their curriculums. Bold visions suggests the possibility of doing the complete advanced degree programs online. While it is not likely that entire accredited clinical training programs will be online in the immediate future, portions of training programs are already being conducted online. For example, I routinely use e-mail for supervision of students, both while they are on campus and when they are off campus on internships, practica, or finishing dissertations. In several cases, entire dissertations were conceived, planned, and executed using the Internet. In many cases, over 2,000 miles separated the student and teacher. E-mail supervision is supplemented by periodic residencies during critical times such as data analysis phase or pre-defense preparation. Proposal meetings and some defenses are held using teleconferencing.

Other programs in a number of disciplines are using e-mail for supervision. Marshall University School of Medicine was one of the early adopters of the Internet for training and supervision. "At the Marshall University School of Medicine students...serve extended rotations (up to nine months in family practice, ob/gyn, pediatrics, surgery, etc.) in rural clinics and hospitals around West Virginia. They submit their patient encounter logs and correspond with their faculty via e-mail who supervise their curriculum" (McCarthy, 1995).

University of Maine's U.S. government funded interdisciplinary program "Training for Health Care for Rural Areas Project," was another early adopter, conducting graduate health professions training via the Internet, using computer conferencing and e-mail (Kovacich, 1995). The astute reader will quickly notice that many of the above examples are from rural areas. And in fact, many of the developing applications are grassroots and born of necessity, or what one colleague called BWCW (Because We Can't Wait) programs (Terry, personal communication, March 16, 1995). In other places, linking people becomes more formalized and may be known as EPSS (employee performance support system) (Brown, 1995).

While e-mail systems are becoming more common in urban and rural settings, e-mail supervision can be of particular importance in remote areas. Recruiting and retaining health-care providers in remote areas is a difficult issue worldwide. In Australia, studies over the past decade have indicated that (a) students from rural secondary schools are less likely than students from metropolitan secondary schools to take undergraduate medical courses and (b) those from rural areas are more likely to enter rural practice than those from metropolitan areas. However, because of the low base rate for students from rural areas, the majority of rural providers originate from urban areas (Jones, 1994). Place of origin notwithstanding, for rural providers, greater isolation and patient needs translates into more continuous hours of coverage, fewer opportunities for respite or continuing education, and increased risk of burnout and compassion fatigue (Office of Technology Assessment, 1991; Stamm, 1998).

Regardless of the background of the provider, the practitioner in an isolated area faces challenges not usually faced by those in urban areas. For example, rural providers may encounter a wider range of problems since they are the primary caregivers for an area. Thus, they may have to practice at the edges of their expertise, or even outside of it simply because they may be the sole caregiver in a region (for example, see Bills, in this volume). The following story, posted to Rural-Care, an Internet discussion list illustrates the point.

...I practiced in Alaska for nearly two years just out of graduate school. While I never attempted to hide the fact that I was a new grad, my age and life experience often thrust me into situations where I was expected to know much more than I did... I am a child and family therapist, and in rural practice, having a specialty often means that there are few (or none) with whom to consult. I have a strong sense of responsibility to the children and parents whom I serve, and in Alaska, I felt isolated and often questioned my knowledge base—finally to the extent that I began looking for post graduate training programs. I left Alaska to obtain more training in child therapy. The fellowship was a meaningful experience and I value what came out of the year I spent; however, if I had had access to e-mail consultation I probably would not have felt the push to move closer to consultation and training (Rawlins, 1995).

In sum, e-mail seems to have an important role to play in the training and supervision of people in many different types of settings. This style of supervision enhances the supervisor's ability to serve student needs and expand the physical training setting, thus allowing the student to work in-vivo without having to move the supervisor to the student. Moreover, advanced training can be provided to the professional in the field from senior colleagues and from people with particular expertise (Stamm & Rudolph, in press). While there are technical and ethical difficulties that must be addressed, the benefits of this type of communication seem to justify solving these difficulties.

Friendships and Mentoring

One of the simplest and most effective elements of self-care is friendships. While it is not likely that online relationships will, or should, replace face-to-face ones, they can be a boon to the professional caregiver. One of the advantages of professional relationships in comparison to personal ones is the shared interest in the professional topic. Online relationships afford the opportunity to discuss professional issues to one's heart's content without boring friends and family members with the details of one's work. In addition, many people have found that their social connections have fallen prey to busy schedules. The advantages of e-mail is that the notes can be written at the convenience of the author and read at the convenience of the recipient. It is not necessary for both people to be online at the same time.

Consulting with one's colleagues and discussing ongoing work is easier. Because of the ease of transferring papers and other materials over the net, peers can provide feedback in a timely and easy manner regarding work in progress. For example, a number of the papers in this book were edited in a matter of days because of electronic transfer. Moreover, these relationships can provide a place to try on ideas about career directions. Because of the egalitarian access, it is also possible for junior colleagues and even students to correspond with senior scholars in a mutually productive interchange combining the senior member's wisdom and the junior member's zeal.

Professional Forums

While private e-mail can be satisfying, sometimes it is helpful to expand the size of your professional community. Discussion lists, also known as Electronic Conferences or Professional Forums, are ongoing online discussions in groups of professionals. Generally these conferences are organized around a particular topic, for example, traumatic stress. Individuals post a statement or question for distribution to all who subscribe to the list. A discussion then ensues as interested parties make comments about the original and subsequent posts. These "conversations" generally are designated as a thread. For example, a recent post to the Traumatic Stress Forum asked for information on structural models of traumatic stress. Several answers were posted to the forum so that all the subscribers saw the responses. In addition, there were "private" posts made to the originator of the thread regarding the questions. The thread continued for several days, with a number of other people entering and leaving the open discussion. After several days of public and private discussion, the originator of the thread distributed a general summary of deliberations to all Traumatic Stress subscribers. One of the interesting outcomes of this particular thread was that there was substantially more research in process on traumatic stress and structural models than the print media (academic journals) would lead one to believe. Multiple respondents indicated that they had papers under review, but faced reluctant publishers, ostensibly due to the "newness" of structural modeling. This interesting information would not have been gleaned easily using other methods of information transfer.

There are other uses of professional forums, such as those that can locate a particular type of resource. During a recent disaster, a person in the affected area (Europe) made a request for help to an Internet list housed in Georgia (that is, the Internet address of the list "resided" on a computer in the United States). This post was picked up in Alaska by me, relayed through New York to a person in Eastern Europe, who then forwarded it to the appropriate European disaster assistance people. This seemingly "roundabout" connection made services available to the peron who requested them less than 24 hours after the original post. Interestingly, the help had been physically close at hand but the person did not know whom to ask. But the electronic relay easily connected the person to help (Note, this story is altered slightly to protect the identity of the people involved.)

Yet another common use of professional forums is announcements of conferences, calls for papers, and RFPs. This is a low-cost, fast way for dissemination of information worldwide. In sum, these ongoing topic-oriented discussions help keep people aware of issues, allow all involved to have an impact on the directions of the field, and provide ongoing continuing education. Moreover, it is quite common for individuals to connect in private conversations, sometimes known as "back-channel" discussions, which often lead to rewarding long-term professional relationships. Suggestions on how to become involved in professional forums are at the end of this chapter.

OTHER TELEHEALTH APPLICATIONS

This section addresses some of the more stable emerging applications of telehealth. While not all of the applications will be directly usable, the concepts driving them will probably influence the overall development of the field of telehealth. A number of the techniques also can be applied in settings outside of health care, such as the application of CHIN technology to university students records.

CHINs

Sometimes the best support of the professional is to make information about the patient readily available. When a professional is trying to render services and information about the patient is not available this can be frustrating, and at times frightening, to the caregiver. One of the solutions to accessing patient records is the Community Health Information Networks (CHIN). These networks allow patient records to be accessed from more than one location. Thus, if a patient sees three caregivers and picks up a prescription in a single day, using a CHIN, each provider can access the complete records of that patient (for more information, see Terry, in this volume). Needless to say, this type of system warrants particular security measures, but it can be an effective method for managing patient records. It can also prevent duplication of services and reduce the risk of lifethreatening complications brought about by counterindicated procedures and prescriptions.

Portable Health Care Technology

There are a multitude of telecommunications adoptions for traditional medical instruments and tests. For example, there are stethoscopes that connect to phone lines so that the sounds can be heard by someone remote to the patient. Originally developed for battlefield applications, the portable health care technology is finding its way into emergency field medicine as well as routine care. This is a suitcase-size kit that contains diagnostic apparatus like an electronic stethoscope, an ekg, heart monitor, blood and chemical testing equipment, etc. All of this diagnostic equipment connects to a phone either through an existing line or through a direct link to a satellite. These kits can be taken into the field, such as a disaster site, or they can be used to monitor chronic patients from their homes. One of the early demonstrations of home health care was a project of the Medical College of Georgia that linked patients to their provider's offices through two-way TV (Sanders, 1995). With recent developments in technology, this can be accomplished with much simpler and less expensive technology that uses existing telephone lines and a television (for example, http://8x8.com). The patient logs in in the morning and sends the provider basic information on their health status. With this increased monitoring, it should be possible to identify variations in the patient's condition before they reach critical levels, allowing for earlier and more conservative treatment.

Teleradiology

Specialty Care
Most areas of health care are incorporating telecommunications technology into their routine practice. Third party reimbursement agencies, including Medicare, have mechanisms for reimbursement of telehealth services. Mental health consultation is

the most common application of telehealth. In 1998, over 7,000 mental health consultations were reported at 43 separate programs in the United States (ATSP, 1999; Grigsby, 1997). Given that these are survey data, the actual numbers are likely much higher. There are emerging guidelines for the use of telehealth in mental health, including those of the American Psychiatric Association (APA Committee on Telemedical Services, 1998).

Other fields also have an established telehealth presence. Teleradiography was an early leader in the telehealth field. In the past two decades, computers have figured prominently in the creation and examination of medical imaging. CT Scans, sonograms, MRIs and even some standard x-ray images are routinely done with computers. This computer enhancement allow images to be rotated, enlarged, and compared to other images. Translating these applications to telehealth requires modest alterations. In the standard application of radiography, images are digitized and then shipped, via telecommunications, to a remote computer. With this equipment, a technician can shoot an image and a radiologist at a remote site can view it nearly instantaneously and make the diagnosis (Agnew, 1995). Dermatology is another area well suited for telehealth. The Internet Dermatology Society maintains a "dermatology teaching and telehealth by providing a primary care residence training dynamic distance learning resource on the Internet" (Drugge, 1995a, Drugge, 1995b). At this time, there is a great deal of energy focused on specialty consultations, however, there is growing interest in management of chronic illness and other home health care as well as in providing care for institutionalized individuals (Stamm, 1998; Magaletta & Ax, 1998). Thus, isolated providers have a range of new options for connecting with their colleagues in a joint effort to provide better care for their patients.

Ethics, Computers and Approaching the Mathematics of Infinity

Harnard (1991) suggests that current developments in technology have important implications for the modern world similar to those which the invention of the printing press fostered during the late Renaissance. Harnard believes the changes wrought by this technology were so immense that he coined the phrase, the "Post Guttenburg World," to denote the importance of the change. From our experience, the extremely rapid pace of change in cyberspace perhaps heralds a technological "marker" equal to the printing press in historical significance. At the very least, these changes can be mind-boggling, especially considering the proliferation of available information. The click of a mouse allows one to search all of cyberspace (population about 100 million users) on any topic of interest. Traffic on the Internet doubles every 100 days. The number of web sites increases daily as does the amount of information catalogued on those web sites. This explosion of information leads us to ask: Is it possible to be responsible for all the information that we can access, just because it is possible?

Is there a limit to our human ability to comprehend the changes? Is technological evolution a more rapid process than human cognitive-affective evolution? Perhaps yes. But, this does not change the probability that the technology will be developed and that we will, most likely, have access to a great deal of it. Given these prospects, what are some of the ethical issues that can be considered in the context of technology and telehealth?

Before computers, research designs focused on identifying and controlling for a "few" variables. Computers, however, have allowed more complex designs and more involved analyses; researchers now address large data sets and vast numbers of variables. At the same time, this increased complexity and technological dependency enhances the probability of producing results without understanding the meaning (Stamm, 1994; Williams, Sommers, Stamm & Harris, 1994). Yet technology is not at issue. The heart of the matter is the meaning that is derived from the use of the technology. So perhaps the most important question is "Can we really 'make sense' of the information produced by technology?" (Christian, Turner & Stamm, 1988; Harris, et al., 1994; Stamm, 1991, 1995b; Williams, Sommer & Stamm, 1993; Williams, Sommer & Stamm, 1992; Williams, Sommers, Stamm & Harris, 1994; Williams, et al., 1992).

Security and Maintenance of Information

Maintaining the security of databases, like those used in research projects, is difficult. Maintaining the security of electronically held personal records databases is even more difficult. Consider patient or student records held in a typical database. These databases offer instantaneous multi-point and multi-user access. While this gives the professional a heretofore unknown ability to provide services for the patient or student, it also extends opportunities for harm. There are two basic categories of risk: (a) risk directly from people and (b) risks from technology.

Risks *to* records *from* people can come from criminal and malevolent intent or from accident or curiosity. Some compromises to security may come from an unauthorized person simply stumbling across information or from curious searching. This is a particular problem in areas with low-population densities or in "closed" systems, such as a university.

For example, what effect could there be if a student trainee in a mental health clinic encounters—whether accidentally or deliberately—the records of a fellow student who has sought treatment at that clinic? While the trainee has not intended to cause harm, the possibility exists for ethical compromise. Consider further that the students are friends. The student trainee knows that the student patient has a diagnosis that, should it be discovered, will prevent them from obtaining a desired internship placement. The student trainee alters the record in order to protect the friend. In this case several compromises have occurred, even though there was no intent to cause harm. First, the student trainee has committed an unauthorized viewing, compromising the confidentiality of the student patient. Second, the student trainee has compromised the integrity of the data by altering it without the permission of the author of the data or the data manager. Finally, by deleting the diagnosis, an important part of the record has been destroyed, compromising the integrity of the database and potentially the patient's care.

Needless to say, criminal access and malevolent intent magnify problems of database security. These types of compromises can be disastrous: there is greater likelihood of more intensive alteration or destruction of records and more widespread invasions of privacy and unauthorized distribution of important confidential information.

Technological risks to a system do not come directly from a person, but from software or computer systems created by people. Some computer viruses, for example, are designed to destroy data and/or to confuse and disorient computer systems. A computer virus in a larger system, especially when that system is connected to other machines via a LAN or the Internet, can wreak havoc on the entire system.

Other potential problems emanate from system programming errors or irregularities in the use of a system. Because computer systems are not intuitively intelligent and cannot always make good judgments with extenuating circumstances, it is possible that an appropriate and approved individual can be denied access to a system. The effects of this denial become vastly more difficult if the access is desired in a medical crisis. Literally, lack of access to information, such as drug allergies, could compromise a patient's safety.

Confidentiality and Encryption

Security issues should be considered when computer-based systems are used for database management and record-keeping. This is particularly salient when the system is used to pass records from one location to another as in a CHIN. Each time a message passes through an Internet computer system, people working in that system can access that message. One solution for record security is *encryption*. There are multiple encryption software programs that can be easily modified for different users. Interestingly, many of these programs are downgraded security technology from previous wars. Encryption and other security measures are the tools for ethical management of data but the foundation is good planning and care of the administration of the database itself.

Perhaps the most important method of maintaining confidentiality is one that is already in use. As professionals know, it is possible to discuss the issues of a case without revealing the details nor the identity of the parties involved. Moreover, from a self-care perspective, it may be vastly more important to discuss the caregiver's *feelings* about the case rather than the details of the case itself. Thus, the writer of the information is the original source of the information and has control over what is shared. A word of caution is appropriate here because security measures on the Internet are still developing. It is a good rule of thumb to write as if others will see your post. In the experience of the author, posts have ended up in places that were unintended, but through human error (usually my own) more frequently than through malice or security breaches. However, it is good to remember that messages can find their way into unintended places.

A Professional's Beginner Guide to the Information Superhighway

In the four years since this chapter was written the population of the Internet has grown from an estimated 25 million (Musler, 1995) to over 100 million (U.S. Department of Commerce, 1998). Connecting people from multiple cultures creates a new culture on the Internet, what is sometimes known as a virtual *Global Village*. Some of the difficulties in this emerging culture are related to who pays and who plays.

Establishing the cost for the use of the Internet is an ongoing battle. Originally a project of the United States government, the Internet has generally been perceived to be free. In the past, most people gained access to the Internet via universities and organizations that paid group fees (unbeknown to the end user). Now, many people access the Internet via online commercial services, which makes costs more visible. Because of the differences between this technology and older, more established technologies, it is impossible to predict how this issue will ultimately turn out.

The emerging Internet culture is unique in the sense that one can make one's voice heard. In many other societies, individuals need power, prestige, or other social accouterments in order to speak or share their thoughts. Because of the different culture of the Internet, anyone can say anything. This is both good and bad. People have a more egalitarian ability to share their views on issues that they perceive to be important. But at times what is said will be offensive to some. Free speech is not without ambiguity and discomfort.

In an effort to make the culture open, but not hostile, general codes of behavior have emerged on the Internet. These guidelines are relatively simple. When you post a message, it is appropriate to include your address at the end of the post and a concise subject line in the address. The subject line is a one-to-five word abstract of sorts that identifies the nature of your comments. When you reply to a message, you should copy only that portion of the message to which you are responding (most software packages make this an automatic task) and delete the remaining text. Your post then consists of the original post plus your reply, with excess information deleted.

One of the difficulties with communication in text only is that it is sometimes difficult to understand the writer's meaning without body language and other social cues. To solve this dilemma, a number of code systems have developed which can show affect, for example, the *smileys*. A :-) is a smiley face turned sideways. This is generally used to denote pleasure or humor. A ;-) is used to denote a wink and a smile. If there is sad affect, the mouth turns down :-(. These smileys can help the reader interpret the feelings of the writer. The following sentence could have multiple meanings depending on the smiley used.

I ran all the way home :-)

I ran all the way home :-(

In the first case, perhaps the writer was anticipating something positive waiting at home and thus could not contain his or her excitement. In the second case, perhaps the writer was afraid and seeking the shelter of his or her home. It is interesting to note that communicating affect via writing requires one to be able to articulate that affect. This is a psychological skill we tend to overlook. Learning to be able to articulate our affect is perhaps a positive side benefit of having to communicate complete thoughts and feelings via text only.

At times people find themselves extremely excited by what they encounter on the *net*. When a person replies without consideration for moderating their affect, it is called a *flame*. Unfortunately, flames are generally personal attacks and may not have any real grounds upon which to reply. In these circumstances, the recipient may reply in like manner in which a *flame war* is begun. These battles can escalate and may include others who have no direct role in the original incident. In the culture of most discussion lists, the approach to flame wars is, in the best behavioral tradition, to ignore them. Without reinforcement to keep flaming, most people will cease and the war will be over. *Flaming* can become a difficult problem for the community. In these circumstances, if the list is managed by a person or team of people, they will generally try in private to persuade the *flamer* to cease his or her behavior. In the most extreme cases, a person may be locked out of access to a particular group.

Some Suggestions

Printed descriptions of Internet operations have built-in limitations. Because of transmission speed and the ease of forwarding messages, the Internet works something like wildfire: hot topics quickly consume respondents' thoughts, but just as quickly die out as other topics surface. Thus, what appears current on the Internet can be passé before it hits the print medium. Moreover, addresses and instructions for electronic resources must be precise; messages are often read by a machine looking for a perfect match. For example, a computer would likely interpret the following two addresses as being different while a human could see their similarity:

yourname@psych.university.edu

your_name@psych.university.edu.

Just to complicate things, electronic addresses and routings can change fairly often as the Internet expands and more people need more information to route messages correctly. Therefore, any information that is as old as print text is subject to having been changed.

That being said, I have included information that is current about some of the resources that I find helpful and interesting and hope that you will be able to locate them. These addresses are current at press time but subject to change. If the addresses have changed, the information will at least put you on the right track to locating resources that intrigue you. The key to using the Information Superhighway is to be bold and to remember that you are in charge: You can always turn off the computer!

Traumatic Stress Informatics: The PILOTS Database

One of the most important online resources for traumatologists is the PILOTS database which contains over 10,000 citations and references from the worldwide traumatic stress literature. PILOTS can be accessed free through the Dartmouth College Library <http://www.dartmouth.edu/dms/ ptsd/PILOTS.html> and is produced by the National Center for PTSD.

PILOTS has many help-screens along the way that can assist the new user. You can also access the PILOTS Database User's Guide at <ftp://ftp.dartmouth.edu/pub/ptsd/PILOTS_User's_ Guide.ascii> or you can obtain a copy from the Superintendent of Documents, U.S. Government Printing Office, PO Box 371954, Pittsburgh PA 15250-7954; stock number 051-000-00204-1. You can also address questions <ptsd@dartmouth. edu> (Lerner, 1995).

General Telehealth Resources

Below are several websites that showcase information about telehealth. The addresses were current at press time but are subject to change. You will need a graphical web browser such as Netscape or Internet Explorer or a text web browser like Lynx to access the sites. You can consult your system operator for more information about how to access the http addresses from your system.

Telehealth Information Exchange (TIE)

TIE is a comprehensive online information exchange for tele-health and telemedicine information. Among the most valuable resources at this site is the searchable bibliographic file. This easy-to-access database contains journal articles as well as citations to newspaper and newsletter articles. There are also databases for programs, funding, and meetings as well as an area devoted to vendor information. TIE is supported in part by the National Library of Medicine. It can be accessed at http://tie.telemed.org or at http://208.129.211.51.

The American Psychological Association

The APA maintains a very large, extremely well cross-referenced site at <http://www.apa.org/>. This site has a combination of member services and public access services. Through a subscription, members can have access to full text of all of the APA journals since 1995, an online version of PsycInfo, and several other professional databases. For non-members, there are both professional and consumer resources, such as a large area for adult consumers at <http://helping.apa.org/>. There is an educational area for children and parents at http://www.kidspsych.org/ and for students of psychology at <http://www.apa.org/ ed/>.

Arent Fox Telemedicine and The Law

Some of the more thorny issues of telehealth are the legal ones. The unquestioned leader of legal information relating to tele-health is the Arent Fox site. They maintain information about federal, state, and case law as well as related articles and reports regarding telehealth. The site may be found at <http://www.arentfox.com/telemedicine.html>.

The US Department of Health and Human Services Office for the Advancement of Telehealth

The Office for the Advancement of Telehealth was created in 1998 to encourage people to use telecommunications for technical assistance, training, and knowledge exchange among health care professionals, particularly for those providing services to underserved and isolated people. The OAT web site archives service, training, and grant information <http://telehealth. hrsa.gov>.

Professional Telehealth/Telemedicine Associations

Two associations have emerged that focus specifically on telehealth and telemedicine. Both are interdisciplinary but they have slightly different focuses. The American Telemedicine Association <http://www.atmeda.org/> is more of a traditional professional scientific organization with individual memberships, while the Association of Telemedicine Service Providers <http://www.atsp.org/> focuses more toward the business of telemedicine with its member unit being organizations. Both maintain websites with important information regarding telehealth.

PROFESSIONAL FORUMS FOR ONGOING DISCUSSION AND PROFESSIONAL COMMUNITY

InterPsych

InterPysch (http://www.InterPsych.org) is an international multi-disciplinary non-profit organization that maintains numerous professional forums (aka mailing lists). Founded in February 1994 by Ian Pitchford of Sheffield, England, these forums allow mental health and behavioral science professionals, students, and interested others to keep up with discourse in their fields, as well as with each other. InterPsych attracted so much attention in its first half-year online that it had to leave the University of Newcastle-on-Tyne because it had outgrown the University's ability to house its growing e-mail traffic. Within a year after its founding, it serves approximately 10,000 subscribers from over 30 countries who represent most fields of behavioral health care. InterPsych is composed of over 40 separate forums, including such topics as child-adolescent-psych, depression, geriatric-neuropsychology, managed-behavioral-health care, mental-health-in-the-media, psyart, psychopharmacology, rural-care, thanatology, transcultural-psychology, and traumatic-stress. Because of the brevity of this chapter, and because of the rapidly growing nature of InterPsych, it is impossible to list all the forums.

However, three InterPsych Forums are particularly relevant to this chapter. Traumatic-Stress, Rural-Care and Secondary-Traumatic-Stress are discussed below with instructions for subscribing.

InterPsych: Traumatic-Stress

Traumatic-Stress is a professional forum run by Charles R. Figley. Since its inception in February 1994, the forum's membership has expanded to about 600 people. The Traumatic-Stress forum promotes the investigation, assessment, and treatment of immediate and long-term psychosocial, physiological, and existential consequences of highly stressful events. Although this is one of the larger InterPsych lists, the load is not burdensome for most. The average number of messages per week is about 20. One of the ongoing topics of discussion of particular interest on this forum is the continuing efforts to identify a cure for PTSD (Figley, 1995). To subscribe to Traumatic-Stress, send a message to <listserv@listp.apa.org> with SUBSCRIBE Traumatic-Stress in the body.

InterPysch: Rural-Care

Rural-Care addresses Self-Care needs and encourages an exchange of ideas, opinions, and information among persons concerned with the delivery of health services to individuals in rural and bush areas. Rural-Care tries to reduce feelings of isolation which rural- and bush-based professionals may feel by providing a professional community at their fingertips. Through Rural-Care, workers in the field can find support from and connections with those professionals who may be located in more urban areas. Some of the issues discussed on Rural-Care are telehealth; appropriateness of treatment; access to referral sources; evaluation of patients and/or service delivery; the unique difficulties in service delivery brought about by geography, weather, local customs, etc.; and the application or misapplication of urban or Western health techniques and ideology in rural/bush settings (Stamm, 1995c). To subscribe to Rural-Care, send a message to <listserv@listp.apa.org> with SUBSCRIBE RURAL-CARE in the body.

InterPsych: Secondary-Traumatic Stress

Secondary-Traumatic-Stress is a closed list for professionals for the discussion of clinical, teaching, and research issues related to the effects of working with individuals who have experienced trauma in their lives. It was founded in 1996 by Laurie Anne Pearlman and B. Hudnall Stamm. This closed list, which requires authentication of credentials in the field of traumatic stress to join, is considerably more intimate than the open traumatic stress list. Discussions generally focus on prevention of STS, referrals for providers seeking assistance with their own STS, or research issues related to studying the phenomenon of STS. To subscribe to Traumatic-Stress, send a message to <listserv@listp.apa.org> with SUBSCRIBE Secondary-Traumatic-Stress in the body.

REFERENCES

Agnew, M. E. N. (1995). *Teleradiology.* in Pearce, F. W., Stamm, B. H., Agnew, M., Reider, R. M., Boucha, K., & Eussen, L. Alaska Telemedicine: *The trail ahead.* Alaska Telehealth Conference, Anchorage, AK.

American Psychiatric Association Committee on Telemedical Services (1998). *APA Resource document on telepsychiatry via videoconferencing.* Washington, DC: Author. Available online at http://www.psych.org/pract_of_psych/tp_paper.html#super.

Association of Telemedicine Service Providers (1999). *1998 Report on U.S. telemedicine activity.* Portland, OR: Author.

Brooks, R. (1995). *Medical Language Translators.* In Pearce, F. W., Stamm, B. H., Agnew, M., Reider, R. M., Boucha, K., & Eussen, L. Alaska telemedicine: *The trail ahead.* Alaska Telemedicine Conference, Anchorage, AK.

Brown, M. (4 April 1995). E-mail/supervision, from a post to Rural-Care <Rural-Care@netcom.com>.

Christian, V., Turner, E., & Stamm, B. H. (1988). *Electronic media and realia in pedagogy in physical education.* The Southern District American Association of Health, Physical Education, Recreation and Dance Convention, Little Rock, AR.

Drugge, R. (4 April 1994a) Teledermatology, from a post to Rural-Care <Rural-Care@netcom.com>.

Drugge, R. (14 April 1994b) Report on Teledermatology to the American Association of Dermatology, Washington, D.C.

Figley, C. R. (1995). The users guide to Traumatic-Stress. Available at Help <Traumatic-Stress-request@listp.apa.org>.

Grigsby, B. (1997). *ATSP report on U. S. telemedicine activity.* Portland, OR: Association of Telemedicine Service Providers. Available: http://www.atsp.org.

Harnad, S. (1991). Post-Gutenberg Galaxy: The Fourth Revolution in the Means of Production of Knowledge. *Public-Access Computer Systems Review 2(1),* 39–53.

Harris, C. J., Stamm, B. H., Munroe, J. F., Shay, J., Sommer, J. F., & Williams, M. B. (1994). *Standards of Practice and Ethical Issues in Trauma.* 10th Annual Conference of the International Society for Traumatic Stress Studies, Chicago, IL.

Hartsough, D. & Myers, D. (1985). *Disaster Work and Mental Health: Prevention and Control of Stress Among Workers.* Washington, D.C.: NIMH, Center for Mental Health Studies Emergencies.

Herman, J. L. (1992). *Trauma and Recovery.* New York: Basic Books.

Janoff-Bulman, R. (1992). *Shattered assumptions: Toward a new psychology of trauma.* New York: Free Press.

Jones, A. (12 April 1995). Rural Based Residencies, from a post to Rural Health Care Discussion List <ruralnet-1@musom01.mu.wvnet.edu>.

Labkoff, S. (1995). Medical PDAs. In Pearce, F. W., Stamm, B. H., Agnew, M., Reider, R. M., Boucha, K., & Eussen, L. Alaska telemedicine: *The Trail Ahead.* Alaska Telemedicine Conference, Anchorage, AK.

Lerner, F. (4 April 1995). The PILOTS Database. E-mail/supervision, from a post to Traumatic-Stress <Traumatic-Stress@netcom.com>.

Magaletta, P. R., Fagan, T. J., and Ax, R. K. (1998). Advancing psychology services through telehealth in the Federal Bureau of Prisons. *Professional Psychology: Research & Practice.* 29(6), 543–548.

McCann, L. & Pearlman, L. A. (1990). Vicarious traumatization: A framework for understanding the psychological effects of working with victims. *Journal of traumatic stress, 3* (1), 131–149.

McCarthy, M. (4 April 1995). E-mail/supervision, from a post to Rural-Care <Rural-Care@netcom.com>.

Musler, B. (10 April 1995). An Internet user's lament. *The Wall Street Journal.*

Nickelson, D. W. (1998). Telehealth and the evolving health care system: Strategic opportunities for professional psychology. *Professional Psychology: Research & Practice.* 29 (6), 527–535.

Office of Technology Assessment (1991). *Health care in rural America* #PB91-104927. Available on-line http://www.wws.princeton.edu/~ota/disk2/1990/9022_n.html.

Pearlman, L. A. & Saakvitne, K. W. (1995). *Trauma and the therapist: Countertransference and vicarious traumatization in psychotherapy with incest survivors.* New York: W. W. Norton.

Rawlins, C. (4 April 1994), Telemedicine, from a post to Rural-Care <Rural-Care@netcom.com>.

Sanders, J. (1995).*The Mobile Medic.* In Pearce, F. W., Stamm, B. H., Agnew, M., Reider, R. M., Boucha, K., & Eussen, L. (1995). Alaska Telemedicine: *The Trail Ahead.* Alaska Telemedicine Conference, Anchorage, AK.

Saranson, I. G., Levine, H. M., Basham, R. B. & Saranson, B. (1983). Assessing social support: The social support questionnaire. *Journal of personality and social psychology, 44,* 127–139.

Sommer, J., Williams, M. B., Harris, C. J., & Stamm, B. H. (1994). The development of ethical principles for post traumatic research, practice, training and publication. In *Handbook of traumatic stress,*

M. B. Williams & J. Sommer, Eds. Westport, CT: Greenwood Publishing Company.

Stamm, B. H. (1991). *From t-test to Discriminant Analysis: Using Multivariate Techniques.* Presented at the International Society for Traumatic Stress Studies, Washington, D.C.

Stamm, B. H. (1993). *Conceptualizing Traumatic Stress: A Metatheoretical Structural Approach.* Dissertation. Laramie, WY.: University of Wyoming.

Stamm, B. H., (1995a). *A Process Approach to Community, Spirituality, Trauma, and Loss.* Trauma, Loss and Dissociation Conference, Washington, D.C.

Stamm, B. H., (1995b). *A Process Approach to the Scientific Method.* Trauma, Loss and Dissociation Conference, Washington, D.C.

Stamm, B. H., (1995c). The users guide to Rural-Care. Available at Help <rural-care-request@listp.apa.org>.

Stamm, B. H. (1998). Clinical applications of telemedicine and telehealth in mental health. *Professional Psychology: Research & Practice 29* (6), 536–542. Available online at http://www.apa.org/journals/pro/pro296536.html.

Stamm, B. H. & Rudolph, J. M. (in press). Changing frontiers of health care: Improving rural and remote practice through professional conferencing on the Internet. *Journal of Rural Community Psychology.* Available online at http://www.marshall.edu/jrcp/index.htm.

Stamm, B. H., Varra, E. M., & Sandberg, C. T. (1993). *When it happens to another: Direct and indirect trauma.* Ninth Annual Conference of the International Society for Traumatic Stress Studies. San Antonio, TX.

Terry, M. J. (16 March 1995). Personal Communication.

Williams, M. B., Sommer, J. F., & Stamm, B. H. (1992). *Developing ethical principles for the International Society for Traumatic Stress Studies.* The First World Conference on Traumatic Stress. Amsterdam, The Netherlands.

Williams, M. B., Sommer, J. F., & Stamm, B. H. (1993). *Developing ethical principles for trauma research, education, and treatment.* Ninth Annual Conference of the International Society for Traumatic Stress Studies, San Antonio, TX.

Williams, M. B., Sommer, J. F., Stamm, B. H., Harris, C. J., & Hammarberg, M. (1992). *Developing ethical principles for the ISTSS-II: Developing comprehensive guidelines.* Symposium presented at the Eighth Annual Conference of the International Society for Traumatic Stress Studies, Los Angeles, CA.

PART FOUR

ETHICAL ISSUES IN SELF-CARE

1 2

Ethical Issues Associated With Secondary Trauma in Therapists

James F. Munroe

James F. Munroe's systematic paper reexamines one of the oldest ethical guidelines in the field, that of the American Psychological Association, in the light of Secondary Traumatic Stress. For many years, we have concentrated exclusively on protecting the client with little or no regard to the caregiver. However, time has shown us that impaired caregivers are not only a loss to the professional community, they are potentially dangerous. This chapter shifts the perspective from being patient-centered to being helper-centered. This is not to reducee the importance of being patient-centered, but to acknowledge the importance of the mental health of the caregiver in his or her ability to give care and to live a productive life.

In recent years, increasing attention has been paid to the effects of trauma therapy on therapists and other professionals who provide care. The trauma literature contains several anecdotal references to therapists suffering such effects as sharing the nightmares of the survivors they were treating (Danieli, 1984; Langer 1987), sharing the hopelessness of clients (Mollica, 1988), having feelings of aggression (Scurfield, 1985), confronting one's own vulnerability and moral attitudes (Haley, 1985), or having feelings of numbing and avoidance (McCann & Pearlman, 1990). Danieli (1984; 1988) proposed that the therapists of survivors of the Holocaust enter into a conspiracy of silence in which the impact of the Holocaust is denied. Herman (1988; 1992) identified the symptoms of incest survivors as being contagious for the therapists who treat them. McCann and Pearlman (1990) referred to such responses as vicarious traumatization and suggested that the effects of trauma therapy on therapists were likely to influence the therapists' personal lives as well as their ability to do therapy. Others have described the effects on therapists as secondary trauma (Catherall, 1992; Figley, 1988; Rosenheck & Nathan, 1985) and more recently a volume by Figley (1995) has identified these effects as compassion fatigue. The common thread among these conceptualizations is that those who do therapy with trauma survivors begin to experience responses that parallel those of their clients.

Secondary effects have long been noted in family members of trauma survivors (Danieli, 1988; Figley, 1988; Milgram, 1990; Nagata, 1990; Solomon, 1990). Empirical studies have demonstrated mixed results on second generation effects, but methodological differences have made it difficult to compare results (Ancharoff, 1994). What does seem to emerge is that although the secondary effects in family members may not reach diagnostic levels, there are still indirect effects from trauma. More recently, several authors have studied these effects more systematically in therapists. Munroe (1991) studied therapists working with combat veterans and found that increasing exposure to PTSD clients was significantly related to higher scores on intrusion and avoidance, and that these effects were distinct from burnout. Kassam-Adams (1995) similarly found higher levels of intrusion and avoidance related to increased therapist exposure to sexually traumatized clients. Chrestman (1994) found that exposure to trauma clients was significantly associated with increased intrusion, avoidance, dissociation, and sleep disturbance in therapists. The overall finding in these studies is that therapists are affected by the trauma work they do and the effects of this work parallel the symptoms of the trauma clients. This raises the question as to whether doing trauma therapy is traumatic in itself. DSM-IV (APA, 1994) criteria for PTSD include being confronted by events that happen to others and experiencing helplessness as a result, as traumatic. Increasingly it appears that the question is not whether therapists will be exposed, but rather, how they will deal with the inevitable results of exposure. If trauma therapy is producing trauma responses in therapists, many substantial ethical questions are raised as to the welfare of therapists and the clients they treat.

The ethical issues in this chapter will draw on the ethical codes for psychologists published by the American Psychological Association (1992); however, ethical codes from other professional organizations reflect similar issues. Where the term "psychologist" is used here, the reader should feel free to substitute appropriate terms, such as therapist, social worker, case manager, counselor, researcher, psychiatrist, administrator, or others who work with trauma survivors. This chapter will not attempt to answer the variety of questions that arise, but seeks mainly to illustrate some of the issues which will have to be dealt with.

THE DUTY TO WARN

If therapists who work with trauma survivors are susceptible to suffering effects from their exposure, we must raise the question of a duty to warn. We are required to warn people if there is an immediate danger, such as a threat to a specific person by a client or when an abusive situation involves children. Since we have reason to believe that harm could come to a therapist as a result of the trauma work they do, this imposes a responsibility to at least warn them of potential damage. A seemingly appropriate time to issue the warning would be when hiring or assigning a new therapist to work with trauma clients (see Figure 1). We may not be able to tell, however, which clients have trauma histories. Perry, Herman, van der Kolk, & Hoke (1990) found that many clients diagnosed as borderline may have undetected trauma histories. Clients who present with substance abuse problems may also be unidentified trauma survivors. It is possible that many clients have significant trauma histories that are not revealed. Munroe, Shay, Fisher, Makary, Rapperport & Zimering (1995) have suggested that transmission of secondary trauma can occur without the content of the trauma being revealed. This indicates that we would be unable to predict which clients would have an effect on therapists, and therefore, it would seem reasonable to warn therapists before they begin working with any clients.

There is also no reason to assume that therapists in the field are sufficiently aware of the danger. Munroe (1991) found that age and experience did not act as a buffer for secondary effects, but that the influence of education level may have been somewhat protective. Kassam-Adams (1995) found that experience and education did not buffer secondary effects. Chrestman (1994) found years of professional experience and higher income were related to fewer effects, but in each of these studies, none of the subjects appeared immune from the effects. It is also possible that some experienced therapists avoid trauma clients and studies which measure secondary trauma, because they serve as reminders of their exposure. It has not been demonstrated that experience or education can prevent secondary effects. Further, we do not know what specific components of education or experience might provide buffering. It might be tempting, and somewhat self protective, to assume that experienced therapists are not susceptible, but there is insufficient data to back up this assumption. The question of cumulative effects, or inoculation effects, is unanswered in primary trauma and as yet unquestioned in secondary trauma. Given this, it again seems prudent to warn all therapists.

FIGURE 1. Proposed Informed Consent Form for Trauma Therapists.

I, _____, have been informed by the staff at _____, that this program works with survivors of trauma, and that I therefore will inevitably be exposed to the effects of secondary trauma. I have been informed that these effects can have beneficial or detrimental results; if dealt with openly, such responses can be viewed as parallels to the clients' trauma responses and as such, are valuable clinical information; if denied or ignored, these same responses can lead to an altered world view which may impede my clinical judgment and interfere with my personal life. I have been informed that my age, experience, or professional training may not provide adequate protection from secondary trauma. I have been informed that the staff expects each member, including myself, to work to understand and act on how this work affects each staff member in the delivery of services to our clients. I have been informed that I may not be a good observer of how this process affects me at any given time. I have been informed that the staff believes all of its actions and interactions related to secondary trauma are considered models for our clients and that each member of the staff is expected to recognize an ethical obligation to model good self care.

Signature   Date

DUTY TO TRAIN

The APA guidelines, under "design of education and training programs," state that such programs should "seek to insure that programs are competently designed, provide for proper experiences" (p. 1607). This suggests that not only should we be concerned about warning candidates of the potential harm of being exposed to trauma, but that we should also train them how to cope with this exposure. We cannot be content to train psychologists who expect to do therapy, but must consider researchers, non-psychologists, and others who will be exposed. Many fields have begun to respond to the exposure of workers to secondary trauma (Gersons, 1989; McCammon, Durham, Allison, & Williamson, 1988; McCammon & Allison, 1995; McFarland, 1986; Talbot 1990). Should course work be required in training programs? Should accrediting bodies require programs to provide such training?

The duty to train does not end with educational or preparatory programs. As with primary trauma, we can expect parallel numbing and denial to show up in secondary trauma. Training students and sending them out into a professional world which denies the effects of secondary trauma will not be very helpful. Is there a duty to train those already in the field? Should employers, administrators, and professional organizations require continuing education on secondary effects?

OCCUPATIONAL HAZARD

Secondary traumatic exposure for therapists and other professionals is part of their job responsibilities. Therapists who have been warned should also be instructed on the importance of balancing their professional and personal lives. Yassen (1995) has pointed out the importance of healthy practices for trauma therapists, and this should be included in training programs. It is not sufficient for employers, however, to instruct therapists to take care of themselves off the job; active preventive measures should also be a regular part of the work environment. Chrestman (1994) found that smaller caseloads and varied assignments reduced exposure. If work is dangerous, employers should strive to provide safe working conditions and reduce risk. An important part of providing such conditions is to work to overcome denial and numbing. If the work environment is not active in this, there is likely to be victim blaming. Those who begin to show signs of being affected will be identified as poorly trained, unable to do the job, or personally flawed. A work environment that denies the existence of these problms will not only prevent such a worker from getting needed support, but will silence other workers, and likely decrease efficiency and effectiveness. If workers are referred out to an employee assistance program (EAP) it may also decrease the likelihood of others responding openly to avoid being stigmatized. Regular debriefing sessions can be helpful, but if these become mandatory, they may defeat the purpose of creating a safe environment for therapists to talk about effects. It may be necessary to have an active ongoing struggle to deal with secondary effects rather than a set plan.

WELFARE OF THE CLIENT

Under "concern for others' welfare" the APA ethical code states, "psychologists seek to contribute to the welfare of those with whom they interact professionally" (p. 1600), and under "social responsibility" states "psychologists are aware of their professional and scientific responsibilities to the community and the society in which they work and live" (p. 1600). If the therapist is being influenced by secondary effects this code may be violated.

Secondary effects will parallel primary symptoms. A therapist who is overwhelmed by the traumatic impact of numerous clients may be in a state of avoidance when a particular client comes in. It is possible that when this client needs to talk about trauma, the therapist will discourage discussion to protect him- or herself. Alternately, the therapist who is in an intrusive phase may insist on getting at the details of a client's trauma when the client is not ready. If the therapist is suffering from disturbed sleep or nightmares he or she may not be attentive to the needs of the client. The therapist's irritability from overexposure may result in the client's being silenced during a session. Overexposed therapists may also be trying to rescue clients who do not need to be rescued, or going on a mission to route out traumatic perpetrators when this is not in the client's best interest. Therapists might also become suspicious of other professionals whom they think do not "understand" the needs of trauma clients, and thereby impede the client from accessing necessary services. Therapists may begin to avoid their trauma clients and misdiagnose them, or they may avoid meetings and supervision. In short, the clients' welfare may be compromised unless professionals recognize the needs of the therapist.

MULTIPLE RELATIONSHIPS

When therapists are overloaded with their clients' traumatic histories and suffering from the effects, it may be obvious to clients before professionals take notice. Many clients are acutely aware of, or concerned about the effects of trauma on others, including therapists (Munroe, Makary & Rapperport, 1990). They see it when they try to talk to family or friends and they know the effects on themselves. Often in therapy clients will comment that they cannot tell their spouses, parents, children, or other therapists about what happened to them because they do not want to harm these people. They will give accounts of how a certain therapist or professional reacted to their stories. Such stories may not be aimed at the people they talk about, but are rather a question to the current therapist about whether he or she will be harmed by the same stories. Therapists will often respond to the story rather than the question. If the client is indeed asking such a question and the therapist does not respond to it, the client may assume that the therapist cannot listen to the trauma material and be unharmed. When the client begins to protect the therapist from the harmful effects of trauma stories, the roles have been switched. The client is now taking care of the therapist, and the therapist has become both therapist and client. This constitutes a dual relationship and an ethical violation. The APA code indicates that a therapist should not be in a relationship if "such a relationship reasonably might impair the psychologist's objectivity or otherwise interfere with the psychologist's effectively performing his or her functions as a psychologist, or might harm or exploit the other party" (p. 1601). If the client has to protect the therapist, it would seem this is both an impairment and an exploitation on the part of the therapist. Additionally, the implied message the therapist is acting out is that trauma should be denied and avoided. This seems hardly an appropriate message for a client who has come for help with traumatic experiences.

The APA code also states, "psychologists are sensitive to real and ascribed differences in power between themselves and others, and they do not exploit or mislead other people during or after professional relationships" (p. 1600). Clients may not ask the implied question of whether the therapist will be affected because of the real or ascribed power differential. A direct question of the therapist may often be countered with an interpretation of the client's questioning behavior rather than a direct response. There is clearly a power differential in who gets to ask questions regarding the other's internal states. When therapists fail to address the issue, whether overt or implied, they may be misleading their clients. The therapist may also be sending a message of superiority, thereby distancing from the client. When therapists imply that they are not affected by the client's trauma story, the client may also assume the therapist is stating that he or she would not have been affected by the same experience. This suggests that the client is somehow defective and unable to handle situations as the therapist would. This may be exactly what the therapist would like to think. The question as to whether the therapist would have handled the trauma any better is a direct confrontation of the therapists' sense of invulnerability. If the therapist cannot face the question of vulnerability to traumatic experiences, the client may well wonder whether the therapist can be of any help. If the therapist cannot handle questions of his or her own vulnerability, is not the client placed in a dual relationship?

STRUCTURING THE RELATIONSHIP

The APA codes also state that "psychologists make reasonable efforts to answer patient's questions and to avoid apparent misunderstandings about therapy" (p. 1605). The question about effects on therapists, even if silenced by power differentials, seems to be one that needs to be answered. Therapists are advised about "avoiding harm" and it seems reasonable for the client to be concerned with the same issue. The code in this section also states that "psychologists discuss with clients or patients as early as is feasible in the therapeutic relationship appropriate issues" (p. 1605). If the issue of therapist vulnerability will determine the client's ability to utilize services, this is an appropriate issue to discuss whether the therapist is comfortable with it or not.

Should the therapist bring up the issue at the beginning of therapy even if the client does not ask? If the therapist does so, it would diminish the impression of superiority by acknowledging that trauma can affect anybody, including therapists. The therapist should then be able to inform the client as to how she or he and their professional colleagues go about protecting and supporting themselves. This would not only relieve the client of the responsibility of caring for the therapist, but would also model methods for coping with trauma, such as a regular consultation with a team to discuss therapist reactions. It could be argued that such a discussion might place an unnecessary burden on a client who might not even be concerned with this issue. It can also be argued that clients may not ask even if they are concerned, and it is therefore the therapist's ethical duty to address the question. Others may argue that putting the therapist in a vulnerable light might be detrimental to clients who need a strong expert image to rely on. It can also be argued that such an invulnerable image is an inappropriate model for clients to look up to. But again, this may be encouraging denial and numbing.

INFORMED CONSENT

The codes state that clients are "informed of significant information concerning the procedure" (p. 1605). The possibility that a therapist's effectiveness may be diminished by the effects of secondary trauma certainly seems significant to clients. Further, it seems significant to inform the client that therapists have adequate resources to deal with such effects. We must also ask ourselves, what if the client already knows or suspects, and we do not address the issue? Clients are frequently concerned about the same effects on their families. Numerous authors have addressed the issue of inter-generational transmission of trauma (Ancharoff, 1994; Danieli, 1984, 1985, 1988; Figley, 1985; Harkness, 1993). A genuine discussion of therapist coping may validate the client's concerns and provide some effective strategies for helping families members cope. Such a discussion necessitates that therapists develop adequate coping strategies for themselves.

PRIVACY AND CONFIDENTIALITY

The codes state that psychologists "discuss the relevant limitations on confidentiality...and the foreseeable uses of the information generated" (p. 1606). Therapists might be very comfortable informing a client that case material will be presented for purposes of diagnosis or treatment planning, but should such a discussion also include the use of case information to assess therapist responses? Again, this would relieve the client of having to care for the therapist and provide a healthy model for coping with trauma. Such consultations would actually deal more with therapist responses and would require no more client information than a more traditional case presentation. The codes do not require that information should not be shared, but only that the limitations be explained. Informing the client might be very reassuring. Too much privacy around trauma stories might also reinforce the client's belief that nobody wants to hear what happened. A therapist who does not share trauma stories and their own responses may be seen as colluding in another conspiracy of silence (Danieli, 1984). Confidentiality can be confused with secrecy. Confidentiality can reside in a team of professionals as well as an individual, as long as the client is informed.

PERSONAL PROBLEMS AND CONFLICTS

The APA codes specify that psychologists "refrain from undertaking an activity when they know or should know that their personal problems are likely to lead to harm....[They] have an obligation to be alert to signs of, and to obtain assistance for, their personal problems at an early stage, in order to prevent significantly impaired performance" (p. 1601). If the therapist knows of a problem that influences therapy, he or she has a choice of what to do, but if a therapist "should know," but does not know, there is a problem. It is entirely possible that when a therapist is being secondarily traumatized, denial becomes a way to cope. If the therapist is in denial then he or she may not know there is a problem even though each therapist should know. There is also the problem of determining when the effects of secondary trauma lead to the therapist becoming "significantly impaired." Is a therapist who is preventing clients from talking about their traumas because of his or her own feelings of being overwhelmed significantly impaired? Is the therapist who is beginning to share the world view of a number of trauma clients able to recognize when he or she is becoming impaired?

The Engagement-transmission model of secondary trauma

(Munroe, 1994) suggests that therapists will usually not be aware of when they are being drawn into re-enactments and secondarily traumatized. Stadler (1990), studying burnout, writes that denial is common in relation to the topic of impaired counselors, and attributes this in part to the myth that training and experience in a mental health professional offers immunity from emotional problems. This suggests that even if therapists know about their secondary reactions they may deny them. In primary trauma many authors have identified the violated sense of invulnerability as a salient factor, but in secondary trauma it may be the myth of professional invulnerability that is significant.

The image of the objective observer and expert, which seems to operate in our professional schema, may lead professionals to believe that they should not have any reactions to their trauma clients. Those who do express their feelings or talk about their reactions may be seen as unprofessional by those who would prefer to deny their own vulnerability. They might be told to seek therapy or get more thorough training. Therapists might be told, as their clients frequently are, to forget about it and get on with their lives. Therapists might also be told that a particular response is a countertransference issue due to some pre-existing condition unrelated to trauma, as their clients are sometimes told. This of course will be of no help to the distressed therapist, not to mention what kind of model it projects for clients. The empirical data on experience and education provides insufficient evidence as to whether these prevent the effects of secondary trauma. In the absence of clear data, and at the risk of allowing "significantly impaired" therapists to practice, it does not seem ethically justifiable to assume any therapist has immunity from secondary effects.

If we begin, however, to search for the point at which a therapist becomes significantly impaired, we will have missed the point. The APA codes require action on impairment only when "there may have been an ethical violation" (p. 1611), but this is too late in the process. The burnout and impairment literature are examples of how efforts to "find the damaged ones" leads to a sort of frenzied searching which will only promote further denial. If we attach the impaired label to therapists who are being secondarily traumatized we end up blaming the victims. On the other hand, if we recognize secondary effects as a normal response to the abnormal occupation of being a trauma therapist, we can begin a dialogue. There is also a tendency to identify new therapists or those who have trauma histories as more susceptible to secondary effects. The literature does not support these ideas so far. Munroe (1991) did not find a difference in secondary effects between therapists who reported a combat history and those who did not. Chrestman (1994) found that trauma survivor therapists show more effects of being traumatized, but it is not clear that these have anything to do with their work as therapists. It could be argued that therapists with a trauma history might be better prepared to deal with secondary effects. This is an old argument about cumulative or inoculative effects which remains unresolved. From an ethical viewpoint, it appears prudent to assume that all therapists are susceptible, and that all therapists should address these issues on a regular basis. This would provide a good model for less experienced therapists even if more seasoned professionals had identified ways to cope effectively.

If all therapists are vulnerable, and both personal and professional interests lead to denial of this vulnerability, this may have a profound impact on trauma therapy. How will therapists be able to determine when their own normal and legitimate responses get to the point of interfering with therapy? If it is the case that the therapist being affected is unlikely to recognize this, then we must ask whether it is ethical to conduct traditional one-on-one psychotherapy with trauma clients. Perhaps individual therapy should only be conducted when a clear support team that is trained to monitor secondary responses is involved. If therapist responses are parallel to those of their clients, these responses can be used as clinical data to enhance the therapy process for clients and buffer the negative effects for therapists (Munroe, Shay, Fisher, Makary, Rapperport, & Zimering, 1995).

WELFARE OF THE THERAPIST

Conspicuously absent from the ethical codes is the welfare of the therapist. Psychologists are instructed to avoid harm "to patients, clients, colleagues, students, research participants, or others with whom they work" (p. 1601). If in fact we do not include ourselves, we are once again providing a damaging model to trauma clients. Survivors of traumas caused by people have been abused by those who deny the importance of the victims' welfare. They often are taught to ignore their own welfare and to sacrifice themselves to the needs of the abusers. When therapists fail to practice adequate self care they reinforce the idea that one should allow oneself to be abused. Such a model may invalidate the help a therapist can offer. The therapist who fails to take lunch breaks, doesn't go on vacations, and works too much overtime to help clients, may in fact be damaging them. Trauma survivors have often been betrayed by words, and if so, they may be much more interested in the actions and behaviors of therapists. They are tuned to what we model and whether we practice what we preach. If we are modeling for our clients, then therapists have an ethical duty to actively demonstrate good self care.

COMPETENCE

Secondary trauma in therapists is a fairly new concept in the trauma field and data is only beginning to emerge. The literature has not yet empirically demonstrated any effective means of prevention. Nonetheless, the codes states "in those areas in which recognized professional standards do not yet exist, psychologists exercise careful judgment and take appropriate precautions to protect the welfare of those with whom they work" (p. 1599). Some authors have proposed what some of these precautions might be (Catherall, 1995; McCann & Pearlman, 1990; Pearlman and Saakvitne, 1995; Munroe, Shay, Fisher, Makary, Rapperport, & Zimering, in 1995), but many more need to be developed.

ETHICAL GUIDELINE PROPOSAL

As a starting point, the following proposals are offered to spur such development: (a) trauma therapists should acknowledge the effects of secondary trauma on themselves and their colleagues and take regular, ongoing actions to insure the welfare of professionals and to preserve their ability to deliver quality services; (b) trauma therapists should not work alone but instead should seek out or create arrangements in which they have regular and open input from other professionals regarding the effects of secondary trauma and its impact on the services they deliver; and (c) trauma therapists should recognize an ethical duty to self care.

CONCLUSIONS

Secondary trauma challenges the field to expand our concepts of ethical practice. Our ability to act ethically in response to this challenge can potentially enhance the wellbeing of both therapists and clients. Failure to do so will diminish us all. The ethical duty to respond will challenge professional organizations, educational institutions, administrators, supervisors, and practitioners, but ultimately each individual will have to confront him- or herself on a regular basis to insure proper ethical behavior. It is hoped that this article will motivate readers to actively challenge themselves with the questions raised.

REFERENCES

American Psychiatric Association. (1994). *Diagnostic and statistical manual of mental disorders* (4th ed.). Washington, D.C.: American Psychiatric Association.

American Psychological Association. (1992). Ethical principles of psychologists and code of ethics. *American psychologist*, 47 (12), 1597–1611.

Ancharoff, M. R. (1994). Intergenerational Transmission of Trauma: Mechanisms for the Transmission of Trauma Effects. Unpublished Ph.D. dissertation, University of Denver, CO.

Catherall, D. R. (1989). Differentiating intervention strategies for primary and secondary trauma in post-traumatic stress disorder: The example of Vietnam veterans. *Journal of traumatic stress*, 2 (3), 289–304.

Catherall, D. R. (1992). *Back from the brink: A family guide to overcoming traumatic stress.* New York: Bantam Books.

Catherall, D. R. (1995). Preventing institutional secondary trauma. In C. R. Figley, (Ed.), *Compassion fatigue: Secondary traumatic stress disorder among those who treat the traumatized.* New York: Brunner/ Mazel.

Chrestman, K. R. (1994). Secondary traumatization in therapists working with survivors of trauma. Unpublished Ph.D. dissertation, Nova University.

Danieli, Y. (1984). Psychotherapists' participation in the conspiracy of silence about the Holocaust. *Psychoanalytic psychology*, 1 (1), 23–42.

Danieli, Y. (1985). The treatment and prevention of long-term effects and intergenerational transmission of victimization: A lesson from Holocaust survivors and their children. In C. R. Figley (Ed.), *Trauma and its wake: The study and treatment of PTSD* (Vol. 1). New York: Brunner/Mazel.

Danieli, Y. (1988). Treating survivors and children of survivors of the Nazi Holocaust. In F. M. Ochberg (Ed.), *Post-traumatic therapy and victims of violence.* New York: Brunner/Mazel.

Figley, C. R. (1988). A five-phase treatment of post-traumatic-stress disorder in families. *Journal of traumatic stress*, 1 (1), 127–141.

Figley, C. R. (Ed.) (1995). *Compassion fatigue: Secondary traumatic stress disorder among those who treat the traumatized.* New York: Brunner/ Mazel.

Gersons, B. P. R. (1989). Patterns of PTSD among police officers following shooting incidents: A two-dimensional model and treatment implications. *Journal of traumatic stress, 2* (3), 247–257.

Haley, S. A. (1985). Some of my best friends are dead: Treatment of the PTSD patient and his family. In W. D. Kelley (Ed.), *Post-traumatic stress disorder and the war veteran patient.* New York: Brunner/Mazel.

Harkness, L. (1993). Transgenerational transmission of war-related trauma. In J. P. Wilson & B. Raphael (Eds.), *International handbook of traumatic stress syndromes.* New York: Plenum Press.

Herman, J. L. (1988). Father-daughter incest. In F. M. Ochberg (Ed.), *Post-traumatic therapy and victims of violence.* New York: Brunner/ Mazel.

Herman, J. L. (1992). *Trauma and recovery.* New York: Basic Books.

Kassam-Adams, N. (1995). The risks treating sexual trauma: Stress and secondary trauma in psychotherapists. Unpublished Ph.D. dissertation, University of Virginia.

Langer, R. (1987). Post-traumatic stress disorder in former POWs. In T. Williams (Ed.), *Post-traumatic stress disorders: A handbook for clinicians.* Cincinnati, OH: Disabled American Veterans.

McCammon, S., Durham, T. W., Allison, E. J., & Williamson, J. E. (1988). Emergency workers: Cognitive appraisal and coping with traumatic events. *Journal of traumatic stress, 1* (3), 353–372.

McCammon, S. & Allison, E. (1995). Debriefing and treating emergency workers. In C. R. Figley, (Ed.), *Compassion fatigue: Secondary traumatic stress disorder among those who treat the traumatized.* New York: Brunner/Mazel.

McCann, I. L. & Pearlman, L. A. (1990). Vicarious traumatization: A framework for understanding the psychological effects of working with victims. *Journal of traumatic stress, 3* (1), 131–150.

McFarland, A. C. (1986). Post-traumatic morbidity of a disaster: A study of cases presenting for psychiatric treatment. *Journal of nervous and mental diseases, 174* (1), 4–14.

Milgram, N. (1990). Secondary victims of traumatic stress: Their plight and public safety. Paper presented at the sixth annual meeting of the Society for Traumatic Stress Studies, New Orleans, LA.

Mollica, R. F. (1988). The trauma story: The psychiatric care of refugee survivors of violence and torture. In F. M. Ochberg (Ed.), *Post-traumatic therapy and victims of violence.* Brunner/Mazel: New York.

Munroe, J. (1991). Therapist traumatization from exposure to clients with combat related post-traumatic stress disorder: Implications for administration and supervision. Ed.D. dissertation, Northeastern University, Boston, MA. *Dissertation abstracts international, 52–03B,* 1731.

Munroe, J. (1994). The engagement transmission model of secondary trauma: Survivors, their families, and the therapists who treat them. Workshop presented at a multi-agency conference on PTSD and The Family: Treatment Approaches to Secondary Trauma. Brockton, MA.

Munroe, J., Makary, C., & Rapperport, K. (1990). PTSD and twenty years of treatment: Vietnam combat veterans speak. Videotape presentation at the sixth annual meeting of the Society for Traumatic Stress Studies, New Orleans, LA.

Munroe, J., Shay, J., Fisher, L., Makary, C., Rapperport, K., & Zimering, R. (1995). Team work prevention of STSD: A therapeutic alliance. In C. R. Figley, (Ed.), *Compassion fatigue: Secondary traumatic stress disorder from treating the traumatized.* New York: Brunner/Mazel.

Nagata, D. K. (1990). The Japanese American internment: Exploring the transgenerational consequences of traumatic stress. *Journal of traumatic stress, 3* (1), 47–70.

Pearlman, L. & Saakvitne, K. (1995). Constructivist self development approach to treating secondary traumatic stress. In C. R. Figley, (Ed.), *Compassion fatigue: Secondary traumatic stress disorder among those who treat the traumatized.* New York: Brunner/Mazel.

Perry, J., Herman, J., Van der Kolk, B., & Hoke, L. (1990). Psychotherapy and psychological trauma in borderline personality disorder. *Psychiatric annals, 20* (1), 33–43.

Rosenheck, R. & Nathan, P. (1985). Secondary traumatization in children of Vietnam veterans. *Hospital and community psychiatry, 36* (5), 332–344.

Scurfield, R. M. (1985). Post-trauma stress assessment and treatment: Overview and formulations. In C. R. Figley (Ed.), *Trauma and its wake.* New York: Brunner/Mazel.

Solomon, Z. (1990). From front line to home front: Wives of PTSD veterans. Paper presented at the sixth annual meeting of the Society for Traumatic Stress Studies, New Orleans, LA.

Stadler, H. A. (1990). Counselor impairment. In B. Herlihy & L. Golden, (Eds.), *AACD ethical standards casebook* (4th ed.). Alexandria, VA: American Association for Counseling and Development.

Talbot, A. (1990). The importance of parallel process in debriefing counselors. *Journal of traumatic stress, 3*(2), 265–277.

Yassen, J. (1995). Preventing secondary traumatic stress disorder. In C. R. Figley, (Ed.), *Compassion fatigue: Secondary traumatic stress disorder among those who treat the traumatized.* New York: Brunner/Mazel.

Self-Care and the Vulnerable Therapist

Mary Beth Williams & John F. Sommer, Jr.

Mary Beth Williams and John F. Sommer, Jr. continue in their tradition of framing standards of practice guidelines for therapy from a distinctly self-care and ethical perspective. Together, from their respective therapy and administrative backgrounds, the authors address pertinent clinical issues, raise questions, and offer possible alternatives. The importance of this chapter cannot be underestimated in this time of uncertainty and change in the trauma treatment field. While Williams and Sommer do not claim to have all the solutions (nor should they), they offer knowledge garnered from years of experience on ethical issues in their work in the International Society for Traumatic Stress Studies and in the U.S. governmental playing field.

There are a significant number of obstacles facing those therapists who have chosen the field of traumatic stress as a career. Until recently, little had been widely published or spoken about the importance of professional support groups, debriefing or ventilating in dealing with countertransference issues. Many therapists felt as if they were burned out;

others began re-experiencing their own demons (particularly in the case of Vietnam veterans, but also in other trauma survivors) and in many instances witnessed by the authors, little was known as to where to turn for help. Although progress has been forthcoming, much more needs to be done.

The establishment of ethical guidelines relating to therapy for traumatic stress is an issue toward which the authors have devoted several years and significant resources. Fortunately interest in this area is growing and emphasis will continue to be placed on the development and implementation of ethical guidelines. These and other subjects are woven through the following chapter in an attempt to illustrate the vulnerabilities experienced by therapists and the importance of addressing these issues on both an individual and collective basis. It is not the intent of the authors to examine these issues in detail but instead to raise the awareness of the reader and to suggest potential areas for later investigation on a more in-depth level.

Webster's (1984) definition of "vulnerable" applies to and should guide efforts at self care for traumatologists. A vulnerable person is one who "can be wounded or physically injured,...open to criticism or attack,...or easily hurt by...adverse criticism [though, perhaps not so easily hurt as we muster forces, gird our loins, and arm ourselves in the breastplates of armor of truth and investigation],...[and] liable to increased penalties and entitled to increased bonuses" (p. 1594). Traumatologists are vulnerable in so many different ways. The purpose of the following sections is to put the vulnerability of those who work with trauma within a framework of ethics and standards of practice, taking into consideration the various aspects of vulnerability that face therapists. The chapter also makes suggestions for acquiring "increased bonuses" (as opposed to suffering "increased penalties") from therapy work.

Therapists, emergency responders, crisis counselors, and others who work with traumatized persons must recognize that they are instruments of healing or hurting. It is therefore important that they are aware of the areas of vulnerability they face as instruments and attempt to use themselves in a manner which maximizes the healing and minimizes the hurting, both for their clients and secondarily for themselves. Each of the following sections examines a potential area of vulnerability and identifies the means to lessen that vulnerability.

THE NEED FOR A STRONG ETHICAL SENSE AND ETHICAL PRINCIPLES OF PRACTICE

Values are the foundations of ethical statements. Persons who work in the trauma field are expected to adhere to values similar to the values espoused by professional organizations such as the American Psychological Association, National Association of Social Workers, and the recently-formed International Association of Trauma Counselors. Values include nonmaleficence (do not harm), beneficence (promotion of the welfare of others about self), justice (fairness), fidelity (honesty and fulfilling commitments), and others.

Ethical statements and beliefs articulate the core values of a profession or group of persons, as well as appropriate rules of conduct and expectations of the group and the individuals belonging to that group (Frankel, 1989; Frankel, 1992). They constitute standards of behavior that are consistent with a view of reality which notes that persons who have been exposed to traumatic events may experience short- and long-term effects from those events, which vary in intensity and phenomenology. Practitioners are vulnerable if they do not have strongly-formed ethical beliefs and values which are consistent with both the profession and the work that they do.

The Need for
Knowledge of Theory
and Ongoing Training

Persons working in the trauma field are particularly vulnerable if they lack a strong foundation in all aspects of trauma theory. It is not enough to read one or two books on the treatment of a certain survivor population or to attend one or two training sessions. The International Association of Trauma Counselors, for example, is establishing broad and comprehensive training standards in order to coordinate, to some degree, clinical practice in the field. The IATC has established three levels of credentialing: Certified Trauma Counselor; Associate in Trauma Support; and Certified Trauma Responder.

Certification as a Certified Trauma Counselor (CTC) requires 2,000 hours of trauma counseling experience and 240 contact hours of required training. This consists of training in PTSD (24 hours), assessment (12 hours), diagnosis (12 hours), case management/treatment planning (12 hours), counseling with individuals/families/groups (36 hours), special populations (18 hours), large-scale disasters (8 hours), community resources/referral (12 hours), criminal justice (12 hours), ethical issues (6 hours), and approved electives (76 hours). In addition a CTC should have at least 50 hours of personal counseling/therapy. The CTC is a professional with an advanced degree.

The Associate in Trauma Support (ATS) has an Associates Degree which combines experience in the field (but without a graduate degree) with a minimum of 32 hours of training/education in the field. A Certified Trauma Responder has similar experience, education and training to the ATS, but also possesses an additional 40 hours of advanced training in disaster response (Salston, 1994).

Some therapists appear to "hang out a shingle" as survivor therapists or traumatologists when they are poorly trained and/or inexperienced. Working with persons who have been traumatized, especially if the traumas have been severe, is not for the inexperienced or beginning therapist, unless that therapist is supervised or mentored very carefully. Combs (1989) aptly noted that the methods a therapist uses in and of themselves are nondynamic; it is the creative use of the self of the therapist as an instrument that brings methods to life. Therapists who work with survivors of trauma therefore need a personalized framework to order their practice of treatment. For diagnostic purposes and insurance requirements, that framework is based on the DSM-IV (American Psychiatric Association [APA], 1994) definition of post-traumatic stress.

However they are also influenced by a variety of renditions of trauma theory. A theory is a guide by which practitioners can make sense of the helping process and is a rationale for what is done in the name of helping (Combs, 1982). It has basic assumptions, offers a structure to illustrate how personality is put together and how it develops, and it has a philosophical element in terms of the values it espouses and the kind of person that is expected to emerge at the end of the process. In short, it provides a cognitive map of organization and an expected course of the process.

Williams and Sommer (1994) have a four-part theory of treatment that includes Encounter/Education; Exploration of the Impact of Trauma and Doing the Work of Processing the Trauma; Skill Building and Client Empowerment; and Evaluation, Integration and Termination. Herman (1992) offers a three-stage theory that essentially combines Williams and Sommer's third and fourth stages. Walker (1994) recently has proposed a similar theory of treatment which she calls Survivor Therapy. The key principles of that therapy method are quite similar to those of Williams and Sommer (1994) and include safety, empowerment, validation, emphasis on strengths, education, expanding alternatives, restructuring clarity in judgment, understanding oppression, and making one's own decisions.

The framework and knowledge base of trauma therapy is constantly changing and expanding. New books describing modifications in theory as well as methods and techniques are appearing in greater numbers (Meichenbaum, 1994; Williams and Sommer, 1994). What makes for a good knowledge base? Knowledge competency includes having up-to-date information about diagnosis and diagnostic instruments, neurobiological aspects of trauma, assessment techniques, research results, cross-cultural issues, bibliotherapy materials, and referral sources, among others. From what sources does a therapist glean information? Examples of sources could be organizations such as the International Society for Traumatic Stress Studies or the International Association of Trauma Counselors, reading the publications of such organizations, attending their annual meetings and/or regional chapter meetings or training institutes, and reading some of the newest books in the field. These examples illustrate ways in which it is possible for the therapist to ensure ongoing exposure to updated materials and knowledge.

THE NEED FOR RESOLUTION OF THE THERAPIST'S OWN ISSUES AND TRAUMA HISTORY

Why do persons become trauma therapists? What is it that draws individuals to the field? For the most part, the motivation is to help others work through their traumas. In some instances, however, therapists have resolved or unresolved trauma histories or have been exposed to the trauma(s) of others and desire to work out personal issues through the lives of their clients. For example, many sexual abuse survivors are drawn to work with other survivors and having a similar history can be a plus. This stance may apply as well to combat veterans who become therapists and work with other veterans. In fact, one folkloric rationale is that "in order to truly understand and empathize with clients, one must have walked in their shoes and similarly suffered." However, it can also be a hindrance if personal issues have not been resolved.

Many persons willingly and sometimes too freely share their own trauma histories with clients, openly acknowledging their own struggles and successes with healing. This is a major ethical concern: how much of the private self should one share in therapy? It may be helpful to allude to one's understanding of a client's pain; but to relate that pain in any great detail can be more therapeutic to the therapist than to the client.

When a trauma therapist has not worked out his or her own primary and secondary traumas relating to past events, then that history may harm the therapeutic process. Briere (1989) noted that a survivor of a particular trauma may be too close to the issues to be clearly objective when treating similarly traumatized survivors. Avoiding one's own issues before entering into the field in earnest can leave one vulnerable to retraumatization and have a negative impact on practice. Therefore, it is important to conduct a thorough analysis of one's own history and construct a trauma timeline of both primary and secondary traumas. It is also important to undertake one's own necessary therapy earlier, rather than later, in one's career.

Persons considering trauma therapy as a career should ask themselves: "What major impacts in my life have led to this work?" These could include involvement in combat, early losses (people, pets, or objects), deaths of significant caretakers, exposure to mental illness or substance abuse in a caretaker, a history of abuse or neglect, living in a household where a parent was a law enforcement officer, growing up in a world where service to others was the only accepted norm, or victimization at the hands of another, to name a few. What values have been affected by these experiences and what motivations underlie the work? To what degree is the desire to help others who have had traumatic experiences motivated by altruism? These are all issues with which a therapist should come to terms and deal with during the educational and training aspects of preparation for a career as a therapist, rather than "on the job."

THE NEED FOR COMPETENCE IN PRACTICE STRATEGIES AND TECHNIQUES

An unskilled therapist, especially in the treatment of stress and trauma, is particularly vulnerable to accusations of incompetence from clients and non-therapists alike. There are a variety of ways to practice therapy, including such techniques as cognitive-behavioral models of thought stopping, in vivo reliving, EMDR, and the use of hypnosis, although some of these methods are coming under attack.

The work relating to most trauma therapy needs to occur in an environment that is safe for clients and therapist alike. Williams (1993a, 1993b) has written extensively on techniques for providing safety in the therapeutic setting. If the therapist's environment is not safe, then avoid trauma work. If the client cannot assure the therapist of a minimal level of personal safety (i.e., that he/she is not going to commit suicide or harm others), then the work cannot go forward.

The work of trauma therapy needs to be carried out in an atmosphere of mutual respect and mutual participation; it is not a therapist-as-authority driven process. The client is the authority and the client's particular phenomenology drives the choice of techniques and strategies, timing and pacing, mode and method. The trauma therapist needs to be flexible in use of strategies as well, choosing what works best from the wide range of treatment options that are now practiced (Wylie, 1989).

Use of techniques involves a deliberate use of self as an instrument of healing. It is a mistake, therefore, to assume that a survivor of trauma will trust the therapist either immediately or after a fairly short period of time. Short-term models of intervention may help a person to deal with symptom release but do not generally work to establish trusting relationships with survivors of trauma, particularly if those traumas involve extreme stress.

The ethical use of self, which involves protection of the client as well as self-protection of the therapist, means that the therapist is committed to the client and is responsible *to* the client, not *for* the client. The therapist must clearly understand the purpose of treatment and must not manipulate the client or use techniques that might be seen as manipulative, leading, or suggestive of traumas that have not occurred. In other words, it is unethical to inform the client that a trauma had to have occurred, based on a trauma symptom "checklist," when the client has no memory of such a trauma. The authors in past years have heard persons say they "know what happened to the client" even though the client does not know. We have quickly cautioned those therapists that such a conclusion should be avoided and must not be voiced to the client. Therapists should make the most ethical and least restrictive diagnosis possible.

Therapists have the responsibility for the organization and the pacing of sessions. For therapy with clients suffering from problems related to post-traumatic stress, a common practice might follow the use of the rule of thirds: one third of the time for present issues, one third for memory/trauma work, and one third for processing (Williams, 1994). Doing ethical trauma work thus requires symptom management.

It is also important for therapists to educate clients about trauma, traumatic stress, and the methods of treatment. Therefore, therapists should avoid some common treatment traps: over-distancing, maintenance of neutrality, lack of caring, avoidance of interpersonal engagement, and extended use of silence (Chu, 1990). Keeping the client informed of the process of therapy lessens therapists' vulnerability to accusations of unethical practice.

The trauma therapist becomes even more vulnerable when issues of commission occur. These issues include pushing too fast for trauma-related material when safety is not established or stability has not occurred, pushing for confrontation with an accused abuser, jumping to the conclusion that abuse has occurred when no evidence thereof is available or deducible, getting caught up in the trauma itself rather than focusing on the client as a person, knowingly developing a surrogate relationship with the client, overlooking pathology, overlooking the danger of a situation, or failing to make a treatment plan that considers issues of hospitalization or commitment when indicated.

The scope of this chapter is not to examine, in detail, the various ethical practices and strategies of the trauma therapist. However, it is important to note that the therapist must establish professional and personal principles concerning the use of touch, power-related issues, transference issues, boundary issues, dual relationships, confidentiality, and other relationship-oriented ethical matters. As one develops a standard of ethical practice, ask if some of the following questions can be of assistance: What guides my actions, knowledge, intuition, self-awareness, theory? How do I evaluate my own effectiveness as a therapist? Do I discourage disclosure of a trauma history or push too early and too fast for disclosure? Thus, awareness of these and other standards can help improve services rendered.

THE NEED FOR AWARENESS OF THE IMPACT OF "THE WORK" ON THE SELF OF THE THERAPIST AND THE WILLINGNESS TO TAKE STEPS TO LESSEN THAT SECONDARY IMPACT

The terms for secondary trauma are many: compassion fatigue (Figley, 1995), vicarious traumatization (McCann & Pearlman,

1990), secondary wounding, event countertransference (Danieli, 1994), and burnout. Although they refer to many differing types of secondary traumatic stress reactions, they all have in common the underlying recognition that trauma work is difficult, challenging, and frequently exhausting for those who undertake it, no matter their profession, gender, age, or level of training and experience. Just how many burned bodies can an emergency workers who works with stressed fire and rescue workers witness or hear descriptions of? How many dozens of bodies of drowned persons can one view as a police psychologist who is a member of a mass casualty Dead Victim Identification team? How many hundreds of stories of rape, molestation, abuse, pain, and suffering can a therapist who works with survivors of sexual abuse hear or imagine before secondary traumatization becomes manifest? Just as trauma exposure heightens the victim's vulnerability to repetitious thoughts, dreams, physical manifestations of events, somatic complaints, transformed meanings, blunted or enhanced affects, abandoned or newly-formed relationships and overadaptive or maladaptive behaviors, secondary exposure to those traumas impacts those who tend to the victims.

How does the work affect the therapist? It impacts in many ways. Listening closely to unfolding atrocities and terror challenges the therapist's world. If one is tired coming into the day's work, then the result may be a gradual numbing and dissociating, particularly if faced with the anger of clients directed against the therapist.

In order to minimize the impact of client material and lessen the vulnerability of therapists to secondary trauma, it is important to examine constantly the toll that conducting the work takes on the self. How has the work affected personal identity, spirituality, sexuality, relationships, dreams or fantasies, and emotional responsiveness? When does work lead to feelings of frustration and hopelessness or to joy and feelings of accomplishment? Identification of personal triggers for secondary wounding is an important part of the self-care process. If there are particular stories or types of traumas that are especially difficult to process, it may be necessary to limit or avoid clients with those histories or stories.

It is also important to recognize what one does to self-soothe. If the self-soothing mechanisms used by the therapist are harmful and impair the practice, then the only ethical course for that therapist is to seek treatment and/or assistance. Having a strong support group with which to share stories, tragedies, and successes is an absolute necessity. Munroe (1994) advises against solo practice. However, for persons who live in rural communities or who have no like-minded colleagues with whom they can link in a group practice, solo practice may be the only option. When this is the case, having phone and face-to-face links with other trauma specialists is essential for maintenance of sanity. It is no small wonder that many trauma therapists have large phone bills, get "on line" quickly, and use conferences and annual meetings to self-soothe, share, unwind, and relax.

In addition, it is important for the trauma therapist to determine how the work has touched his or her own personal schemas or beliefs and expectations concerning safety, trust, power, esteem, and intimacy of self and others (McCann & Pearlman, 1990). To determine the impact of the work on one's sense of safety, the therapists can ask themselves, How vulnerable do I feel to harm? How do I protect myself from the effect of this work? Where is my safe place? How hypervigilant am I? What, if anything, gives me an adrenalin high when I do this work? To what risky situations does this work expose me? What needs for security do I have?

When examining the impact of the work on one's beliefs about trust in self and others, therapists might ask themselves the following questions: Do I have a support system which backs me? Whom do I trust or mistrust? Do I trust my intuition, my knowledge, or both? What makes me a trustworthy person? Do I believe in the existence (and power) of evil? When

I self-examine the impact of the work on my beliefs about power and control, what is my personal locus of control? Do I ever force or try to manipulate others to feel helpless? Do I feel helpless and, if so, when and where? Do I ever get into power struggles with clients? How do I react to those struggles? How do I react to maladaptive expressions of power in my clients (e.g., suicide gestures or self-mutilation)? How do I increase my own sense of personal power? Do I have fantasies that are power related? What would I do if a client attacked me or threatened me?

When examining the impact of the work on one's sense of self esteem, therapists might consider, Do I value myself? Do I devalue myself? If so, when? Do I feel responsible for events that happen in the lives of my clients? Do I ever consider myself a victim of trauma? Am I a cynical person or am I hopeful and optimistic? What personal resources do I have to protect me from secondary traumatization? What beliefs protect me and give me strength? Finally, when examining the impact of the work on one's sense of intimacy, therapists might ask the questions, Do I feel connected to others? Where and from whom do I get support? Has the work made me feel closer to, or more distant from, others?

To resolve secondary traumatization, or at least to lessen its impact, the authors of this chapter suggest that the trauma therapist may undertake the following measures:

1. Get supervision from someone who understands the dynamics of PTSD and its impact as well as methods of treatment of PTSD.

2. Clarify one's own sense of meaning and purpose in life.

3. If one feels overwhelmed in a therapy-related matter, break the task(s) down into manageable components; apply case management strategies.

4. Identify one's own personal and social resources and supports and then plan strategies for their use.

5. Diversify interests to include balance, including materials

read or workshops attended, and between personal and professional lives.

6. Play.

7. Laugh.

8. Be creative and use one's intuitive side.

9. Develop one's spiritual side as a grounding tool.

10. Take care of oneself physically; use physical means to find adrenalin highs.

11. Develop personal rituals to ensure safety and empowerment.

12. Dream.

13. Journal.

14. Modify one's own work schedule to fit one's life (Colrain & Steele, 1990).

15. Identify those triggers which may cause one to experience vicarious traumatization (images, actions).

16. Get therapy if personal issues and past traumas "get in the way."

17. Maintain a high-energy level through proper diet, sleep, exercise, etc.

18. Use one's own self-soothing capacities in a positive manner.

19. Know one's own limitations.

20. Have hope in the ability of people to change, heal, grow.

21. Admit it when one does not know an answer or makes a mistake.

22. Keep the boundaries one sets for self and others.

23. Develop strategies to stay "present" during therapy sessions, even when hearing or seeing the horror others have experienced.

24. Maintain an ability to see "gray."

25. Know one's own level of tolerance.

CONCLUSIONS

As in any profession or field of work, there are some therapists who cross ethical boundaries and who do not set an example others should follow. On the other hand there are a large number of trauma therapists who are overworked and, until recently, hard-pressed to know exactly how to take care of their own counter transference issues. Fortunately, there are organizations such as the International Society for Traumatic Stress Studies and the International Association of Trauma Counselors that provide information and training on these and numerous other subjects relating to the treatment of traumatized populations. Dedicated therapists involve themselves in the annual meetings and regional conferences of these and other reputable organizations relating to the field of mental health. They are constantly seeking additional information and training.

The disorders addressed in this chapter are, for the most part, two that are widely recognized. Post-traumatic Stress Disorder (PTSD) was first recognized in the American Psychiatric Association's Diagnostic and Statistical Manual, third edition (1980). Multiple Personality Disorder was initially recognized in DSM-III-R (1987) and is now known as Dissociative Identity Disorder in DSM-IV (1994). Significant progress in understanding post-traumatic stress has transpired over the past 15 or so years, but there is much more to be done. In order to continue making gains in knowledge and treatment, and for competently trained therapists and counselors to continue to diagnose and work with those who are suffering from traumatic events, it is necessary to educate the public and its representatives to various legislative bodies about the reality of the disorders we have discussed, as well as their related symptoms. In the opinion of these authors, it is also important to educate therapists to care for themselves in order to provide the best standards of care for those suffering individuals, communities, and nations.

REFERENCES

American Psychiatric Association. (1980). *Diagnostic and statistical manual of mental disorders* (3rd ed.). Washington, D.C.: American Psychiatric Association.

American Psychiatric Association. (1987). *Diagnostic and statistical manual of mental disorders* (3rd ed. rev.). Washington, D.C.: American Psychiatric Association.

American Psychiatric Association. (1994). *Diagnostic and statistical manual of mental disorders* (4th ed.). Washington, D.C.: American Psychiatric Association.

Briere, J. (1989). *Therapy for adults molested as children: Beyond survival.* New York: Springer Publishing Co.

Chu, J. (1990). Ten traps for therapists in the treatment of trauma survivors. *Dissociation,* 1, 24–32.

Combs, A. (1982). *A personal approach to teaching: Beliefs that make a difference.* Boston: Allyn & Bacon.

Combs, A. W. (1989). *A theory of therapy: Guidelines for counseling practice.* Newbury Park, CA: Sage Publications.

Danieli, Y. (1994). Countertransference and trauma: Self healing and training issues. In M. B. Williams & J. F. Sommer (Eds.), *Handbook of post-traumatic therapy.* Westport, CT: Greenwood Press.

Figley, C. G., (Ed.). (1995). *Compassion fatigue: Coping with secondary stress disorder in those who treat the traumatized.* New York: Brunner/Mazel.

Frankel, M. S. (1989). Professional codes: Why, how, and with what impact? *Journal of business ethics,* 8, 109–115.

Frankel, M. S. (1992). Taking ethics seriously: Building a professional community. Keynote Address, American Dental Hygienists Association Conference, Louisville, KY.

Guralnik, D. B. (Editor in Chief) (1984). *Webster's new world dictionary of the American language* (2nd. ed.). New York: Warner Books.

Herman, J. L. (1992). *Trauma and recovery.* New York: Basic Books.

McCann, I. L., & Pearlman, L. A. (1990). Vicarious traumatization: A framework for understanding the psychological effects of working with victims. *Journal of traumatic stress,* 3, 131–149.

Meichenbaum, D. (1994). *A clinical handbook/practical therapist manual for assessing and treating adults with post-traumatic stress disorder (PTSD).* University of Waterloo: Ontario, Canada.

Salston, M. (Winter, 1994). Certification standards. *Frontline Counselor: IATC Newsletter,* p.4.

Steele, K., & Colrain, J. (1991). Abreactive work with sexual abuse survivors: Concepts and techniques. In M. Hunter (Ed.), *The sexually abused male: Application of treatment strategies*. New York: Lexington.

Walker, L. E. A. (1994). *Abused women and survivor therapy*. Washington, D.C.: American Psychological Association.

Williams, M. B. (1993). Establishing safety in survivors of severe sexual abuse in posttraumatic stress therapy. *Treating abuse today*, 3 (l), 4–11.

Williams, M. B. & Sommer, J. F. (Eds.) (1994). *Handbook of posttraumatic therapy*. Westport, CT: Greenwood Press.

Wylie, M. S. (March/April, 1989). Looking for the fence posts. *Networker*, 23–33.

1 4

No Escape from Philosophy in Trauma Treatment and Research

Jonathan Shay

Long known by his colleagues for being an independent thinker, Jonathan Shay asked that this paper be kept in the voice in which it originated; readers will notice immediately that it is a transcript of a spoken work. The paper, printed here in a slightly altered form, was originally given at the 1994 International Society of Traumatic Stress Studies meeting. In his talk, as well as in this chapter, Shay challenges us with his clarity of vision of what the classics can teach us about trauma. It is a unique perspective, one that has received much acclaim in Shay's 1994 book, Achilles in Viet Nam, *and will appear again in his future works. It takes us from our usual modes of thinking into a new and invigorating perspective.*

The conference organizer told me I have 20 minutes for all of philosophy. Great! Considering the amount of time most people devote to the voluntary study of philosophy as adults, that's probably far too much time. My goal for this talk is to make a number of appeals:

1. To recall that virtually all of our academic disciplines evolved out of and differentiated from philosophy within the last few centuries—*often from only one side of an unsettled philosophical dispute.* The fact that one side won, institutionally speaking, does not necessarily mean that it had the stronger case and the dispute was settled by victory for that side. Never forget the power of a social group {and academic and professional disciplines are indeed multigenerational social groups} to construct a reality for its members.

2. To accept as a lifelong task strengthening capacities for ethical perception and deliberation;

3. To skeptically monitor the social construction of reality in our own worlds;

4. To become more alert to those ideas that are so pervasive as to be invisible;

5. To take our own lives seriously and not leave these tasks to the "experts" and the "professionals."

Some writers, following the line of Aristotle's famous lecture series "Ethics," say that it is the branch of philosophy that deals with how to live well, how to achieve human flourishing (Nussbaum, 1986; Broadie, 1991). When someone gives such a definition, readers generally glaze over and nod and pay not the slightest attention to the fact that just yesterday, we might have heard that a colleague was hauled before a professional ethics board—I guess by that definition to be sternly admonished that he or she had not been living well, had failed to flourish.

The internationally prominent French philosopher Paul Ricoeur wants us to reserve the word ethics for philosophizing about living well and the word morals for philosophizing about our duties. But as Ricoeur also points out the Greek word "*ethos*" and the Latin word "*mores*" mean exactly the same thing—the customs, habits, way of life of an individual or group (Ricoeur, 1992, 170). So this does not really help at all. If I succeed at what I am doing, you will leave this chapter with not one piece of philosophical jargon, with no hundred-dollar words like "deontology" or "deictic," nor with hair-splitting distinctions between the words "ethics" and "morals," but rather with a greater curiosity to just plain figure out what people are talking about when they throw these words around.

Long-dead philosophers are usually the source of pervasive, invisible—therefore unconscious—"truths" that get built into our institutions, our "common sense," and our emotional reactions to events. Controversies as fresh as whether to admit to the possibility of post-traumatic personality changes in the DSM-IV version of PTSD goes back to ancient roots. (This was, as you know, *rejected* by the Anxiety Disorders Committee and thus does not appear in the DSM-IV.)

So that this sweeping claim doesn't hover in the bloodless world of abstraction, I want to give you this example that is central to the field of trauma, particularly to severe, prolonged trauma under effective conditions of captivity, such as political torture, domestic battering, combat, incest—trauma bad enough to produce what Judy Herman (1992) calls "complex PTSD," what the DSM-IV Field Trials awkwardly called Disorders of Extreme Stress Not Otherwise Specified [DESNOS], and what ICD-10 calls "Enduring Personality Change after Catastrophic Experience" (W.H.O., 1992). Here is this example, in the form of a question: *Can any workings of bad luck produce cruel or evil actions in a good person?*

Plato (*Apology*, 41d) has Socrates say, in his famous defense before the court that condemned him to death, "nothing can harm a good man either in life or after death," and again in the *Republic* we hear extensively argued that the good person cannot be harmed by the world. For Plato, the notable quality that a good man has is inextricably bound up with good breeding, in particular aristocratic lineage. By the time we get to the Roman Stoics, however, this possibility of unshakable goodness, now called virtue, has been democratized so that even a slave could possess it, having acquired it by good upbringing in childhood. In this form Christianity took up the idea and clothed it with the doctrine of God's grace. By the late 18th Century it had been set in stone by Immanuel Kant, who said that which is truly deserving of ethical praise, blame, or true moral worth cannot be augmented or diminished by fortune. In the 20th Century, psychoanalysis offered us as a "scientific" result what the culture had already embraced, that no bad events could shake good character, once formed in childhood. When a previously good person engages in horrible acts, we must have been deceived; there had been a hidden flaw, a *diathesis*—give it a Greek name and that makes it more true than if you say it in plain English—a word incidentally that harks right back to Plato's *Republic*.

Because of the presence of such "heavies" as Plato, the Stoics, and Kant, you may be wondering—well, maybe they're right after all, maybe it's "truth." It's hard to buck that kind of authority, especially if you are unaware of the fact that this reflects only *one* tradition and don't know who's on the other side of the issue or what they have to say.

Plato's contemporaries thought of him as a crank, not a philosopher, a word they reserved for the tragic poets like Sophocles, Euripides, Aeschylus, and above all, Homer. All of the tragic poets presented the destruction of good character by external events, particularly betrayal and bereavement. Among those whom subsequent ages also called philosophers, Aristotle undercut Plato's position most powerfully, although there are times that Aristotle appears to endorse it, and people argue and argue about where he really stood.

So as much as I hate to, I'm going to have to drop this line of discussion and move on because of time and just leave you again with slogans:

1. No escape from philosophy!
2. There are many unsettled questions in ethical philosophy.

Table 1

THE PROFESSIONAL VALUE PATTERN IN OUR SOCIETY

	UNIVERSALISM	FUNCTIONAL SPECIFICITY	COLLECTIVITY ORIENTATION	ACHIEVEMENT	AFFECTIVE NEUTRALITY
DEFINITION OF PATTERN VARIABLE NOW NORMATIVE FOR THE PROFESSIONAL	Rule-based orientation to patient as subsumable example of abstractly defined category; relationship based on transcendent standard	Significance of patient limited to diagnosis and specific role in treatment, discipline-based orientation toward patient; division of labor, specialization	Defines role/value in relation to institution and profession; fear of institutional sanctions; legitimate gratifications only from institutional and professional rewards, including pay and public esteem	Professional's role /value based on performance competency conceived as learnable, transferable technique, not as personal to the professional	Personal detachment; situation assessed in light of reason, not emotion; delay and restriction of gratifications to those given by the institution and profession
DICHOTOMOUS OPPOSITE	PARTICULARISM	DIFFUSENESS	SELF-ORIENTATION	ASCRIPTION	AFFECTIVITY
DEFINITION OF DICHOTOMOUS OPPOSITE	Orientation to patient on the basis of the particularity of his/her situation, history; immanence	Whole patient seen as significant; no prior limits to interest or concern for patient	Role/value defined in relation to patient; satisfaction derived from relation to patient	Professional's role/value based on personal characteristics	Situation assessed in light of emotions and personal gratifications
INSTITUTIONAL-IZATION OF PATTERN VARIABLE	Diagnosis-based access, treatment, work organization, claims on resources	Licensure, departmental and professional organization along disciplinary lines	Titles; institutional power; differential compensation	Credentials; licensure examinations; training program criteria, training program curricula	Disciplinary codes against exploitation and abuse of patients
VOICE OF COMMON SENSE	"If we don't know the diagnosis, how are we going to know what to do?"	"You do your job and I'll do mine, and together we'll get the job done." "I'm the doctor, so shut up."	"You've lost your objectivity." "Get with the program." "Everyone wants to get ahead [in their institution and/or profession]"	"Of course you can trust me; I've trained many years for this work." "I'm the doctor, so shut up."	"You can't let your feelings get involved." "Just stick to the facts." "Don't drag your personal stuff into this."
ADVANTAGES OF CURRENTLY NORMATIVE PROFESSIONAL VALUE PATTERN	Predictability; fairness; elimination of nepotism, bribery, exploitation; organizational discipline	Predictability; fairness; goal-attainment, insofar as competency is real; is claimed to promote efficiency	Predictability; is claimed to prevent exploitation, but may just shift beneficiary of the exploitation; is claimed to put patient's needs first	Predictability; fairness; is claimed to promote competency; elimination of hereditary, racial, ethnic, gender privilege	Personal self-discipline; is claimed to put patient's needs first; prevents exploitation and abuse of patients
EXAMPLES OF HOW OBSTRUCTS TRAUMA RECOVERY	Rules were often the direct source or legitimization of the trauma; survivor can't trust rule-dominated person	Promotes splitting	Careerism sometimes source of trauma; requires that patient trust the institution, not the person; promotes splitting	Confusion of credentials with competence; abuse of institutional power was source of trauma	No communialization of trauma; obstructs trust; blocks awareness of important clinical information
EXAMPLES OF HOW NORM OBSTRUCTS THERAPIST SELF-CARE	Normative failure to attend to particularity of therapist's own experience of the patient's narratives and reenactments; "I'm fully trained, so...."	Limits growth and job satisfaction; can obstruct team community building; reduces team communication	Normative illusion that institution and profession provide all the social support that is needed to do the work safely; myth of professional invulnerability	Normative illusion that technical proficiency is adequate to hearing trauma narratives and engagement in trauma reenactments; myth of professional invulnerability	Myth of professional invulnerability; loss of signal function of emotions; blocks necessary social support; feared loss of colleague esteem; feared loss of job

3. Let's learn to recognize when one side of an unsettled philosophical controversy is presented as conclusive truth.

Now I want to direct your attention to Table 1. The ethos or value pattern of the professions (Parsons, 1951) you see laid out in Table 1 represents the product of millennia of philosophic and social struggle. This value pattern is deeply embedded in our common sense, our institutions, our social ideologies. The final two rows of the table point out that this value pattern often leads us astray in our work with trauma survivors and in our practices of self-care in doing this work.

Each component of the professional value pattern has a long history and is the product of many centuries-long struggles that we take pride in as social progress. They are not only deeply rooted in ourselves as internalized ideals, but are just as deeply institutionalized in the formal structures and processes of our mental health workplaces. These value orientations speak to us usually in voices of "common sense," so pervasively "true" that that we often fail to notice their presence. The professional value pattern contains many solid virtues, which when absent we note to our horror as exploitation, corruption, and abuse. The positive side of these value orientations is given in the top row labelled "advantages of currently normative professional value pattern." The two final rows sketch out the obstacles that these value orientations throw up to our clinical work and describe how they obstruct therapist self-care.

I want briefly to draw your attention to a number of very interesting questions about how we know what we know and what degree of trustworthiness and permanence we attribute to this knowledge. Here are some of the questions that seem important to me:

1. Is it possible to escape the moral dimension of trauma in our "scientific" studies of it?

2. When we demonstrate that something has "psychometric properties" does this mean that we have discovered something

that is "real?" In what sense is it real—does this mean not culturally and historically constructed? There is an important sense in which the human heartbeat (or the feline heartbeat, for that matter) is not culturally constructed, likewise the mineral, bauxite. When we demonstrate that something has "psychometric properties" have we discovered something like bauxite?

3. Is there a conflict in trauma research between the epistemological standard of the double blind study and the ethical requirement for informed consent? Can someone whose capacity for social trust has been destroyed by repeated betrayal and prolonged abuse give informed consent?

Each of these questions could be a chapter in itself.

Therapist self-care is the final topic that I want to devote time to before I stop—*what is the ethical standing of the needs of the trauma therapist?* Let us take an undramatic and familiar example: What ethical standing does the good of my night's sleep have when set against the good of my patient's finding comfort when he (all of my patients are men) feels despair in the middle of the night? In fact, our philosophical tradition is extraordinarily weak in its ability to deal with the problem of competing, incommensurable goods. Utilitarian ethics, institutionalized in modern America as cost/benefit analysis, is genuinely useful when you can meaningfully define competing goods in a common coinage, but leaves you utterly at sea when no common coinage can be found. I challenge you to find a convincing way to make the good of my patient's comfort in nocturnal despair commensurable with the good of my night's sleep. We have many rich and varied ways of thinking about conflicts of good and evil, but few to help us in conflicts of good and good. So in our practical deliberations, such as what to do when called in the middle of the night, we tend to fall back on notions of moral duty, and on Christian praise of self-sacrifice.

Duty entered Hellenistic philosophy through the Stoics and then merged very powerfully with the stream of "Thou Shalts" and "Thou Shalt Nots" from the Bible. In modern times Immanuel Kant set the question What is my Duty? at the top of everyone's agenda.

We ask, what is our duty when a patient calls in the middle of the night? What I want you to notice here is that there is a large void when we attempt to answer the question of the affirmative ethical standing of the self, the self of the therapist, in this situation. By framing it in terms of duty, we are usually pushed to a limited number of alternatives:

1. We can deny that the telephone call really represents a good for the patient, or is such a negligible good that the patient's ethical claim is negligible. Therefore we have no duty to pick up the phone.

2. We can admit that it *is* a good for the patient, but declare that good to be tainted by illegitimate means, such as lying about suicidal intent to gain comfort in despair. This allows us to redefine the conflict from being the clash of two goods to being the clash of good and evil.

3. We convince ourselves that refusing the patient's phone call promotes a *higher* good of the patient, and that thus refusing it becomes part of our duty as therapists. Much supervisory instruction is devoted to the subject of "setting limits," "role-modeling appropriate boundaries" for the benefit of the patient, etc.

4. We shift the duty to someone else through "coverage" arrangements in the form of phone answering machine instructions to call someone else.

5. We perceive some threat to health or safety (Kant, 1991, no. 5, 19–20) in accepting the phone call, which for the first time gives the therapist any ethical standing and allows the mobilization of righteous indignation at the violation of rights, shifting somewhat the perspective away from duties.

In general we lack confidence of our capacities for practical deliberation in situations of conflicting goods. Very possibly you have paid a therapist or outside supervisor for years in search of this confidence. I'm here to tell you that the lack, dear reader, is not necessarily in yourself, but in our philosophical heritage.

What is notably absent from all of the alternatives we come up with in the middle of the night is the calm, assured, affirmative respect accorded to the self of the therapist that therapists routinely accord to patients. The pressures that our patients mobilize in the middle of the night depend to some extent on the ethical vacuum that our culture creates around the self of the therapist.

So that I can perhaps dispel suspicions that professional philosophers would hold their noses at this account, I just want to briefly quote from a recently published symposium of ethical philosophers: "over a large range of cases our ordinary thinking about morality assigns no positive value to the well-being or happiness of the moral agent of the sort it clearly assigns to the well-being or happiness of *everyone other than the agent*." (Slote, 1993, p. 441). And "if I am faced with someone who has a valid claim of need, I cannot appeal to facts of self-interest in deliberating whether I should offer help, because self-interest *per se* cannot rebut a moral presumption" (Herman, 1993, p. 319).

This is an unresolved issue—the ethical standing of the self—in our philosophy, an invisible lacuna, if you wish. I make no claim to fill it here today, but merely to point it out, to make the invisible visible. However, I want to close by pointing to the obvious fact that therapist self-care most readily acquires an affirmative ethical standing if it is strongly valued and supported by a *community*, in particular, the community of the therapist's co-workers. This positive value is raised to an exponent if there is actual community among the *patients,* and if that community of patients values and supports therapist self-care as very much in its self-interest. However much of the ethos of the professional presumes, and frequently promotes, an isolated *individual* as the patient, and contemplates neither the existence nor ethical standing of community among patients.

REFERENCES

Broadie, S. (1991). *Ethis with Aristotle*. New York: Oxford University Press.

Herman, B. (1993). Obligation and performance: A Kantian account of moral conflict. In O. Flanagan and A. O. Rorty (Eds.), *Identity, character, and morality: Essays in moral psychology*. Cambridge: MIT Press.

Herman, J. L. (1992). *Trauma and recovery*. New York: Basic Books.

Kant, E. (1991). *The metaphysics of morals* (M. Gregor, trans). New York: Cambridge University Press.

Nussbaum, M. (1986). *The fragility of goodness: Luck and ethics in Greek tragedy and philosophy*. New York: Cambridge University Press.

Parsons, T. (1951). *The social system*. New York: Free Press.

Plato. *Apology*. 41d.

Ricoeur, P. (1992). *Oneself as another* K. Blamey (trans). Chicago: University of Chicago Press.

Slote, M. (1993). Some advantages of virtue ethics. In O. Flanagan and A. O. Rorty (Eds.), *Identity, character, and morality: Essays in moral psychology*. Cambridge: MIT Press.

World Health Organization. (1992). *The ICD-10 classification of mental and behavioral disorders*. World Health Organization.

The Germ Theory of Trauma:
The Impossibility of Ethical Neutrality

Sandra L. Bloom

This final chapter is likely to be the most provocative. Sandra L. Bloom argues from a feminist-theoretical perspective that we have collectively created violence and that this violence is like an infection that is destroying our humanity. While some will not be able or willing to take on Bloom's perspective, others will likely cry out in relief to read it. It is not a chapter that can be responded to lightly. It challenges our thinking and invites quantitative questions. I invite you to read this chapter and see for yourself how you will be affected by the material.

To study psychological trauma means bearing witness to horrible events....When the traumatic events are of human design, those who bear witness are caught in the conflict between victim and perpetrator. It is morally impossible to remain neutral in this conflict. The bystander is forced to take sides.

> Judith Lewis Herman
> from *Trauma and Recovery*

Before Pasteur's discovery that it was microbes that were causing infections, people generally thought that the source of disease came from within, a manifest form of inner corruption, an expression of the punitive wrath of God, or demon possession. The germ theory showed that the infectious agent came from outside the person and if the person was vulnerable an infection would ensue (Schwartz, 1995). As the science of microbiology grew, it became apparent that some bacterial agents were so virulent that they could overwhelm the defenses of virtually everyone and that some social conditions like poor nutrition and improper sanitation were known to increase the likelihood of infection universally. The public health profession grew upon the premise that infectious agents killed and maimed the innocent and the guilty and could only be kept at bay by the enforcement of public policy that applied to all. Protecting the health of the nation's most valuable resource—human labor—was considered a social, moral, and economic responsibility.

In some meaningful ways, trauma theory is the psychological version of the germ theory. We now have an understanding of the connection between pathogenic forces in the external world and the internal pathology of the person. We know a great deal about how the body, mind, and soul of the victim interact with the body, mind and soul of the perpetrator (Davidson & Foa, 1993; Janoff-Bulman, 1992; van der Kolk, 1988, 1989, 1993; van der Kolk, Greenberg, Boyd & Krystal, 1985; Wilson & Raphael, 1993; Wolf & Mosnaim, 1990). But what impact does this profound shift in perspective have on us? In this chapter I want to extend the infection metaphor to our entire socio-cultural milieu and present an argument to the reader that the current epidemic of violence is a major public health problem. As clinicians who deal with the immediate and long-term effects of violence, we are part of the extended public health system. In this capacity we have a critical, but challenging role to play that may be vitally important to our attempts to care for ourselves as well as our patients. To understand where we are going, let us dwell for a minute, on where we have been.

The greatest significance of Pasteur's observations was that he was able to establish a cause-and-effect relationship between pathogens and disease. Once a causal connection could be established, efforts could be undertaken to combat the causal agent and to increase the resistance of the host to disease. In contrast, until now the etiological basis for mental disorders has been insubstantial to nonexistent. This is reflected in the DSM categorization schemes, which are descriptive accounts of symptom complexes. As a consequence, psychiatry has never been able to achieve the same level of respectability as the other medical professions which are based on a the cause-and-effect relationship between disease, external pathogenic factors, and the state of the targeted organism.

Unfortunately, the focus of attention for psychiatric dysfunction has, for the most part, remained firmly fixed within the individual, a century after the focus expanded outwards for physical disorders. In earlier times, the individual psychiatric defect revolved around original and internal corruption, punishment by God, or possession by demons (Ellenberger, 1970; Porter, 1987; Zilboorg, 1941). Over time the demon theory as well as the punishment-by-God theories lost momentum, but the locus of the problem still remained within the individual whether it was due to Freudian theories of arrested psychosexual development or faulty brain neurotransmitters. As a consequence, the individual model of treatment has prevailed and mental health has never really caught on as a major public health concern or social responsibility.

Among some biological psychiatrists, the individual model has been reduced even further to a total preoccupation with brain function, divorced from any outside pathogenic agent. In the last several decades, this approach has been so influential, that in some circles psychotherapy is considered an unnecessary luxury, if not a waste of time, while we wait for medications to be discovered that will wipe-out mental illness (Mender, 1994). Some psychiatric programs have become so reductionistic that little meaningful emphasis is placed on the skills involved in developing relationships, working through transference, and managing countertransference reactions. Since, in this model, mental health problems are largely a result of individual neurotic, psychotic, or character problems, the political and moral values of the patient's contextual frame are largely irrelevant, and the therapist, physician, or psychiatrist therefore has no real moral responsibility to do anything except follow a standard set of long-standing professional ethics. In political and moral terms, "the actions dictated by those who focus on individual pathology are carefully claimed to derive from no moral or political base; ordered to no social goal beyond that of patching the wounded" (Armstrong, 1994).

The individualistic approach is analogous to the practice of pre-Pasteur medicine. Since physicians could not see microbes and could not, therefore, see the relational aspects of disease, the measures they took could not be grounded in an understanding of microbial function. If they were compassionate and intuitive, they would recommend kindness, concern, and compassion on the part of others, but this was not a requirement for healing, rather a sign of benevolence on the part of the healers. If they washed their hands or took any sanitary measures, it was because they preferred it that way, not because it was known to be necessary. And because their practices were based on unsound theory, some of the things they did were downright harmful, like continuous bleeding and the administration of herbs and potions that were sometimes poisonous.

When the great microbiology discoveries began to occur the enthusiasm for antibiotic treatment grew. In the early heydays of antibiotic treatment many thought that the elimination of infectious disease was just around the corner. Enormous strides were made in conquering disease that had plagued humans since the beginning of time. But nothing is ever that "easy" and nature has a way of fighting back. Now we know that infectious agents tend to mutate readily, are difficult to eradicate, and that our "scorched earth" policy in regards to infectious agents may be dangerous in the long-term, as microbes rapidly develop resistance to our usual antibiotic regimens. Consequently, more attention is being paid to increasing the resistance of the host to infection, promoting other factors that lead to healing, and decreasing the external factors that foster disease (Goldberg Group, 1994).

Public health officials have sometimes been forced, often against their wishes, to enter the realms of politics, social values, and ethics as it has become increasingly clear that social factors play a large role in the spread or containment of various diseases, most recently, for example, AIDS. In trying to liberate us from these scourges, some people have lost a great deal in the struggle, as the culture refuses to break through its own denial about the relationship between disease processes and social disorder. Trauma theory provides the theoretical framework to bring psychiatry into a much better alignment with medicine, as the health care field gears up for the new century and a new paradigm. Trauma theory proposes that the origin of a significant proportion of physical, psychiatric, and social disorder lies in the direct and indirect exposure to external traumatogenic agents. Trauma causes chronic, infectious, multigenerational, and often lethal disease. Although some traumatic events are highly likely to create post-traumatic effects in anyone, the more usual interaction is between the strength and persistence of the stressor and the vulnerability of the stressed. Van der Kolk (1989) points out that traumatization occurs when ones' combined internal and external resources are insufficient to cope with the impending external threat. Certain environments are clearly more likely to provide a fertile breeding ground for traumatogenic events than others.

Just as bacteria and viruses are the usual infectious agents, the perpetrators of violence are the carriers of the trauma infection. The more destructive the perpetrators are, the less the chances of survival for their victims. The more intense the level of contact, the greater the likelihood that the victims will suffer from the long-term consequences of the perpetrators' disease. The poorer the health of the victim—physical, psychological, and social—the greater the likelihood of exposure. The infection even takes on a pseudo-genetic form of transmission as the effects and patterns of violence are passed from parents through children, both through what is done that is negative and what is not done that is positive. But bacteria have relatively few friends among people. The carriers of the infection of violence traditionally have been men, the men that women and their children love, need, respect, and obey.

For hundreds of generations, fathers and mothers have carefully and dutifully prepared our boy children to become the carriers of violence so that they would fight and defend the survival of the species. Violence administered in childhood was used almost as an inoculation to prepare boys for the inevitable violence of manhood. That boy children may be more hormonally predisposed to violence and therefore more trainable may be true. But ascribing violence largely to biology is a cop-out. Our cultural training of boys is far too methodical, pervasive, and insistent to ascribe anything but a relatively small role to biological predisposition. As long as people were strung out in small numbers around the globe, and as long as our weapons were limited to stones, clubs, and even knives, the most violent of our species—our infectious agents—could live in relative harmony with the rest of us. Similarly, under normal circumstances, thousands of microbial varieties live within our bodies in such a state of relative harmony with each other because of a balance of power between them and our immune system. Many microbes serve a beneficial purpose in furthering our existence. Violent males used to have alternatives less available now. There was always a frontier to be settled, an indigenous people to be conquered. Likewise, there were women and children to be protected from the danger of others. But under changing conditions, when the balance is lost, a microbe that has been previously harmless or even beneficial, can become a killer. AIDS victims do not die from the AIDS virus, they die from what the AIDS virus does to the internal microbial balance.

Our human balance of power with our "violence microbes" has been lost as well. It is as if the infectious agent carrying violence has mutated and the infection has become so virulent that it no longer serves any master except the Grim Reaper. The causes for this increased virulence are complex—increasing world population, diminishing resources, loss of frontiers, urbanization, increased destructive power of weapons—some of the same circumstances that lead to the increase in other forms of disease as well. Whatever the cause, we do not appear able to contain the infection. People are coming down with the disease faster than we can treat them, and for many the damage is so profound that our best efforts to save them are stymied. Our entire society has been infected by an AIDS-like virus that has destroyed our capacity to resist violence. In fact, we long for it, seek it, profit from it, enjoy it, get sexually aroused by it, and deliberately expose our children to it. The social forces that previously held violence to sustainable limits have been shattered in this century. Our capacity for violence has outstripped our ability to limit it. The infection is out of control and we now have an epidemic. It is not enough to look for increasingly potent antibiotics—we cannot afford to imprison or kill the large percentage of the population that it would be necessary to isolate from others if we were to focus on perpetrator behavior alone. While we try to contain the most virulent strains and take steps to decrease the virulence of the rest, we must provide the conditions that improve our ability to resist the infection of violence. This is a public health emergency.

Few of us who stumbled upon trauma theory ever intended to become public health clinicians and therein lies one of the chief difficulties in achieving adequate self-care. One of the many consequences of the shift in perspective towards a trauma-based approach for the mental health professions is to place us in the uncomfortable position of recognizing the validity of the long-standing feminist aphorism that the personal is political. The problems of our patients are not entirely their own. Even if they are now "sick," their sicknesses spring from their injuries. They have been unable to protect themselves from the infection of violence, and no one else was effective at providing the necessary protection. Now they appear to need our protection—in reality or in symbols. The results of this recognition can be professionally and personally confusing, disorganizing, even disastrous. "Victims invite us to violate the basic tenets of psychotherapy—to suspend value judgments, moralizing, and therapeutic activism. The desire to take a moral stance, to actively side with positive action, interpersonal connections, and empowerment, puts a great strain on our capacity to take a passive, listening stance from which we can help our patients figure out how the trauma has affected their inner world and outer expressions" (van der Kolk, 1994).

So what happens to us? We listen to stories of pain, loss, and despair every day. We watch our injured patients, children and adults, struggle to overcome the devastating legacies of their past. Our minds and our bodies are affected by their pain, as we use our natural human empathic skills to provide the bridge back to safe human contact. We are therapists who are supposed to bring healing to the sick. But we are also bystanders to the events they reveal, to the infection to which they have succumbed and which they now carry in their souls. We often help promote the circumstances in which healing can occur and provide the empathy, support, guidance, and education that each survivor needs in order to transform pain and destruction into meaning and creation. As a result of hard work, they are often able to free themselves from the infection of violence and turn to helping others to free themselves as well.

But we make a living off this pain and infection. We are all part of the matrix of abuse, oppression, and violence that characterizes our culture. It is an intrinsic and usually undiscussed paradox of the entire psychiatric profession. Without suffering, we could not survive. When the problem could be laid at the door of the individual patient's vulnerability, perversity, obstinacy, or stupidity, we could pride ourselves on our patience, perseverance, wisdom, and compassion. Now it is hard to avoid feeling vaguely guilty, not just survivor guilt, but guilt by association, guilt by complicity. When we focus exclusively on our patients, we fail to fulfill our public health function of at least notifying someone about the source of the infection, the violent perpetrators. They frighten us, they overwhelm us, we do not know what to do about them. If we get near them, they are very likely to infect us as well. As a result, we have an endless stream of infected people to treat, while the "typhoid Marys" of the infection of violence are left to wander where they will. Louise Armstrong has addressed this in her powerful book about the politics of sexual abuse:

> Psychiatry and psychology on either side, believing or disbelieving women and children, defuses the issue by medicalizing it. That, in removing it from the political sphere to that of individual pathology, it is an excellent vehicle for problem management rather than for social change....The therapeutic ideology readily leads to not change but imaginary change. Not to an assault on the root cause of rape but to the building of endless treatment centers for a predictably endless supply of the wounded who, in their public display of anguished neediness, are taken to suffer from diminished capacity - to be humored....Their illness is what is to be studied, debated, named, and renamed; their defects are focal (Armstrong, 1994).

One of the reasons that the trauma model is so disturbing is that it forces us to confront our own hypocrisy, denial, and rationalization if we are to be effective in helping our patients to face the truth of their own lives. They were the victims and cannot change the past. They have been infected by the disease of violent perpetration. It is not necessarily a lethal infection. But, if they do not die from the effects of violence, either as a direct result of injuries inflicted by the perpetrator or injuries inflicted as they turn the violence inward, then they are quite likely to spread the infection to others, either by acting violently themselves, or by failing to protect those in their care. In the face of this horror, we have weekly, daily, sometimes hourly choices to make. We can, if we wish, choose to become a part of the ancient "conspiracy of silence," the term used initially to describe the typical interaction of Holocaust survivors and their children with psychotherapists when Holocaust experiences were mentioned, and more generally used to describe the pervasive social denial of the effects of human violence (Danieli, 1994). This dark conspiracy of silence has permitted the infection of violence to reach epidemic proportions, exposing us all to ever-increasing risks. If we wish to stop colluding with this silence, then we must determine how we can bear witness to what we see and what we know without damaging the therapeutic relationship. What is our responsibility in actively advocating for changes in the social forces that contribute so largely to creating environments that are traumatogenic—poverty, illiteracy, patriarchal domination, inadequate health care, poor childcare, unemployment, corporal punishment, racial and gender discrimination, abuse of power, corruption in government, and criminal capitalism?

It is very tempting to take the side of the perpetrator. All the perpetrator asks is that the bystander do nothing. He appeals to the universal desire to see, hear, and speak no evil. The victim, on the contrary, asks the bystander to share the burden of pain. The victim demands action, engagement, and remembering....In order to escape accountability for his crime, the perpetrator does everything in his power to promote forgetting. If secrecy fails, the perpetrator attacks the credibility of his victim. If he cannot silence her absolutely, he tries to make sure that no one listens....The more powerful the perpetrator, the greater is his prerogative to name and define reality, and the more completely his arguments prevail (Herman, 1992).

The trauma model goes a long way towards resolving the mind/body dichotomy that has divided psychiatry from the rest of medicine. Biological and clinical researchers are providing us with a way of understanding and visualizing many points of contact between the threat of harm, the responses of the body to that threat, and the long-term emotional, cognitive, and physical effects of those responses. But in doing so, they are also providing the justification for a greatly enlarged public health system. Traumatic experience, particularly early trauma, places human beings at greatly expanded risk of premature death, disease, social maladjustment, and psychological distress. For every adult patient that we take the time, energy, and money to treat, there are simultaneously hundreds of children who are being placed at risk for the very same problems as they become adults (Garbarino, Dubrow, Kostelny & Pardo, 1992; National Victim Center, 1992; Sherman, 1994). This is no longer speculation or hypothesis. We who deal with the devastating effects of trauma know this to be true.

And therein lies the dilemma for many of us. We can take time off, be good to ourselves, get our own therapy when we need it, obtain routine consultation to help work through countertransference issues, and follow all the other excellent guidelines for self-care. But what are we going to do about the moral burden of knowing what we now know? In our individual work with our patients, we can be very clear about the political nature of their oppression, remain neutral enough to be that sounding board that they need, while conveying a therapeutic stance of "ethical nonneutrality" (Agger & Jenson, 1994). But therapists now are being roundly criticized for trying to do too much, for interfering in family matters, for crossing over the boundaries between therapy and politics in their practice. Many of these critics are supporting the development of a "Mental Health Consumer Protection Act" which claims as its mission the protection of the public from the adverse consequences of mental health practitioners. Part of the development of this legislation is to be a "legal analysis comparing fraudulent and politicized psychotherapists to drunk drivers" (Barden, 1994). Some therapists have become overinvolved, much to their ultimate detriment, in trying too hard to bring about change in individual patients for whom the only solution is self-empowerment. But in many cases, this is the result of misplaced moral concern. We cannot bring about social change via individual therapy without doing damage to the necessary bonds of trust, confidentiality, and safety that the individual requires for healing. But we also cannot turn away from our moral obligation to provide testimony to our culture about what we have witnessed.

This crossover point of connection between the individual patient, the therapist, and the society has perhaps been best discussed by those who have treated victims of trauma under conditions of state terrorism, torture, and political repression, as in the case of therapists working in Chile during the right-wing, military dictatorship.

> The development of the concept of the 'committed bond' between therapist and patients seems very significant to us. In this way subjectivity was integrated into political discourse, and countertransference could become a medium for social change, for example, through therapists' prosocial commitment to denouncing human rights violations....This bond implied a therapeutic stance of 'ethical nonneutrality' toward the patient. This attitude followed naturally from the organizational setting of therapy, which was offered in institutions that were in opposition to the government and its human rights violations. Without this commitment, basic

trust and empathy could never have been established....The experiences from Chile seem, then, to demonstrate that the problem of the wounded healer cannot be discussed only from the perspective of the intrapsychic dynamics of the therapist. In a context of human rights violations, this problem must also be related to the political context. To be on a survivor's mission in Chile was not only a question of one's own survival but also of the survival of democracy and human dignity" (Agger & Jensen, 1994).

In the treatment of victims of violence, particularly as a result of childhood violence, we know now that we are not dealing with the safe ground of individual pathology. We are confronting the results of years of civil rights violations for whom no one is held accountable, violations that go largely unchecked. There is insufficient public will to truly act to protect the rights of children from abuse and neglect. From the 1990 Board Report of the U.S. Advisory Board on Child Abuse and Neglect:

> Child abuse and neglect in the United States now represents a national emergency...in spite of the nation's avowed aim of protecting its children, each year hundreds of thousands of them are still being starved and abandoned, burned and severely beaten, raped and sodomized, berated and belittled....The system the nation has devised to respond to child abuse and neglect is failing....It is not a question of acute failure of a single element of the system but instead, the child protection system is plagued by chronic and critical multiple organ failure (U.S. Advisory Board, 1990).

What are we supposed to do in the face of this disaster? Why do so few people notice that we are feeding on our own young? If we do not blow the whistle, who will?

When we serve in our professional role of therapist, we are duty bound to protect boundaries for the sake of our patients and ourselves. But as citizens, there is no justification for our participation in the conspiracy of silence about child abuse. Neither scientist nor psychotherapist can remain morally "neutral" (Weaver, 1961). There is no such reality. If we do not become more socially and politically engaged and organized, then we are simply bystanders. Who is a bystander? If you are not a victim or a perpetrator, you are a bystander. Bystanders are the audience. They are all those present at the scene of an incident who provide or deny support for a behavior. The victim and perpetrator form a linked figure and the bystanders form the ground against which perpetration is carried out or prevented. It is of vital interest to note that among many acts of perpetration which have been studied, it is the behavior of the bystanders that determines how far the perpetrators will go in carrying out their behavior:

> Bystanders, people who witness but are not directly affected by the actions of perpetrators, help shape society by their reactions. If group norms come to tolerate violence, they can become victims. Bystanders are often unaware of, or deny, the significance of events or the consequences of their behavior. Since these events are part of their lifespace, to remain unaware they employ defenses like rationalization and motivated misperception, or avoid information about the victims' suffering. Bystanders can exert powerful influence. They can define the meaning of events and move others toward empathy or indifference. They can promote values and norms of caring, or by their passivity or participation in the system they can affirm the perpetrators (Staub, 1989).

In this concept lies the key to interrupting the victim-perpetrator cycle of violence that is destroying our social safety. History attests to the fact that once violence is tolerated and supported as a group norm, an increasing number of bystanders become victims and/or perpetrators until it becomes progressively more difficult to make clear differentiations among the three groups. It is time to turn our attention away from our exclusive preoccupation with the pathology of the victim and the pathology of the perpetrator and begin planning how to activate the bystanders, including the bystander in each one of us. It is time for us to augment the level of health and well-being in the population so that the infectious agent has some limits, some containment. Perpetrators can only spread their infection when they are allowed to do so, when the vulnerable remain unprotected. Violence is currently the most critical public health problem facing this nation and as clinicians who know this, we have a professional, personal, political, and moral responsibility to say so.

An important part of self-care is being able to look ourselves in the mirror in the morning without shame. It is being able to create for ourselves and our patients a climate of not just biological, psychological, and social safety, but moral safety as well (Bloom, 1994). But this is a course of action that is fraught with danger. Again, clinicians who have confronted state terrorism have the most immediate experience of the dangers involved.

> It appeared that therapists were exposed to the same kinds of trauma as their patients. They were exposed to direct and indirect repression, to social and individual marginalization, and to primary, secondary, and tertiary traumatization. Their work, which helped the enemies of the regime, was fraught with danger and could bring on traumatization by direct actions from the regime. The work could per se be traumatizing without an adequate safe-holding environment. The work could, however, also be experienced as healing for therapists because of the commitment to a higher goal, the struggle for prosocial change and human rights" (Agger & Jensen, 1994).

As trauma therapists, we too are routinely working with victims of torture. Sometimes we are asked to provide guidance to victims of political terrorism and torture, of combat, of disasters. But they come to us, here in the United States as refugees, seeking and finding sanctuary. We do not know their torturers, or may already perceive them as enemies. We do not share the values of their perpetrators. The stories of their suffering are less likely to trigger our specific childhood memories. But what about the torment that we see here that occurred not in a totalitarian dictatorship, was not inflicted by strangers, and was not endured as an adult. It occurred in a free and democratic country in which children are supposed to be protected by law, it occurred at the hands of primary caretakers who usually displayed both love and hatred for their children, and it was endured during the helplessness and dependency of childhood. It happened at the hands of people we see everyday, who work side-by-side with us, who enjoy the same movies, read the same newspapers, watch the same sports, who share many of our same values. The fact that a significant proportion of the United States population has been traumatized in childhood indicates that the problem of the abuse of power is as problematic here as in many totalitarian regimes—but the abuse of power is in the home, if not in the state. This being the case, we can expect that any meaningful therapeutic challenge to this power will be poorly received. And it has been. For an increasing number of therapists, self-care now extends to attempting to master the constant concern about lawsuits, worries about being picketed, and fears that those whom they see may be secretly taping interviews hoping to bring legal action against a therapist (Doehr, 1994).

It is not only the patients but also the investigators of posttraumatic conditions whose credibility is repeatedly challenged. Clinicians who listen too long and too carefully to traumatized patients often become suspect among their colleagues, as though contaminated by contact. Investigators who pursue the field too far beyond the bounds of conventional belief are often subjected to a kind of professional isolation. To hold traumatic reality in consciousness requires a social context that affirms and protects the victim and that joins victim and witness together in a common alliance...For the larger society, the social context is created by political movements that give voice to the disempowered. The systematic study of psychological trauma therefore depends on the support of a political movement (Herman, 1992).

We look around and the "enemy" is not across the sea. The enemy is in our schools, in our government, our police force, our churches, our homes. Many of us sleep with the enemy; some of us see the enemy every morning in the mirror or across the breakfast table. The enemy is us, our very own, and the enemy is sick. The need to control, to dominate, to avoid experiencing the full range of emotions, to be unable to put feelings into words, to experience relief in hurting other people, to watch and participate in other people's suffering without compassion, to deny reality, to deny committing wrongful deeds—these are signs of a virulent and life-threatening, infectious disease called violence. But even those of us who are not directly inflicting the violence are infected as well. The most recognizable sign of infection in us is fear and compliance with a system we know is dealing death. We collude with the violence by allowing it to determine our behavior without steady and insistent protest against the freedom that we consequently lose. We collude with it by failing to consistently and actively and loudly protest against the situations that promote violence within the family. We collude with it whenever we maintain the pretense that the individual model of treatment can possibly address the enormous social problems that play such a role in guaranteeing that violence will increase, not decrease.

Part of our self-care must revolve around saying just this, saying what all of us are terrified to say. The long-term, multigenerational effects of trauma comprise the worst infection known to humanity. Our species can only be free when we have learned ntrol this infection. The balance of health must be restored the social body by permitting less exercise of power by those already badly infected. The 20th Century plague of violence must be contained and as witnesses to the debilitating results of this disease, we must speak out. This public health emergency requires our active and vocal participation in an organized, financed, nonviolent, grassroots, multiracial, bi-gendered social protest. Part of self-care is achieving some acceptable measure of moral integrity and this we cannot do alone.

References

Agger, I. & Jensen, S. B. (1994). Determinant factors for countertransference reactions under state terrorism. In J. P. Wilson & J. D. Lindy (Eds.), *Countertransference in the treatment of PTSD*. New York: Guilford.

Armstrong, L. (1994). *Rocking the cradle of sexual politics*. Reading, MA: Addison Wesley.

Barden, R. C. (1994, August). A proposal to finance preparation of model legislation titled Mental Health Consumer Protection Act. Hoffman Estates, IL: Illinois FMS Society.

Bloom, S. L. (1994). The Sanctuary model: Developing generic inpatient programs for the treatment of psychological trauma. In M. B. Williams & J. F. Sommer, Jr. (Eds.), *Handbook of post-traumatic therapy: A practical guide to intervention, treatment, and research*. New York: Greenwood Publishing.

Burton Goldberg Group (1994). *Alternative medicine: The definitive guide*. Puyallup, WA: Future Medicine Publishing.

Danieli, Y. (1994). Countertransference and trauma: Self-healing and training issues. In M. B. Williams and J. F. Sommer, Jr. (Eds.), *Handbook of post-traumatic therapy: A practical guide to intervention, treatment, and research*. Westport, CT: Greenwood.

Davidson, J. R. T. & Foa, E. B. (1993). *Posttraumatic stress disorder: DSM-IV and beyond*. Washington, D.C.: American Psychiatric Press.

Doehr, E. (1994). Inside the false memory movement. *Treating abuse today*, 4 (6), 5–12.

Ellenberger, H. E. (1970). *The discovery of the unconscious: The history and evolution of dynamic psychiatry.* New York: Basic Books.

Friedman, M. J. (1990). Interrelationships between biological mechanisms and pharmacotherapy of posttraumatic stress disorder. In M. E. Wolf & A. D. Mosnaim (Eds.), *Posttraumatic stress disorder: Etiology, phenomenology and treatment.* Washington, D.C.: American Psychiatric Press.

Garbarino, J. H., Dubrow, N., Kostelny, K. & Pardo, C. (1992). *Children in danger: Coping with the consequences of community violence.* San Francisco: Jossey-Bass.

Herman, J. L. (1992). *Trauma and recovery.* New York: Basic Books.

Janoff-Bulman, R. (1992). *Shattered assumptions: Towards a new psychology of trauma.* New York: Free Press.

Mender, D. (1994). *The myth of neuropsychiatry: A look at paradoxes, physics, and the human brain.* New York: Plenum Press.

National Victim Center (1992). *Crime and victimization in America: Statistical overview.* Arlington, VA: National Victim Center.

Porter, R. (1987). *A social history of madness.* New York: Weidenfeld & Nicolson.

Schwartz, M. (1995, January 24). Radio interview with Maxim Schwartz, Executive Director, Pasteur Institute. *BBC Worldwide Services,* National Public Radio.

Sherman, A. (1994). *Wasting America's future: The Children's Defense Fund report on the costs of child poverty.* Boston: Beacon Press.

Staub, E. (1989). *The roots of evil: The origins of genocide and other group violence.* New York: Cambridge University Press.

U.S. Advisory Board on Child Abuse and Neglect (1990). *Child abuse and neglect: Critical first steps in response to a national emergency.* Washington, D.C.: U.S. Government Printing Office.

van der Kolk, B. A. (1994). Foreword in J. P. Wilson & J. D. Lindy, *Countertransference in the treatment of PTSD.* New York: Guilford.

van der Kolk, B. A. (1989). The compulsion to repeat the trauma: Re-enactment, revictimization, and masochism. *Psychiatric clinics of North America, 12* (2), 389–411.

van der Kolk, B. A. (1988). The trauma spectrum: The interaction of biological and social events in the genesis of the trauma response. *Journal of traumatic stress, 1,* 273–290.

van der Kolk, B. A., Greenberg, M., Boyd, H. & Krystal, J. (1985). Inescapable shock, neurotransmitters, and addiction to trauma: Toward a psychobiology of post traumatic stress. *Biological psychiatry*, *20*, 314–325.

van der Kolk, B. A. & Saporta, J. (1993). Biological response to psychic trauma. In J. P. Wilson & B. Raphael, *International handbook of traumatic stress syndromes*. New York: Plenum Press.

Weaver, W. (1961). The moral un-neutrality of science. *Science 133*, 3448: 255–262.

Zilboorg, G. (1941). *A history of medical psychology*. New York: W. W. Norton.

Maximizing Human Capital: Moderating Secondary Traumatic Stress through Administrative & Policy Action

Joseph M. Rudolph, M.A. & B. Hudnall Stamm, Ph.D.

T he more we learn about Secondary Traumatic Stress, the more we realize the importance of recognizing the needs of the helpers (including clinicians, teachers, and researchers) as well as the needs of those we seek to help. While this seems plain, it is not necessarily easy to identify, understand, or address the problems or the solutions. Moreover, the effects of secondary trauma may be less apparent to supervisors, administrators, and state or federal policy makers who may be removed from the terror of the people with whom we work. Yet, after decades of downsizing and budget cuts, corporations and government agencies are opening to the idea of an organization's value coming not only from goods and services, but from the employees. This is most noticeable in the United States, Japan, and the European Economic Community, where an increasing number of governmental and corporate policies address the impact of the worker's work on his or her whole life. In the corporate world, there is a growing trend toward expanding capitalization, not through things alone, but through people; a trend called "maximizing human capital" (cf. Arthur Anderson, 1998). Thus, with the growing knowledge of the costs of caring, it seems not only increasingly important, but feasible, to develop social and professional support networks, understanding administrative structures, and organizational, local, state and federal policies that support the well-being of workers in our field.

This book and others (Figley, 1995; Pearlman, 1995) chronicle different ways that helpers are affected by and can be fortified against the impacts of Secondary Traumatic Stress. Most of the information comes from those who are on the front lines, not from the policy world. Ironically, many of the probable solutions can be implemented most effectively at the administrative or political level. Certainly applying what we have learned to administrative procedures, policy decisions, and legal and regulatory areas can help decision makers create policy that supports us in the ways that we most need to be supported. To do this, it is necessary for us to "step across the aisle" and join with the administrators and governmental officers who determine the organizational, national and international policies under which we must operate (DeLeon, Frank, & Wedding, 1995).

Bridging the Gap

Most administrators and policy makers face severe challenges in making decisions that adequately meet the needs of all parties involved (Anderson, 1994; DeLeon et al., 1995; Lindbloom & Woodhouse, 1993; Patton & Sawicki, 1993). Policy makers are often asked to make decisions without sufficient information or time to gather it. They may never have the luxury of systematically detailing the systems in which we work. They may not have the time or support to understand how policies would affect the work we do. It is important to remember that changes are generally made to systems that are not working and the pressure to solve problems, whether it be from the organizational bottom or the top, can be intense. Moreover, every decision has to be "managed" so that those it will affect have an opportunity to judge its merits, rather than reject it simply because it is unfamiliar (Guba & Lincoln, 1989; Patton & Sawicki, 1993; Rossi & Freeman, 1993; Shadish, Cook, & Leviton, 1991).

Administrators and policy makers are pragmatic people. Whether we realize it or not, they are tasked from both sides— by their superiors (or in the case of legislative personnel, their constituents) as well as by the workers they affect—to maximize the performance and minimize the costs of their organizations. Most are not trained practitioners of the fields they administrate, and thus do not have direct knowledge of the challenges in providing services, teaching, or doing research. Decision makers in the regulatory and legislative process have limited direct contact with health care and educational organizations and must rely on research, professional and consumer testimony, and constituent concerns (Anderson, 1994; DeLeon et al., 1995; Lindbloom & Woodhouse, 1993). Information can be difficult to obtain because most researchers, educators, and practitioners are not active in the political arena. Policy makers have to rely on information they are given, which is more likely to come from business and financial researchers than from those doing the work under consideration (Anderson, 1994; Lindbloom & Woodhouse, 1993).

To complicate matters, few workers who deal with traumatic stress are familiar with the larger administrative structures of the organizations for which they work (DeLeon et al., 1995). Undoubtedly, the complexity of the policy process can be as off-putting to us as the intricacies of scientific research are to policy makers. Perhaps because of this, few follow the legal and regulatory changes that occur at the global, federal, and state levels. Most of us are familiar with the emergence of a global economy and the current international mode of fiscal frugality, yet how many of us follow the business trends that drive the fiscal realities of our employers or reimbursement authorities? Beyond the vicissitudes of the global economy, for many trauma workers, war and ethnopolitical conflicts determine the number, traumatic content, and access to people in need of their services.

At the heart of this gap is the very way in which the respective fields view information. Science deals in probabilities. In the scientific world, upon which health care and education alike firmly perch, answers are hypotheses with greater or lesser statistical support. In policy, answers must be definable, absolute, and unambiguous so that they can be translated into actions. Thus, science must be willing to commit to taking a stand, even if it is based on probabilities, and policy makers must be willing to realize that outcomes are not always predictable.

This is a good time to try to close the gap. At the close of this millennium, there is a resurgence of addressing the value of the worker to the organization that is consonant with the prevention and treatment of Secondary Traumatic Stress. In 1997, the National Alliance of Business 29th Annual Workforce Conference theme was "Investing in our Human Capital." Similarly, a growing number of scholars are focusing on the quality of life and mental health of workers in assessing business trends. For example, Gaddy (1996), in large part, based his analysis of market reform in Russia on the mental health of the workers. He argued that for Russia to succeed, it must maximize its human capital by supporting good matches between people's personal attributes and their work. Surely if the economy of Russia rests on the quality of relationship between the worker and his or her work, there is room for addressing the impact of those who work around traumatized individuals and the impact of this work on them.

To support administrative and policy changes, we must first educate ourselves about the policy process (DeLeon, et al., 1995). Secondly, we need to develop carefully crafted policy agendas that are firmly grounded in research (Guba & Lincoln, 1989; Patton & Sawicki, 1993; Rossi & Freeman, 1993; Shadish, et al., 1991). Third, we need to present these agendas to the administrators and policy makers in a cooperative spirit; we need to help decision makers understand our needs (Anderson, 1994; Lindbloom

& Woodhouse, 1993). We need compelling demonstrations of the positive fiscal and ethical implications of maximizing human capital within organizations. Fourth, we have to recognize that some change is inevitable (Kennedy, 1993; Reich, 1993). Rather than waiting for funding cuts or administrative policies designed by people not familiar with our work, we should develop innovative and viable alternatives to current practices or structures. Fifth, we need to recognize the nature of administrative and policy change (Patton & Sawicki, 1993; Rossi & Freeman, 1993). Policy is a slow cyclical process that is affected by an inestimable number of political, social, and economic pressures. Compromise, perseverance, and respect for small changes are requisite skills. We need to pick our battles well, know when to make concessions, and recognize the challenge in developing administrative structures and policy.

A MODEL OF ADMINISTRATIVE AND POLICY CHANGES

Administrators and policy makers, like scientists, have field-specific ways of organizing and using information (Anderson, 1994; Lindbloom & Woodhouse, 1993). Increasingly, the language of science and the language of policy overlap. Nowhere is this more evident than in the proliferation of "outcomes based" programs. These programs are evaluated on how well they meet the specified outcome. Many of us are trained in program evaluation and even in cost-benefit analysis, two skills often used in policy analysis. To facilitate understanding of the policy process, we present a simple conceptual model presenting some of the key terms that appear in policy analysis.

There are four general terms used in our sample policy analysis. The first term is *effectiveness*: does this policy suggestion reduce the risk of STS? The second term, *efficiency*, refers to the cost-benefit ratio. The third, *administrative feasibility*, addresses the fiscal and implementation ramifications of the suggested policy. The final term, *political feasibility*, addresses the political realities of the policy. Are there legislative and regulatory changes that need to be made and if so, how likely are you to gain support for the changes? Each of these terms is amplified below.

Effectiveness

Effectiveness is the policy concept recognized by most clinicians, researchers, or educators. In the simplest terms, it refers to the capacity to address the issue at hand, in this case Secondary Traumatic Stress. Does the proposed strategy provide a solution that will moderate or reduce Secondary Traumatic Stress among the staff? The answer to this question is generally established through research. As with any research, it is essential to clearly state the problem to be addressed and to have a good justification for the proposed intervention or program. As the research base of STS grows, the quality of our ability to address the effectiveness of our policies will increase. Similarly, as policies are implemented, it is important to track their impact and make appropriate changes.

Efficiency

Efficiency asks what are the pros and cons of this intervention or program? Typically administrative and policy analyses are based on the idea of cost benefit ratios. They identify the positive benefits to the organization or staff and the costs, in money, equipment, supplies and staff time. Both categories are translated into dollars and then compared. If the benefits outweigh the costs the program may be adopted. It is especially important at this stage to identify all aspects from both sides. To legitimately evaluate the positive and negative aspects of the program or intervention, it would be ideal to have at least one benefit that counters each cost to the organization. While accounting for benefits in terms of dollars is less important, it is essential that the benefits are clearly thought out and well justified. This will not only increase the odds of getting the program approved but it will also help you understand the true limitations of your program. One method for justifying benefits has come to be known as a "cost offset." Cost offsets show for every $Xs spent on the program, $Ys are saved down the line. Preventive health care is a quintessential example of a medical cost offset. For example, say on average, for every $1 spent in childhood immunizations, $26 could be saved in health care costs during the child's life. Clearly immunization would be a good investment. In STS, cost offsets could be calculated for more effective treatment, reduced turnover, malpractice insurance, etc.

Administrative Feasibility

The third area to examine is the Administrative Feasibility of the proposed intervention or program. This includes all the tangible aspects of the program or intervention that you are asking of your organization. In this case, fiscal refers to all of the financial burden of the program, such as increased or decreased revenue, costs to implement and maintain the program, the cost of resources necessary to run the program, and salary of staff committed to the program. The details will vary depending on the kind of program or intervention and the kind of organization. Administrative issues include all of the changes—additions or subtractions—to the current administrative structure. What tasks will be associated with the implementation and maintenance of the program and what is the burden on the staff? While we have only included fiscal and administrative categories as examples, there are many other categories that may be added depending on the mission, goals, and performance measures of your organization. Cost offset information may be helpful here as well.

Political Feasibility

Political feasibility has two facets, internal to an organization and external to an organization. Internally, political feasibility refers to the various policies, procedures, and practice standards that relate to a specific program or intervention. This information may help justify the implementation or allocation of funds using the specific administrative and organizational language. For example, before embarking on a program change, it is important to learn what organizational mechanisms exist to address change. Understanding these mechanisms helps identify the right path for processing your suggestions and serves to increase your understanding of the administrative structure and functioning of your organization.

The external aspect of political feasibility can be used to identify the different groups and issues that will be affected by the proposed program or policy. It is especially important in policy development to know which groups may support or oppose your efforts. What other organizations are likely partners or competitors? You should identify all groups with an interest in the topic including related professionals, consumer groups, and financially related organizations such as third-party payers or financiers. Some changes must take place in the legislative or regulatory arena at which time the scope of those reviewing your efforts increases fantastically.

Regardless of whether you are working with internal or external political feasibility, you need to understand your scope of influence and the range of impact that your proposal will have. Change can run the gamut from small adjustments in a treatment team to alterations of federal law or international policy. The scope of influence is critical to identifying the groups that may be involved. As the scope of influence grows, so grows the number of groups to be considered. Some projects become high profile, making it imperative to interact with the media in such a way that your message is conveyed as you intend.

POLICY AGENDA FOR ADDRESSING STS

In table 1, we present six policy changes implied by the chapters in this book and review them in the four areas mentioned above. The six policy changes we summarized from this book are (a) lower caseloads, (b) telehealth support, (c) increased staff time, (d) increased leave time, (e) mental health care, and (f) supervision. Each of these examples is based on the theory and research presented by the authors in this book. These chapters provide a framework from which to develop theoretical models for the policy changes suggested. In most of the examples there is some crossover between the categories of the analysis.

Our first example is lowering clinical caseloads. The theory suggested by Chrestman, Kassam-Adams, Pearlman, and Munroe, is that lower caseloads will reduce the overall level of exposure to traumatized clients and allow the clinicians more time between clients to process and complete administrative tasks. Building from this theory, the benefits of the program have been stated, lower exposure and more time. Alternatively the costs to the organization are fewer clients and less revenue. Fewer cases would also reduce the administrative burden, because there would be fewer insurance claims. Finally, from a political perspective, we could use the ethical and practice guidelines from professional organizations like the American Psychological Association. Additionally we would need to understand the institutional standards, contracts, and certification standards. If, for example, our proposal would decrease the number of patients to 75 where the institution needed 100 to maintain its Federal funding, then such a proposal would be untenable.

Our second suggestion is telehealth support. This was taken from the Stamm chapter describing telehealth as a way to increase access to resources and develop professional relationships. One benefit is that telehealth is easily accessible. Accessibility is enhanced due to the large computer networks used by health care organizations to store clinical notes and billing information. The costs would be largely borne in training, possibly minor changes to the technology. Administratively it seems fiscally possible depending on the quality of the equipment, access to the internet, and the competence and workload of the

Table1

	Effectiveness[1]	Efficiency[2]		Administrative Feasibility[3]		Political Feasibility[4]
		Benefit	Cost	Fiscal	Administrative	
Lower Caseloads	YES: Chrestman, Kassam-Adams, Pearlman, Munroe	• Fewer cases • More time, resources, & energy	• Fewer clients • Less revenue	• Less revenue • Less turnover	• Less turnover • More providers • Fewer cases	• Ethics practice limits • Institutional Standards • Institutional Cert. Requirements
On-Line Usage	MAYBE: Stamm	• Access to resources & professionals • Accessible	• Training • Hard/Software	• Hard/Software • Provider • Training cost • Training time	• Depends on equipment • Depends on competence	• Available of Telecommunication Technology
Increased Staff Time	YES: Pearlman, Catherall, Munroe	• Team work • Support staff • Attend to problems	• Fewer contact hours • Fewer Clients	• Hrs per wk staff time	• Scheduling	• Ethics: supervision • Institutional Standards • Institutional Cert. Requirements
Leave Time	YES: Pearlman, Munroe	• Satisfaction • Less tired/ • Leisure time	• Fewer contact hours • Leave pay	• Leave pay	• Scheduling	• Institutional Standards • Institutional Cert. Requirements • State/Federal labor laws
Mental Health Care	YES: Catherall, Pearlman, Munroe	• Reframing stressor	• Stigma • Service cost	• Service cost	• Access • Avail to all • Confidential	• Institutional Standards • Institutional Cert. Requirements • State/Federal labor laws
Supervision	YES: Catherall, Munroe, Pearlman	• Training • Soc support • Empathy • Resources	• Staff time • Time from services	• Increased support	• Hrs per wk • Scheduling • Access • Confidential	• Licensure requirements • Ethics supervision • Institutional Standards • Institutional Cert. Requirements

[1]Effectiveness: Does this lower Secondary Traumatic Stress?
[2]Efficiency: What is the cost-benefit ratio?
[3]Administrative Feasibility: What are the fiscal implications of this policy? What are the administrative implications of this policy?
[4]Political Feasibility: What are the legislative changes that need to be made?

network managers. Adding telehealth would also require the organization to develop policies and procedures to ensure the security of the records and the use of the Internet while on company time. Politically the primary issue would be related to public utilities and access to the Internet.

Conceptually, increased staff time and supervision are very similar. Increased staff time speaks to Pearlman, Catherall, and Munroe's conception of having supportive organizations. Increasing staff time means providing regular time to discuss the day to day operations of the organization. This should provide time for consultation or debriefing difficult cases in a supportive collegial environment. Supervision refers to the provision of regular professional clinical and/or administrative support from a senior staff member. This serves both to enhance professional development and to deal practically and emotionally with difficult cases. For increased staff time and for supervision, the primary benefit to the staff is ongoing training, increased social support, and an arena in which to handle difficult cases. Increased staff time may also serve to identify administrative or clinical problems and their solutions. Supervision allows the staff to continue their professional development. The costs for both of these interventions are reduced patient loads and salary costs associated with non-billable hours. Administratively, mechanisms would have to be developed to handle scheduling changes and to ensure the confidentiality of cases. Politically, in most professional organizations both staff time and supervision can be counted as forms of supervision. These additions can also be used to ensure internal quality assurance monitoring. Instituting these practices could increase the quality of care by in creasing the resources available to the providers.

Leave time can be construed as part of an employee's benefit package. Leave time (Munroe and Pearlman) here refers to providers having access to adequate amount of vacation, sick, and family leave time. Providers need variety in their lives including having a life outside of work. The primary benefits are increased employee well-being and satisfaction with their work. If people are able to relax and spend time with their families they will be less tired and generally more satisfied with work. The primary costs are financial—paying for leave time. The administrative challenge is largely in scheduling, both in managing around leave time and in tracking the amount of leave time used. Politically, many leave standards are set by legislative rules and institutional policy. In this case it would be particularly important to know both the institutional and federal or state guidelines.

Finally, mental health care (Catherall, Munroe, Pearlman) is defined as having access to professional mental health services outside the employing organization. This would be considered part of the benefits package or similar to, although separate from, clinical supervision. This particular example would allow providers to seek short-term mental health care to deal with problems that are impeding their ability to work. The care provided in this plan could be limited to work related incidents or expanded to include family mental illnesses or marital therapy. The theory, as presented by Catherall, Munroe, and Pearlman, is to help people attend to particularly difficult cases or situations in a way that does not stigmatize them in their work setting. Additionally, it provides a way to help workers manage other stress in their lives that may impact their ability to do their jobs. The primary costs are financial, that is, paying for the services. Other associated costs are social. As Catherall reminds us, many organizational cultures are steeped in traditions that do not allow acknowledging that providers are affected by their work. Furthermore, these cultures do not acknowledge the impact of one's personal life on work. In such organizations, it would be difficult to gain approval for this policy. Even if it is possible to change the corporate mentality, there are many federal, state, and institutional policies governing the provision of benefits.

While these six example interventions are minimally addressed and represent a wide range of scope and kind, the general discussion illustrates a way of thinking from which to build political and administrative changes in your organizations. Each recommendation would need to be thoroughly explored in the context of any particular organization and documented before being suggested as a policy change. While this model may be new to some, the basic elements of good project design, well-developed and supported theories, and complete and accurate presentation of information should be familiar to all clinicians, researchers, and educators. Addressing policy merely requires us to focus our talents in a slightly different direction, toward the organization rather than the student, client, or research participant.

CLOSING THOUGHTS

Experience has shown us that impaired providers have an impact on the consumers, clinicians, and administrative staff of an organization. While it is valuable and necessary to understand and recognize the impacts of Secondary Traumatic Stress, it is a whole other thing to intervene when a colleague and friend is having a tough time. Unfortunately, the concept of STS is sufficiently new that we often do not have existing administrative structures to support interventions. We need to begin building structures that contain safety nets for impaired professionals and moderating structures that support people in all aspects of their work. We will not be able to completely prevent workers from being affected by their work with the traumatized, but we can build better environments to support workers when they are affected. We can build structures that help ensure that those who are affected can heal as quickly as possible and continue to function as productive workers. To build such structures will take vision and action beyond a personal understanding of STS and its effects. It requires the administrative and policy structures to recognize the costs of caring, the challenges of providing care, and the support necessary to counteract those costs.

REFERENCES

Anderson A. (1998). *HR Director: The Arthur Andersen Guide to Human Capital.* New York: Author.

Anderson, J. E. (1994). *Public Policymaking: An Introduction.* (Second ed.). Boston: Houghton Mifflin.

DeLeon, P. H., Frank, R. G., & Wedding, D. (1995). Health psychology and public policy: The political process. *Health Psychology,* 14(6), 493–499.

Figley, C. R. (Ed.). (1995). *Compassion Fatigue: Coping with Secondary Traumatic Stress Disorder in Those Who Treat the Traumatized.* New York: Brunner Mazel.

Gaddy, C. (1996). No turning back market reform and defense industry in Russia: Who's adjusting to whom? *The Brookings Review,* 14 (3), 30–33.

Guba, E. G. & Lincoln, Y. S. (1989). *Fourth Generation Evaluation.* Newbury Park: Sage Publications, Inc.

Kennedy, P. (1993). *Preparing for the Twenty First Century.* New York: Random House.

Lindbloom, C. E. & Woodhouse, E. J. (1993). *The Policy-Making Process.* (3rd ed.). Englewood Cliffs: Prentice-Hall, Inc.

Patton, C. V., & Sawicki, D. S. (1993). *Basic Methods of Policy Analysis and Planning.* (2nd ed.). Englewood Cliffs: Prentice-Hall, Inc.

Pearlman, L. A. & Saakvitne, K. W. (1995). *Trauma and the Therapist: Countertransference and Vicarious Traumatization in Psychotherapy with Incest Survivors.* New York: W. W. Norton.

Reich, R. B. (1993). *The Work of Nations: Preparing Ourselves for 21st Century Capitalism.* New York: Alfred P. Knopf.

Rossi, P. H. & Freeman, H. E. (1993). *Evaluation: A Systematic Approach.* (5th ed.). Newbury Park, CA: Sage Publications, Inc.

Shadish, W. R., Cook, T. D., & Leviton, L. C. (1991). *Foundations of Program Evaluation.* Newbury Park, CA: Sage Publications, Inc.

Published Works in Secondary Traumatic Stress

The references below are compiled and arranged purely for convenience' sake. In several instances, references appear more than once. In order to give a better view of the literature, I have listed the major texts in the field and then by appropriate chapter below. In other cases, if a paper clearly fit more than one group, I included it more than once. I categorized as theory those papers that were trying to define the field (whether or not they used data). This section includes papers that refer to the ethics issues involved in STS and papers that address organizational psychology—how can the organization be arranged to help prevent STS. The remaining papers are grouped by the type of occupations to which they refer: public service/crisis workers, health care providers and child protection workers, researchers, teachers, and a final category for other jobs. I followed the general convention of including Emergency Medical Service (EMT/EMS) workers with public safety workers and disaster responders rather than with health care givers. There was no clear place to include those who work with refugees and torture. I included them as best I could with health care provider or crisis workers, depending on their training background.

Comprehensive Texts

Figley, C. R. (Ed.). (1995). *Compassion fatigue: Coping with secondary traumatic stress disorder in those who treat the traumatized*. New York: Brunner/Mazel. Introduces the concept of compassion fatigue as a natural and disruptive by-product of working with traumatized and troubled clients. Provides theory for assessment and treatment, discusses difference between compassion fatigue PTSD and burnout. Includes information about prevention and treatment.

Figley, C. R. (Ed.). (in press). *Treating compassion fatigue*. New York: Brunner/Mazel. This edited book focuses on responses to compassion fatigue.

Paton, D. & Violanti, J. (Eds.). (1996). *Traumatic stress in critical occupations: Recognition, consequences & treatment*. New York: Charles C. Thomas. This book describes how working in critical occupations can affect the well-being of professional groups such as police officers, firefighters and emergency medical service workers. It discusses the processes and mechanisms which underpin occupational and traumatic stress reactions.

Pearlman, L. A. & Saakvitne, K. W. (1995). *Trauma and the therapist: Countertransference and vicarious traumatization in psychotherapy with incest survivors*. New York: W. W. Norton. Discusses the theoretical underpinnings of countertransference and vicarious traumatization and explains contructivist self development theory and trauma therapy. Covers work with incest survivors, gender roles and countertransference, working with sexual abuse patients, risks of vicarious traumatization for therapists, and issues of professional development, supervision, consultation with respect to vicarious traumatization.

Saakvitne, K. W. & Pearlman, L. A. (1996). *Transforming the pain: A workbook on vicarious traumatization*. New York: W. W. Norton. This is the first workbook to address vicarious traumatization and is designed helpers to help assess, address, and transform one's own vicarious traumatization.

Stamm, B. H. (Ed.). (1995/1999). *Secondary traumatic stress: Self-care issues for clinicians, researchers, and educators*. Lutherville, MD: Sidran Press. Covers a wide range of issues in secondary traumatic stress, including definitions, understanding the cost of caring, risks of treating sexual trauma, self care models and suggestions, secondary trauma in the classroom, organizational concerns, and use of telemedicine to ameliorate secondary traumatic stress, ethical problems, & theories & philophy of secondary traumatic stress.

Wilson, J. P. & Lindy, J. D. (1994). *Countertransference in the treatment of PTSD*. New York: Guilford Press. This is a book about what we go through as we listen to and work with our trauma patients and how our own experiences may help or hinder the recovery process for victims of violent or sexual assault. Issues include countertransference and indirect trauma.

General Theory Papers

Agger, I. & Jensen, S. B. (1994). Determinant factors for countertransference reactions under state terrorism. In J. P. Wilson & J. D. Lindy (Eds.), *Countertransference in the treatment of PTSD*. New York: Guilford Press. The authors describe their work with Chilean therapists who attempt to carry out professional responsibilities in an environment in which state terrorism uses the internment and torture of political dissidents as a commonplace tool of oppression. This oppression extends to mental health professionals, who work at great risk, in secret, to aid those who have been victimized by the system.

Bloom, S. L. (1995). The germ theory of trauma: The impossibility of ethical neutrality. In B. H. Stamm (Ed.), *Secondary traumatic stress: Self-care issues for clinicians, researchers, and educators*. Lutherville, MD: Sidran Press.

Catherall, D. R. (1995). Preventing institutional secondary traumatic stress disorder. In C. R. Figley (Ed.), *Compassion fatigue: coping with secondary traumatic stress disorder in those who treat the traumatized*. New York: Brunner/Mazel. This chapter focuses on institutions that are vulnerable to acts of violence or other sources of traumatic stress, and how to prepare for potential stressful exposure.

Dunning, C. (1994). Trauma and countertransference in the workplace. In J. P. Wilson & J. D. Lindy (Eds.), *Countertransference in the treatment of PTSD*. New York: Guilford Press. The author discusses trauma and countertransference in the workplace and the "ripple effect" that draws fellow employees, supervisors, and administrative personnel into the wake of traumatic events.

Dutton, M. A. & Rubinstein, F. L. (1995). Working with people with PTSD: research implications. In C. R. Figley, (Ed.). *Compassion fatigue: Coping with secondary traumatic stress disorder in those who treat the traumatized*. New York: Brunner/Mazel. This chapter reviews the literature to develop an understanding of the trauma worker's secondary traumatic stress (STS) reactions, which are the psychological effects of exposure to traumatic events through contact with survivors and perpetrators of trauma.

Figley, C. R. (1995). Compassion fatigue as secondary traumatic stress disorder: An overview. In C. R. Figley (Ed.), *Compassion fatigue: Coping with secondary traumatic stress disorder in those who treat the traumatized*. New York: Brunner/Mazel. This chapter introduces the compassion fatigue designation, the symptoms associated with it, and a theoretical model that accounts for and predicts the emergence of compassion stress and compassion fatigue among professionals working with traumatized people.

Figley, C. R. (1995). *Compassion fatigue: Coping with secondary traumatic stress disorder in those who treat the traumatized*. New York: Brunner/Mazel.

Figley, C. R. (1995). Compassion fatigue: Toward a new understanding of the costs of caring. In B. H. Stamm (Ed.), *Secondary traumatic stress: Self-care issues for clinicians, researchers, and educators*. Lutherville, MD: Sidran Press. Discusses the emergence of information that forms the basis of our understanding of Compassion Fatigue and Compassion Stress and the necessity to help caring (health) professionals overcome the costs of caring.

Harris, C. J. & Linder, J. G. (1995). Communication and self care: Foundational issues. In B. H. Stamm (Ed.), *Secondary traumatic stress: Self-care issues for clinicians, researchers, and educators*. Lutherville, MD: Sidran Press.

Howard, G. (1995). Occupational stress and the law: me current issues for employers. *Journal of Psychosomatic Research*, 39(6), 707–719. Discusses various interpretations of legal issues with respect to occupational or traumatic stress, with cross-cultural comparisons between the UK and the United States.

McCann, I. L. & Pearlman, L. A. (1990). Vicarious traumatization: A framework for understanding the psychological effects of working with victims. *Journal of Traumatic Stress*, 3(1), 131–149. Within the context of their new constructivist self-development theory, the authors discuss therapists' reactions to clients' graphic & painful traumatic material, the ways that therapists can transform and integrate this material to provide the best services to clients, and how therapists can protect themselves against the serious harmful effects of vicarious traumatization.

Munroe, J. F. (1995). Ethical issues associated with secondary trauma in therapists. In B. H. Stamm (Ed.), *Secondary traumatic stress: Self-care issues for clinicians, researchers, and educators*. Lutherville, MD: Sidran Press.

Pearlman, L. A. & Saakvitne, K. W. (1995) *Trauma and the therapist: Countertransference and vicarious traumatization in psychotherapy with incest survivors*. New York: W. W. Norton.

Richards, D. (1994). Traumatic stress at work: A public health model. *British Journal of Guidance & Counselling*, 22(1) 51–64. Reviews the prevalence and natural history of post-traumatic stress and describes the new public health movement as a potential framework for managing traumatic stress in the workplace.

Shay, J. (1995). No escape from philosophy in trauma treatment and research. In B. H. Stamm (Ed.), *Secondary traumatic stress: Self-care issues for clinicians, researchers, and educators*. Lutherville, MD: Sidran Press.

Simon, B. (1993). Obstacles in the path of mental health professionals who deal with traumatic violations of human rights. *International Journal of Law and Psychiatry*, 16(3–4), 427–440. This paper discusses the obstacles in the path of mental health professionals becoming more involved in issues of human rights violations, especially cases involving children.

Stamm, B. H. (in press). Measuring compassion satisfaction as well as fatigue: Developmental history of the Compassion Fatigue and Satisfaction

Test. In C. R. Figley (Ed.), *Treating compassion fatigue*. Philadelphia: Taylor and Francis. This chapter discusses the logic of addressing both negative and positive reactions to working with people who have been traumatized and reviews the psychometric properties of the Compassion Fatigue and Satisfaction Scale.

Stamm, B. H. (Ed.). (1995/1999). *Secondary traumatic stress: Self-care issues for clinicians, researchers, and educators*. Lutherville, MD: Sidran Press.

Valent, P. (1995). Survival strategies: A framework for understanding secondary traumatic stress and coping in helpers. In C. R. Figley, (Ed.), *Compassion fatigue: Coping with secondary traumatic stress disorder in those who treat the traumatized*. New York: Brunner/Mazel. The model presented in this chapter helps to categorize and conceptualize traumatic stress reactions as a context for understanding the nature and role of survival strategies.

Williams, M. B. & Sommer, J. F., Jr. (1995). Self-care and the vulnerable therapist. In B. H. Stamm (Ed.), *Secondary traumatic stress: Self-care issues for clinicians, researchers, and educators*. Lutherville, MD: Sidran Press.

Specific Populations

Exposure Due to Emergency Service Provision
(Police, EMS, Crisis Workers, Graves Registry, etc.)

Alexander, D. A. (1990). Psychiatric intervention after the Piper Alpha disaster. *Journal of the Royal Society of Medicine, 84*(1), 8–11.

Bartone, P. T., Ursano, R. J., Wright, K. M., & Ingraham, L. H. (1989). The impact of a military air disaster on the health of assistance workers: A prospective study. *Journal of Nervous and Mental Disease, 177*(6), 317–328. This study, an examination of the aftermath of the Gander, Newfoundland airplane crash which killed 248 people, aimed to: a) identify the major stress areas for disaster family assistance workers; b) examine the relation between degree of exposure to these stressors and health; and c) locate risk factors, or resistance resources that might modulate any ill effects of exposure.

Beaton, R. D. & Murphy, S. A. (1995) Working with people in crisis: Research implications. In C. R. Figley (Ed.), *Compassion fatigue: Coping with secondary traumatic stress disorder in those who treat the traumatized*. New York: Brunner/Mazel. The authors assert that crisis workers are at risk for secondary trauma stress, which may result in unintended and deleterious effects such as relationship problems and substance abuse.

Beehr, T. A., Johnson, L, B., & Nieva, R. (1995). Occupational stress: Coping of police and their spouses. *Journal of Organizational Behavior, 16*(1),

3–25. Police and their spouses reported using four coping activities in response to their own stressors: problem focused, emotion focused, religiosity, and rugged individualism. Three potential police strains previously noted in non-empirical literature were given special attention; divorce potential, drinking behavior, and suicide thoughts.

Bradford, R. & John, A. M. (1991). The psychological effects of disaster work: Implications for disaster planning. *Journal of the Royal Society of Health, 111*(3), 107–110. The paper focuses on the psychological consequences of disaster work, including the issue of identifying staff who may be more vulnerable to psychological distress and planning for the aftermath of disasters.

Burkle, F. M. (1996). Acute-phase mental health consequences of disasters: Implications for triage and emergency medical services. *Annals of Emergency Medicine, 28*(2), 119–128. This article focuses on building an EMS system framework for recognition and response to psychological problems in the acute phase of disaster.

Cohen, R. E. (1989). Educacion y consultor'a en los programas de intervencion despues de desastres. [Education and consultation in post-disaster intervention programs]. In B. R. Lima & M. Gaviria (Eds.), *Consecuencias psicosociales de los desastres: La experiencia latinoamericana* [*Psychosocial consequences of disasters: The Latin American experience*]. Chicago: Hispanic American Family Center. Describes education and consultation as the most important activities when assisting organizations and personnel at the scene of a disaster.

Davis, J. A. (1996). Sadness, tragedy, and mass disaster in Oklahoma City: Providing critical incident stress debriefings to a community in crisis. *Accident and Emergency Nursing, 4*(2), 59–64. Following the bombing of the Alfred P. Murrah Federal Building in Oklahoma City, crisis response teams of the National Organization for Victim Assistance provided critical incident stress debriefing, education and crisis intervention, and one-to-one services to firefighters, police, and emergency personnel, and to citizens, children and families. This article describes the objectives and activities of the crisis response teams and offers general guidelines for the debriefing process.

Dunning, C. (1988). Intervention strategies for emergency workers. In M. Lystad (Ed.), *Mental health response to mass emergencies: Theory and practice.* New York: Brunner/Mazel. Dunning focuses on services to disaster workers: police, fire, and emergency medical personnel. She is concerned that organizational plans should focus on: (1) the development of mechanisms to enhance workers' ability to perform optimally at the disaster site; (2) the reduction of the negative impact of disaster management on future organizational functioning; and (3) organizational responsibility for ameliorating negative consequences of disaster work.

Durham, T. W., McCammon, S. L., & Allison, E. J. (1985). The psychological impact of disaster on rescue personnel. *Annals of Emergency Medicine*, *14*(7), 664–668. Reports on the survey of 79 rescue, fire, and medical personnel and police officers who treated victims of an apartment building explosion, which reveals their levels of PTSD symptoms, types of coping behavior, and general psychological impact of participation in the rescue.

Erasonen, L. & Liebkind, K. (1993) Coping with disaster: The helping behavior of communities and individuals. In J. P. Wilson & B. Raphael (Eds.), *International handbook of traumatic stress syndromes*. New York: Plenum Press. As noted by other authors in this Handbook, a disaster is often a traumatic experience for emergency workers. However, where disaster relief organizations adequately prepare, train, and debrief (i.e., facilitate the stress recovery progress) the emotional reactions can be diminished and effectively.

Evans, R. C. & Evans, R. J. (1992). Accident and emergency medicine II. *Postgraduate Medical Journal*, *68*(804) 786–799. During mass casualty events psychological trauma is an important cause of morbidity among survivors and rescue personnel, and there is always a need for crisis intervention following a disaster.

Farberow, N. L., et al. (Eds.). (1978, reprint 1986). *Training manual for human service workers in major disasters*. U.S. National Institute of Mental Health. Disaster Assistance and Emergency Mental Health Section. Washington: Government Printing Office. Topics treated: introduction; before the training begins; training the trainers; training the human service workers; special risk groups; self-awareness session; health service worker information form; training program evaluation form; client information form; examples of disaster-related emotional problems.

Follette, V. M., Polusny, M. M., & Milbeck, K. (1994). Mental health and law enforcement professionals: Trauma history, psychological symptoms, and impact of providing services to child sexual abuse survivors. *Professional Psychology: Research and Practice*, *25*(3), 275–282. A survey of 558 mental health and law enforcement professionals assessed current and past trauma experiences, exposure to traumatic client material, and the sequelae of both of those types of personal and professional trauma experiences. Results indicated that 29.8 percent of therapists and 19.6 percent of officers reported experiencing some form of childhood trauma.

Foreman, C. (1992). Disaster counseling. *American Counselor*, *1*(2), 28–32. A member of the trauma team that responded to Northern California's 1989 Loma Prieta earthquake tells of efforts to counsel rescue and recovery workers to prevent the onset of PTSD.

Foreman, C. (1994). Immediate post-disaster treatment of trauma. In M. B. Williams & J. F. Sommer (Eds.), *Handbook of post-traumatic therapy*. Westport, Connecticut: Greenwood Press. Certain features of traumatic events contribute to the greater likelihood of the development of PTSD among survivors and rescue workers.

Genest, M., Levine, J., Ramsden, V., & Swann, R. (1990). The impact of providing help: Emergency workers and cardiopulmonary resuscitation attempts. *Journal of Traumatic Stress*, 3(2), 305–313. Although anecdotes suggest that emergency medical technicians themselves often must cope with severe trauma because of their work, most empirical work has been concerned with the aftermath of disaster. The authors examine the psychological aftermath of rescue workers following resuscitation attempts.

Harris, C. J. (1995). Sensory-based therapy for crisis counselors. In C. R. Figley (Ed.), *Compassion fatigue: Coping with secondary traumatic stress disorder in those who treat the traumatized*. New York: Brunner/Mazel. This chapter identifies various assessment and treatment paradigms appropriate for helping crisis workers who suffer from secondary traumatic stress (STS) or secondary traumatic stress disorder (STSD).

Hartsough, D. M. (1985). Stress and mental health interventions in three major disasters. In D. M. Hartsough & D. G. Myers (Eds.), *Disaster work and mental health: Prevention and control of stress among workers*. Rockville, MD: National Institute of Mental Health. The monograph is organized around stress theory, which states that certain external events (stressors) can put extra demands on the individual (stress) that can lead to physical and/or emotional wear and tear (strain). Emergency workers are subject to a variety of stressors, arising out of the disaster itself, death, and different aspects of the job, such as time pressures or conflicts.

Hodgkinson, P. E. & Shepherd, M. A. (1994) The impact of disaster support work. *Journal of Traumatic Stress*, 7(4), 587–600. This study attempts to examine the impact of disaster-related stress on helpers offering psychological support to victims of two major disasters, and to identify potential moderating factors.

Jiggetts, S. M. & Hall, D. P. (1995). Helping the helper: 528th Combat Stress Center in Somalia. *Military Medicine*, 160(6), 275–277. This article describes the use of critical incident stress debriefings as a means to reduce distress in the wake of mass-casualty care.

Kaufmann, G. M. & Beehr, T. A. (1989). Occupational stressors, individual strains, and social supports among police officers. *Human Relations*, 42(2), 185–197 A survey of 121 police officers of a Midwestern state found that occupational stressors (under-utilization of skills, quantitative workload, and job future ambiguity) and several types of social support are related to individual psychological strain.

Leach, J. (1994). *Survival psychology*. New York: New York University Press. This volume is a primer in survival psychology and is written primarily for those who may handle victims or to plan for potential victims—military personnel, rescue services, medical and health workers, design engineers, seamen and aircrew, offshore and field workers, explorers and adventurers, disaster and civil defense planners.

Lesaca, T. (1996). Symptoms of stress disorder and depression among counselors after an airline disaster. *Psychiatric Services*, 47(4), 424–426. Psychological symptoms of 21 therapists who provided counseling to individuals affected by the crash of a commercial airliner were compared with those of 20 therapists from the same mental health center who did not participate in the disaster relief efforts.

Lum, G., Goldberg, R. M., Mallon, W. K., Lew, B., & Margulies, J. (1995). A survey of wellness issues in emergency medicine (part 2). *Annals of Emergency Medicine*, 25(2), 242–248. This is the second in a series of three annotated bibliographies on wellness issues and their relation to the practice of emergency medicine and focuses on the issues of stress in internship and residency, stress and burnout, stress management, and critical incident stress debriefing.

Marmar, C. R., Weiss, D. S., Metzler, T. J. & Delucchi, K. L. (1996). Characteristics of emergency service personnel related to peritraumatic dissociation during critical incident exposure. *American Journal of Psychiatry*, 153(7, Festschrift Supplement), 94–102. The aim of this study was to identify characteristics of emergency services personnel related to acute dissociative responses at the time of critical incident exposure; a phenomenon designated "peritraumatic dissociation."

Marmar, C. R., Weiss, D. S., Metzler, T. J., Ronfeldt, H. M., & Foreman, C. (1996). Stress responses of emergency service personnel to the Loma Prieta earthquake Interstate 880 freeway collapse and control traumatic incidents. *Journal of Traumatic Stress*, 9(1), 63–85. Compares 3 groups of relief workers in the Loma Prieta earthquake Interstate 880–freeway collapse in terms of their psychological reactions.

McCammon, S. L. & Allison, E. J. (1995). Debriefing and treating emergency workers. In C. R. Figley (Ed), *Compassion fatigue: Coping with secondary traumatic stress disorder in those who treat the traumatized*. New York: Brunner/Mazel. Emphasizes the importance of promoting trauma resolution and healthy coping strategies in emergency workers and suggests several of these strategies.

McCammon, S. L. & Long, T. E. (1993) A post-tornado support group: Survivors and professionals in concert. *Journal of Social Behavior and Personality*, 5, 131–148 (1993). Describes the development and course of a post-tornado support group in a rural setting.

McCammon, S. L., Durham, T. W., Allison, E. J., & Williamson, J. E. (1988). Emergency workers' cognitive appraisal and coping with traumatic events. *Journal of Traumatic Stress*, 1(3), 353–372. Police, fire, emergency medical, and hospital personnel were surveyed following two disasters in the same county: an apartment building explosion followed 1 year later by a devastating tornado.

Mega, L. T. & McCammon, S. L. (1992). Tornado in eastern North Carolina: Outreach to school and community. In L. S. Austin (Ed.), *Responding to disaster: A guide for mental health professionals*. Washington, DC: American Psychiatric Press. The authors document community and professional response to an unpredicted natural disaster, including two survivor outreach and assessment programs.

Miles, M. S., Demi, A. S., & Mostyn-Aker, P. (1984). Rescue workers' reactions following the Hyatt Hotel disaster. *Death Education*, *8*, 315–331. The workers and volunteers who participated in the rescue activities from the collapsed skywalk of the Hyatt-Regency Hotel in Kansas City were exposed to numerous stressors that made them at risk for physical and emotional sequelae. The purpose of this study was to describe the physical and emotional reactions and the help-seeking behaviors of these rescue workers.

Miller, L. (1995). Tough guys: Psychotherapeutic strategies with law enforcement and emergency services personnel. *Psychotherapy*, *32*(4), 592–600. This article describes the types of stresses and problems experienced by police officers, firefighters, and paramedics, and outlines the psychotherapeutic strategies that may prove most effective in helping the helpers.

Moran, C. C. & Britton, N. R. (1994). Emergency work experience and reactions to traumatic incidents. *Journal of Traumatic Stress*, *7*(4), 575–585. The present study examined the association between volunteer emergency work experience, personality, and reactions to a past traumatic incident. The data did not support the idea that emergency workers are hardier than most, or have particular coping styles.

Myers, D. G. (1985). Helping the helpers: A training manual. In D. M. Hartsough & D. G. Myers (Eds.), *Disaster work and mental health: Prevention and control of stress among workers*. Rockville, Maryland: National Institute of Mental Health. The manual is intended primarily for trainers who are mental health professionals with training responsibilities related to local disaster plans and personnel.

Paton, D. & Violanti, J. (Eds.). (1996). *Traumatic stress in critical occupations: Recognition, consequences & treatment*. New York: Charles C. Thomas. This book describes how working in critical occupations can affect the well beginning of professional groups such s police officers, firefighters, and emergency medical service workers. It discusses the processes and mechanisms that underpin occupational and traumatic stress reactions.

Raphael, B. (1986). *When disaster strikes: How individuals and communities cope with catastrophe*. New York: Basic Books. When a great disaster strikes a community it will reverberate through it: all will feel to me degree the death, fear, loss, and devastation that the assault comprises. Many members of the community are victims and many are helpers. These roles and experiences may be changed and interwoven that the distinction between victim and helper has little meaning.

Raphael, B., Meldrum, L., & O'Toole, B. (1991). Rescuers' psychological responses to disasters. *British Medical Journal, 303*(6814), 1346–1347. Discusses the fact that valuable research has been done to clarify the impact of disasters (including PTSD) on rescue workers and suggests ways of preventing long-term morbidity.

Raphael, B., Singh, B. S., & Bradbury, L. (1986). Disaster: The helper's perspective. In R. H..Moos (Ed.), *Coping with life crises: An integrated approach*. New York: Plenum Press. This chapter draws attention to the stresses experienced by the "helpers" and the needs they may have for psychological support and preventive services.

Raphael, B., Singh, B., Bradbury, L., & Lambert, F. (1983–1984).Who helps the helpers? The effects of a disaster on the rescue workers. *Omega, 14*(1), 9–20. This paper reports the results of a questionnaire survey conducted one month after the Granville rail disaster on 95 of the personnel involved in the rescue work and a follow-up on 13 of them one year later.

Shepherd, M. & Hodgkinson, P. E. (1990). The hidden victims of disaster: Helper stress. *Stress Medicine, 6*(1), 29–35.The article reviews the effects of disaster work on helpers, both of the emergency service type (rescue, recovery, and identification personnel) and those who offer psychological support.

Skolnick, A. A. (1995). First complex disasters symposium features dramatically timely topics. *Journal of the American Medical Association, 274*(1), 11–12. A brief report on the first Harvard University Symposium on Complex Disasters (Boston, 1995) which brought together an interdisciplinary group of experts to examine the ethical and logistical problems that follow disaster.

Sloan, I. H., Rozensky, R. H., Kaplan, L., & Saunders, S. M. (1994). A shooting incident in an elementary school: Effects of worker stress on public safety, mental health, and medical personnel. *Journal of Traumatic Stress, 7*(4), 565–574. The effects of impact of event and five categories of worker stress were studied with 140 police, fire, medical, and mental health personnel who were involved in emergency service work following a shooting in an elementary school.

Stearns, S. D. (1993). Psychological distress and relief work: Who helps the helpers? *Refugee Participation Network, 15*, 3–8. Much attention has been devoted to the negative psychological effects of violence, war, famine and torture on refugees. The psychological difficulties helpers face may shape interactions between them and the people they endeavor to assist. Models from disaster relief literature may be used to explore methods for countering stressful or traumatic events.

Sutker, P. B., Uddo, M., Brailey, K., & Allain, A. N. (1992). *Operation Desert Shield/Storm (ODS) Returnee Evaluation, Debriefing, And Treatment Program report*. West Haven, Connecticut: Northeast Program Evaluation Center. Report on a treatment project for 6,000 Louisiana-based U.S. reservists and National Guard personnel who were deployed to the Persian Gulf.

Sutker, P. B., Uddo, M., Brailey, K., & Allain, A. N. (1993). War-zone trauma and stress-related symptoms in Operation Desert Shield/Storm (ODS) returnees. *Journal of Social Issues*, 49(4), 33–50. Studied the relationship of Operation Desert Shield/Storm (ODS) participation and symptoms of psychological distress in a comparison of 215 Army National Guard and Army Reserve troops who were activated to service in the Persian Gulf and returned to the States without seeking mental health treatment services and 60 troops from these same units who were activated but not deployed overseas. Negative psychological outcomes were measured within four to ten months from homecoming in three domains.

Sutker, P. B., Uddo, M., Brailey, K., Allain, A. N., & Errera, P. (1994). Psychological symptoms and psychiatric diagnoses in Operation Desert Storm troops serving grave registration duty. *Journal of Traumatic Stress*, 7(2), 159–171. This clinical report describes symptoms of psychological and physical distress and psychiatric disorder in 24 Army Reservists who served war zone graves registration duty in support of Operation Desert Storm.

Sutker, P. B., Uddo, M., Brailey, K., Vasterling, J. J., & Errera, P. (1994). Psychopathology in war-zone deployed and nondeployed Operation Desert Storm troops assigned graves registration duties. *Journal of Abnormal Psychology*, 103(2), 383–390. Early psychopathology outcomes were compared in troops mobilized for Persian Gulf graves registration duty but differentiated by war-zone deployment.

Taylor, A. & James W. (1989). Survival and development. In A. Taylor & W. James, (Eds.), *Disaster and disaster stress*. New York: AMS Press. There are lessons that survivors can learn and put to good use when, rather than if, other disasters arise. Topics treated: social issues; support groups; emergency services; reactions of emergency personnel; police self-help groups; professional involvement; monitoring personal stress.

Taylor, A. & James W. (1989). The matrix of human factors. In A. Taylor & W. James, (Eds.), *Disaster and disaster stress*. New York: AMS Press. Disaster stress is the outcome of a combined matrix of factors that involves people and their environment. This matrix sets out the sequential stages of disasters from which, if there is sufficient warning beforehand, a sufficient number of survivors and an adequate quantity of supplies afterwards, some positive outcome can be expected.

U.S. National Institute of Mental Health. Emergency Services Branch.

(1987). *Prevention and control of stress among emergency workers: A pamphlet for workers*. Rockville, MD: National Institute of Mental Health. This pamphlet discusses approaches that have been found to be helpful to workers in dealing with disaster-related stress. It suggests interventions that may be helpful before, during, and after disaster.

Ursano, R. J., Fullerton, C.S., Wright, K. M., McCarroll, J. E., Norwood, A. E., & Dinneen, M. M. (1992). *Disaster workers: Trauma and social support*. Bethesda, MD: Department of Psychiatry, F. Edward Hebert School of Medicine, Uniformed Services University of the Health Sciences. This volume reviews the initial data collected from two disasters which occurred in 1989: the crash of United Flight 232 near Sioux City, Iowa and the explosion in the gun turret aboard the USS Iowa. The focus of these studies is on the short- and long-term reactions of workers who helped in the aftermath of these calamities.

Violanti, J. M. (1995). Survivors' trauma and departmental response following deaths of police officers. *Psychological Reports, 77*(2). 611–615. It was hypothesized that satisfaction with supportive reactions of the police department following the on-duty death of an officer helps to ameliorate traumatic stress in surviving spouses. A secondary analysis was conducted of data obtained from 162 surviving police spouses. Analysis indicated that spouses' reported satisfaction with the department was significantly associated with lower trauma stress scores.

Violanti, J. M. (1996). The impact of cohesive groups in the trauma recovery context: Police spouse survivors and duty-related death. *Journal of Traumatic Stress, 9*(2), 379–386. This paper examines the impact of surviving spouse social interactions on psychological distress following the death of a police officer.

Wagner, D., Heinrichs, M., & Ehlert, U. (1998). Prevalence of symptoms of posttraumatic stress disorder in German professional firefighters. *American Journal of Psychiatry, 155*(12) 1727–1732. Investigated the prevalence of posttraumatic stress disorder (PTSD) and comorbid symptoms among professional firefighters in Germany, and examined both primary and secondary traumatic stress disorder experienced by those Ss exposed to the sufferings of others.

Weaver, J. D. (1995). *Disasters: Mental health interventions*. Sarasota, Florida: Professional Press. This volume will provide a practical overview of the Disaster Mental Health field and the many opportunities it offers to those who are willing and able to assist others in times of disaster. Significant background literature is reviewed, with emphasis on material published by the Center for Mental Health Services (CMHS), formerly called the National Institute of Mental Health (NIMH). Sections cover subjects including crisis intervention, screening, support, consultation, preparedness planning, bereavement, supervision, working with the media, PTSD, burnout, and survival techniques relevant to both victims and helpers.

Weiss, D. S., Marmar, C. R., Metzler, T. J., & Ronfeldt, H. M. (1995). Predicting psychosomatic distress in emergency services personnel. *Journal of Consulting and Clinical Psychology, 63*(3), 361–368. This study identified predictors of psychosomatic distress in emergency services (EMS) personnel exposed to traumatic critical incidents. A replication was performed in 2 groups.

Health Care & Social Service Providers
(Therapists, Physicians, Nurses, etc.)

Acker, K. H. (1993). Do critical care nurses face burnout, PTSD, or is it something else?: Getting help for the helpers. *Clinical Issues in Critical Care Nursing, 4*(3), 558–565. The Adaptation Process Phenomenon describes a sequence of behavioral patterns and responses during stressful situations, perceived or not, that can result in negative behavioral responses to stress. For critical-care nurses, negative responses can impair the ability to care for patients and families.

Agger, I. & Jensen, S. B. (1994). Determinant factors for countertransference reactions under state terrorism. In J. P. Wilson & J. D. Lindy (Eds.), *Countertransference in the treatment of PTSD*. New York: Guilford Press.

Astin, M.C. (1997). Traumatic therapy: How helping rape victims affects me as a therapist. *Women & Therapy, 20*(1) 101–109.

Barker P., Reynolds B., Whitehill, I., & Novak V. (1996). Working with mental distress. *Nursing Times, 92*(2), 25–27. The notion of 'health checks' for staff is fraught with complications. Not only might it be impossible to isolate nurses who are 'unhealthy,' but the measures might discourage nurses from admitting to psychological problems. Most important, the therapeutic relationship between nurses and those in their care might be threatened.

Bills, L. J. (1995). Trauma-based psychiatry for primary care. In B. H. Stamm (Ed.), *Secondary traumatic stress: Self-care issues for clinicians, researchers, and educators*. Lutherville, MD: Sidran Press.

Blanchard, E. A. & Jones, M. (1997). Care of clinicians doing trauma work. In M. Harris & C. L. Landis (Eds.), *Sexual abuse in the lives of women diagnosed with serious mental illness*. India: Harwood Academic Publishers. This chapter addresses STS issues for clinicians working with seriously, mentally ill female survivors of sexual abuse.

Booth E. W. (1991). Compassion fatigue [letter; comment]. *Journal of the American Medical Association, 266*(3), 362.

Brende, J. O. (1991). When post traumatic stress "rubs off." *Voices, 27*(1–2), 139–143. Brende briefly outlines his 12-point outpatient program which he initially developed in response to the needs of himself and other staff members of a Veterans Administration hospital who were suffering from various PTSD symptoms that their patients exhibited.

Brown, D., Carn, J., Fagin, L., Bartlett, H., & Leary, J. (1994). Mental health: Coping with caring. *Nursing Times*, 90(45), 53–55.

Carbonell, J. L. & Figley, C. R. (1996). When trauma hits home: Personal trauma and the family therapist. *Journal of Marital & Family Therapy*, 22(1), 53–58.

Catherall, D. R. (1995). Coping with secondary traumatic stress: The importance of the therapist's professional peer group. In B. H. Stamm (Ed.), *Secondary traumatic stress: Self-care issues for clinicians, researchers, and educators*. Lutherville, MD: Sidran Press.

Cerney, M. S. (1995). Treating the "heroic treaters." In C. R. Figley (Ed.), *Compassion fatigue: Coping with secondary traumatic stress disorder in those who treat the traumatized*. New York: Brunner/Mazel, (1995). Cerney notes that therapists who work with traumatized patients are especially vulnerable to secondary traumatic stress (STS) and secondary traumatic stress disorder (STSD).

Charney, A. E. & Pearlman, L. A. (1998). The ecstasy and the agony: The impact of disaster and trauma work on the self of the clinician. In P. M. Kleespies (Ed.), *Emergencies in mental health practice: Evaluation and management*, 418–435. New York: The Guilford Press. Focuses on the impact and unique challenges that disaster and trauma work impose on the self of the helping professional who works in the area of disaster/crisis intervention.

Chrestman, K. R. (1995). Secondary exposure to trauma and self reported distress among therapists. In B. H. Stamm (Ed.), *Secondary traumatic stress: Self-care issues for clinicians, researchers, and educators*. Lutherville, MD: Sidran Press.

Cohen, L. M., Berzoff, J. N., & Elison, M. R. (Eds.). (1995). *Dissociative identity disorder: Theoretical and treatment controversies*. Northvale, NJ: Aronson.

Courtois, C. A. (1993). Vicarious traumatization of the therapist. *Clinical Newsletter*, 3(2), 8–9. Vicarious traumatization is conceptualized as a special form of countertransference stimulated by exposure to the client's traumatic material.

Courtois, C. A. (1997). Healing the incest wound: A treatment update with attention to recovered-memory issues. *American Journal of Psychotherapy*, 51(4) 464–496. Discusses treatment issues such as the effect on the therapist.

Coyle A. & Soodin, M. (1992). Training, workload and stress among HIV counsellors. *AIDS Care*, 4(2):217–221.

Creagan, E. T. (1993). Stress among medical oncologists: The phenomenon of burnout and a call to action. *Mayo Clinic Proceedings*, 68(6), 614–615.

Crothers, D. (1995). Vicarious traumatization in the work with survivors of childhood trauma. *Journal of Psychosocial Nursing and Mental Health Services*, *33*(4), 9–13. Staff members suffer through issues similar to those that patients suffer through during the course of the patient's hospital stay.

Cunningham, M. (1997). Vicarious traumatization: Impact of trauma work on the clinician. *Dissertation Abstracts International Section A: Humanities & Social Sciences*, *57*(9–A), 4130.

Davidson, P. & Jackson, C. C. (1985). The nurse as a survivor: Delayed post-traumatic stress reaction and cumulative trauma in nursing. *International Journal of Nursing Studies*, *22*(1), 1–13. Little attention has been directed to the persistence of certain long-standing hidden symptoms of trauma in nurses. It is postulated that findings from recent studies on delayed post-traumatic stress reaction in Vietnam veterans, victims of natural disaster, and survivors of the holocaust, delineate symptoms which are al found in stress-prone nurses utilizing maladaptive coping strategies in response to hospital-related traumatic episodes.

de Jonge, J., Janssen, P., & Landeweerd, A. (1994). Effecten van werkdruk, autonomie en sociale ondersteuning op de werkbeleving van verplegenden en verzorgenden. [Effect of work stress, autonomy and social support on the work experience of nurses and caregivers]. *Verpleegkunde*, *9*(1), 17–27. This paper describes a study on the relationship between job characteristics, health and well-being of health care professionals from various sectors (N = 249).

Deiter, P. J. Pearlman, L. A. (1998). Responding to self-injurious behavior. In P. M. Kleespies (Ed.), *Emergencies in mental health practice: Evaluation and management*. New York: The Guilford Press. Discusses treatment as best for the client and effects on the treater. Describes a model to understand, prevent, and treat therapists contracting traumatic stress disorders themselves when working with families experiencing traumatic stressors.

Dutton, M. A. (1992). *Empowering and healing the battered woman: A model for assessment and intervention*. New York: Springer.

Editor's post script (1993). Thoughts on therapist self-care from Jacob Lindy, Christine Courtois, Janet Yassen, Joe Ruzek, Matthew Friedman, and Dudley Blake. *Clinical Newsletter*, *3(2)*, 20.

Everett, S. R. (1997). Stress, vicarious traumatization, and coping: Therapists' efforts to manage the stress of treating sexual trauma. *Dissertation Abstracts International: Section B: the Sciences & Engineering*, *57*(10–B), 6568.

Figley, C. R. (1995). Systemic traumatization: Secondary traumatic stress disorder in family therapists. In R. H. Mikesel, D. D. Lusterman, & S. H. McDaniel (Eds.), *Integrating family therapy: Handbook of family psychology and systems theory*. Washington, DC: American Psychological Association.

Figley, C. R. & Kleber, R. J. (1995). Beyond the "victim": Secondary traumatic stress. In R. J. Kleber, C. R. Figley, & B. Gerson (Eds.), *Beyond trauma: Cultural and societal dynamics*. New York: Plenum Press. Shows that the experiences of a traumatized person affect those of other members of a social system in many ways, including family, friends and helpers.

Follette, V. M., Polusny, M. M., & Milbeck, K. (1994). Mental health and law enforcement professionals: Trauma history, psychological symptoms, and impact of providing services to child sexual abuse survivors. *Professional Psychology: Research and Practice, 25*(3), 275–282. A survey of 558 mental health and law enforcement professionals assessed current and past trauma experiences, exposure to traumatic client material, and the sequelae of both of those types of personal and professional trauma experiences. Results indicated that 29.8 percent of therapists and 19.6 percent of officers reported experiencing some form of childhood trauma.

Fox, R. & Cooper, M. (1998). The effects of suicide on the private practitioner: A professional and personal perspective. *Clinical Social Work Journal, 26*(2) 143–157. Discusses the impact of suicide and burnout and vicarious traumatization in psychotherapy with chronically suicidal patients.

Friedman, M. J. (1996). PTSD diagnosis and treatment for mental health clinicians. *Community Mental Health Journal, 32*(2), 173–189. This article focuses on 4 issues: PTSD assessment, treatment approaches, therapist issues, and current controversies.

Funk, J. R. (1995). Burnout among "healers." *American Journal Hospital Palliative Care, 12*(3), 27–30.

Gabriel, M. A. (1994). Group therapists and AIDS groups: An exploration of traumatic stress reactions. Special Issue: The challenge of AIDS. *Group, 18*(3), 167–176. Examines how multiple AIDS-related deaths of group members exert a traumatizing effect on group therapists (GPTs), creating vicarious traumatization. Explores therapeutic interventions for GPTs coping with multiple deaths.

Garside, B. (1993). Physicians mutual aid group: A response to AIDS-related burnout. *Health & Social Work, 18*(4), 259–267. Physicians providing primary health care to people with AIDS are exposed to the same stressful experiences as other AIDS caregivers. Although mutual aid groups have proved useful in relieving stress for AIDS caregivers in general, physicians as a professional group present particular problems that impede their access to mutual aid. This article describes the origins and functioning of a physician's mutual aid group facilitated by the author.

Good, D. A. (1996). Secondary traumatic stress in art therapists and related mental health professionals. *Dissertation Abstracts International Section A: Humanities & Social Sciences, 57*(6–A), 2370.

Haley, S. A. (1974). When the patient reports atrocities: Specific treatment considerations of the Vietnam veteran. *Archives of General Psychiatry*, 30(2), 191–196. The Vietnam combat veteran who reports atrocities presents a special therapeutic challenge. The therapist's countertransference and real, natural response to the realities of the patient's experience must be continually monitored and confronted.

Harbert, K., & Hunsinger, M. (1991). The impact of traumatic stress reactions on caregivers. *Journal of the American Academy of Physician Assistants*, 4(5), 384–394. Trauma affects victims and caregivers. Many caregivers eventually encounter a traumatic event to which they react with severe inner turmoil. The response of the caregiver varies: many fully recover within days or weeks of the event; a few may be overwhelmed that their ability to function at work and in relationships with family members and friends is jeopardized.

Harris, C. J. (1995). Sensory-based therapy for crisis counselors. In C. R. Figley (Ed.), *Compassion fatigue: Coping with secondary traumatic stress disorder in those who treat the traumatized*. New York: Brunner/Mazel.

Hartman, C. R. & Jackson, H. C. (1994). Rape and the phenomena of countertransference. In J. P. Wilson & J. D. Lindy (Eds.), *Countertransference in the treatment of PTSD*. New York: Guilford Press. The authors discuss rape and countertransference.

Hartsough, D. M. & Myers, D. G. (1985). *Disaster work and mental health: Prevention and control of stress among workers.* Rockville, MD: National Institute of Mental Health. This monograph focuses attention on emergency worker needs, specifically to (1) increase understanding of the problems faced by emergency workers and the likely health and mental health impact on the workers; (2) encourage emergency organizations to address these needs before, during, and after a disaster; and (3) provide a model training package for teaching emergency organizations and their workers how to prevent, ameliorate, and treat mental health problems arising out of emergency work.

Hollingsworth, M. A. (1993). Responses of female therapists to treating adult female survivors of incest. *Dissertation Abstracts International*, 54(6–B), 3342.

Hover-Kramer, D, Mabbett, P., & Shames, K. H. (1996). Vitality for caregivers. *Holistic Nursing Practice*, 10(2), 38–48. Changes such as increased patient acuity, shorter hospital stays, workplace reorganization, revision of the nursing role, and the development of home care services all contribute to high stress rates for health care workers. Research results on vitality are presented from three nursing professionals with backgrounds in education, psychotherapy, holistic nursing, and energy-based practice.

Johnson, C. N. E. & Hunter, M. (1997). Vicarious traumatization in counselors working in the New South Wales Sexual Assault Service: An exploratory study. *Work & Stress*, *11*(4) 319–328. 2 groups of counselors, were compared on a number of measures. The results indicate that sexual assault counselors experience greater emotional exhaustion and use more escape/avoidance coping strategies.

Joinson, C. (1992). Coping with compassion fatigue. *Nursing*, *22*(4), 116, 118–119, 120.

Kassam-Adams, N. (1995). The risks of treating sexual trauma: Stress and secondary trauma in psychotherapists. In B. H. Stamm (Ed.), *Secondary traumatic stress: Self-care issues for clinicians, researchers, and educators.* Lutherville, MD: Sidran Press.

Kinzie, J D. (1994). Countertransference in the treatment of Southeast Asian refugees. In J. P. Wilson & J. D. Lindy (Eds.), *Countertransference in the treatment of PTSD.* New York: Guilford Press. The author describes the psychiatric treatment program for Cambodian victims of the Marxist Pol Pot regime (the Khmer Rouge), Vietnamese refugees, and many others at the Oregon Health Sciences University in Portland, Oregon. Over 70 percent of this population suffer from PTSD and comorbid states.

Kluft, R. P. (1994). Countertransference in the treatment of multiple personality disorder. In J. P. Wilson & J. D. Lindy (Eds.), *Countertransference in the treatment of PTSD.* New York: Guilford Press. This chapter presents an extensive review of the phenomena of countertransference in clinical work with disociative disorders, especially multiple personality disorder (MPD).

Lansen, J. (1993). Vicarious traumatization in therapists treating victims of torture and persecution. *Torture*, *3*(4), 138–140 (1993). It has become clear during recent years that therapists exposed to traumatic "material" run the risk of becoming traumatized themselves: vicarious traumatization. In order to get an impression of the extent of this phenomenon among therapists who work with torture victims, a questionnaire was sent to many centers in the world involved with this work. About 10 percent of the therapists seem to be affected.

Lindy, J. D. & Wilson, J. P. (1994). Empathic strain and countertransference roles: Case illustrations. In J. P. Wilson & J. D. Lindy (Eds.), *Countertransference in the treatment of PTSD.* New York: Guilford Press. In this chapter we examine and illustrate a range of countertransference roles and reactions and their management at different points in the treatment process.

Lyon, E. (1993). Hospital staff reactions to accounts by survivors of childhood abuse. *American Journal of Orthopsychiatry*, *63*(3), 410–416. Staff reactions to hospitalized patients' accounts of their abuse were found to resemble symptoms of PTSD.

Maltz, W. (1992). Caution: Treating sexual abuse can be hazardous to your love life. *Treating Abuse Today*, *2*(2), 20–24.

Marvasti, J. A. (1992). Psychotherapy with abused children and adolescents. In J. R. Brandell (Ed.), *Countertransference in psychotherapy with children and adolescents*. Northvale, NJ: Aronson. Chapter describes a variety of countertransference reactions and responses in clinical scenarios involving abused and neglected children and their families.

Matsakis, A. (1994). Other professional and therapeutic concerns. In A. Matsakis, *Post-traumatic stress disorder: A complete treatment guide*. Oakland, California: New Harbinger Publications. This c covers aspects of the therapist-client relationship and concerns specific to the therapist as a person and a mental health professional. These include the major transference and countertransference issues that occur in work with trauma survivors, assessment of PTSD for nonclinical purposes, and the issue of false memories.

Maxwell, M. J. & Sturm, C. (1994). Countertransference in the treatment of war veterans. In J. P. Wilson & J. D. Lindy (Eds.), *Countertransference in the treatment of PTSD*. New York: Guilford Press. This chapter represents an outgrowth of collective clinical experience with veterans of World War II, Korea, Vietnam and the Persian Gulf, treated in U.S. Department of Veterans Affairs (VA) Medical Center, Veteran Readjustment Centers (VA Counseling or "Vet" Centers), and private practice settings.

McCann, I. L. & Colletti, J. (1994). The dance of empathy: A hermeneutic formulation of countertransference, empathy, and understanding in the treatment of individuals who have experienced early childhood trauma. In J. P. Wilson & J. D. Lindy (Eds.), *Countertransference in the treatment of PTSD*. New York: Guilford Press. The first section of this chapter explores and explains the importance of managing countertransference reactions with patients who report early childhood trauma. A hermeneutic formulation of the relationship between countertransference, empathy, and understanding in treating individuals who have experienced early childhood trauma and abuse is presented.

Meyers, T. W. (1997). The relationship between family of origin functioning, trauma history, exposure to children's traumata and secondary traumatic stress symptoms in child protective service workers. *Dissertation Abstracts International Section A: Humanities & Social Sciences*, 57(11–A), 4931.

Munroe, J. F., Shay, J., Fisher, L. M., Makary, C., Rapperport, K., & Zimering, R. T. (1995). Preventing compassion fatigue: A team treatment model. In C. R. Figley (Ed.), *Compassion fatigue: Coping with secondary traumatic stress disorder in those who treat the traumatized*. New York: Brunner/Mazel. The authors suggest that isomorphic characteristics of compassion fatigue and PTSD, and the intensity and duration of exposure by clients, is predictive of responses. The authors assert that no therapists are immune to these effects. The chapter deals with the thorny ethical questions in traumatology: the duty to inform, educate, and act in connection with compassion fatigue among colleague therapists.

Nader, K. (1994). Countertransference in the treatment of acutely traumatized children. In J. P. Wilson & J. D. Lindy (Eds.), *Countertransference in the treatment of PTSD*. New York: Guilford Press. This chapter discusses countertransference in the treatment of acutely traumatized children.

Neumann, D. A. & Gamble, S. J. (1995). Issues in the professional development of psychotherapists: Countertransference and vicarious traumatization in the new trauma therapist. *Psychotherapy, 32*(2), 341–347. Psychotherapy with survivors of chronic childhood trauma poses unique challenges to therapists. This article describes countertransference responses that are common to work with survivors.

Occupational Health Safety. (1993).Workplace stress rated for AIDS caregivers [news]. *Occupational Health Safety. 62*(1), 12–14.

Op den Velde, W., Koerselman, G. F., & Aarts, P. G. (1994). H. Countertransference and World War II resistance fighters: Issues in diagnosis and assessment. In J. P. Wilson & J. D. Lindy (Eds.), *Countertransference in the treatment of PTSD*. New York: Guilford Press. This chapter discusses the phenomena of countertransference in those who are professionally responsible for the treatment, psychotherapy, and medico-legal examination of survivors of Nazi persecution during World War II in the Netherlands.

Parson, E. R. (1994). Inner city children of trauma: Urban violence traumatic stress response syndrome (U-VTS) and therapists' responses. In J. P. Wilson & J. D. Lindy (Eds.), *Countertransference in the treatment of PTSD*. New York: Guilford Press. This chapter highlights the reality of violent traumatic stress in the daily lives of urban children and explores the complexities of treating these children from the perspective of using therapists' human dynamic responses to promote healing in the child.

Pearlman, L. A. & Mac Ian, P. S. (1995). Vicarious traumatization: An empirical study of the effects of trauma work on trauma therapists. Special Section: Trauma, disaster planning, and psychological services. *Professional Psychology: Research & Practice, 26*(6) 558–565. This study examined vicarious traumatization in 188 self-identified trauma therapists.

Pearlman, L. A. & Saakvitne, K. W. (1995). Treating therapists with vicarious traumatization and secondary traumatic stress disorders. In C. R. Figley (Ed.), *Compassion fatigue: Coping with secondary traumatic stress disorder in those who treat the traumatized*. New York: Brunner/Mazel. The authors emphasize those who treat adult survivors of childhood sexual abuse. Pearlman and Saakvitne have observed that these therapists find that their inner experiences of "self" and "other" transform in ways that parallel the experience of the trauma survivor.

Pearlman, L. A. (1995). Self-care for trauma therapists: Ameliorating vicarious traumatization. In B. H. Stamm (Ed.), *Secondary traumatic stress: Self-care issues for clinicians, researchers, and educators*. Lutherville, MD: Sidran Press. Those who voluntarily engage empathically with survivors to help them resolve the aftermath of psychological trauma open themselves to a deep personal transformation. This transformation includes personal growth, a deeper connection with both individuals and the human experience, and greater awareness of all aspects of life. The darker side of the transformation includes changes in the self that parallel those experienced by survivors themselves.

Pickett, M., Brennan, A. M., Greenberg, H. S., Licht, L. & Worrell, J. D. (1994). Use of debriefing techniques to prevent compassion fatigue in research teams. *Nursing Research*, 43(4), 250–252.

Pilkington P. (1993). Who cares for the carers? [editorial]. *Journal of Advanced Nursing*, 18(12), 1855–1856.

Riordan, R. J. & Saltzer, S. K. (1992). Burnout prevention among health care providers working with the terminally ill: A literature review. *Omega*, 25(1), 17–24. This article presents a review of the literature on burnout and its prevention among caregivers to the dying.

Roberts, G. L., O'Toole, B. I., Lawrence, J. M. & Raphael, B. (1993). Domestic violence victims in a hospital emergency department. *Medical Journal of Australia*, 159(5), 307–310. The authors attempt to determine the prevalence and predictors of domestic violence victims among attenders at the emergency department at Royal Brisbane Hospital in 1991.

Rosenbloom, D. J., Pratt, A. C., & Pearlman, L. A. (1995) Helpers' responses to trauma work: Understanding and intervening in an organization. In B. H. Stamm (Ed.), *Secondary traumatic stress: Self-care issues for clinicians, researchers, and educators*. Lutherville, MD: Sidran Press.

Rozelle, D. (1997). Trauma and the therapist: Visual image making, countertransference, and vicarious traumatization. *Dissertation Abstracts International: Section B: Sciences & Engineering*, 58(4–B), 2136.

Ruzek, J. (1993). Professionals coping with vicarious trauma. *Clinical Newsletter*, 3(2), 12–13, 17. Discusses adaptive and maladaptive coping methods employed by professional helpers in responding to the difficulties associated with their job.

Saakvitne, K. W. & Carnes, B. A. (1992). Caring for the professional caregiver: The application of Caplan's model of consultation in the era of HIV. *Issues in Mental Health Nursing*, 13(4), 357–67. This article describes the development and implementation of a psychosocial support program, based on Caplan's (1973) model of mental health consultation, for nursing staff impacted by the HIV epidemic.

Saakvitne, K. W. & Pearlman, L. A. (1996). *Transforming the pain: A workbook on vicarious traumatization*. New York: W. W. Norton.

Saakvitne, K. W. (1995). Therapists' responses to dissociative clients: Countertransference and vicarious traumatization. In L. M. Cohen, J. N.

Berzoff, & M. R. Elison (Eds.), *Dissociative identity disorder: Theoretical and treatment controversies*. Northvale, NJ: Aronson.

Schauben, L. J. & Frazier, P. A. (1995). Vicarious trauma: The effects on female counselors of working with sexual violence survivors. *Psychology of Women Quarterly, 19*(1), 49–64. The primary purpose of this study was to assess the effects on counselors of working with sexual violence survivors. Counselors who had a higher percentage of survivors in their caseload reported more disrupted beliefs (particularly about the goodness of other people), more symptoms of PTSD, and more self-reported vicarious trauma.

Simonds, S. L. (1997). Vicarious traumatization in therapists treating adult survivors of childhood sexual abuse. *Dissertation Abstracts International: Section B: Sciences & Engineering, 57*(8–B), 5344.

Slover, C. A. (1998). The effects of repeated exposure to trauma on volunteer victim advocates. *Dissertation Abstracts International: Section B: Sciences & Engineering, 58*(8–B), 4473.

Sorrells-Jones, J. (1993). Caring for the caregivers: A wellness and renewal project. *Nursing Administration Quarterly, 17*(2), 61–67.

Spellmann, M. E. (1993). Direct and vicarious trauma and beliefs as predictors of PTSD. *Dissertation Abstracts International, 54*(5–B), 2773.

Stamm, B. H. (1999). Creating virtual community: Telehealth and self care, updated. In B. H. Stamm (Ed.), *Secondary traumatic stress: Self-care issues for clinicians, researchers, and educators*. Lutherville, MD: Sidran Press. This chapter discusses telemedicine as a way of addressing community in order to create friendships and to empower our caregiving to our clients, patients, ourselves, and our professional peers.

Steele, K. (1991). Sitting with the shattered soul. *Treating Abuse Today, 1*(1), 12–15 Therapists can experience their own form of PTSD in response to working with survivors of severe abuse.

Terry, M. J. (1995). Kelengakutelleghpat: An Arctic community-based approach to trauma. In B. H. Stamm (Ed.), *Secondary traumatic stress: Self-care issues for clinicians, researchers, and educators*. Lutherville, MD: Sidran Press. This paper is an outgrowth of an Alaska Native health-care program that has now become a model for health care delivery systems from rural and inner-city America to the frontiers of developing nations. In the face of overwhelming primary and secondary traumatic stress, a critical incident stress management program was revised to emphasize collaboration and traditional Native values.

Truman, B. M. (1997). Secondary traumatization, counselor's trauma history, and styles of coping. *Dissertation Abstracts International Section B: Sciences & Engineering, 57*(9–B), 5935.

Vachon, M. L S. (1987). Team stress in palliative/hospice care. In L. F. Paradis (Ed.), *Stress and burnout among health care providers caring for the terminally ill and their families*. New York: Haworth Press. Using data gathered as part of a larger study of occupational stress, the subset of hospice health care provider was analyzed to ascertain the stressors and manifestations of stress they encountered in their work.

Valent, P. (1995). Survival strategies: A framework for understanding secondary traumatic stress and coping in helpers. In C. R. Figley (Ed.), *Compassion fatigue: Coping with secondary traumatic stress disorder in those who treat the traumatized.* New York: Brunner/Mazel. The model presented in this chapter helps to categorize and conceptualize traumatic stress reactions as a context for understanding the nature and role of survival strategies. The author notes that whereas PTSD describes the reliving and avoidance of traumatic stress responses, there is a need for a framework for the great variety of such responses, some of which may even be contradictory (such as courage and fear).

Van De Water, R. C. (1996). Vicarious traumatization of therapists: The impact of working with trauma survivors. *Dissertation Abstracts International Section B: Sciences & Engineering, 57*(3–B), 2168.

van der Veer, G. (1992). *Counselling and therapy with refugees: Psychological problems of victims of war, torture and repression.* Chichester, England: John Wiley & Sons. This book offers a practical guide to the treatment of the psychological problems encountered by refugees. It brings together the author's own experience and the available scientific literature and thereby builds a bridge between theoretical knowledge about the problems of refugees and clinical practice.

Vesper, J. H. (1998). Mismanagement of countertransference in posttraumatic stress disorder: Ethical and legal violations. *American Journal of Forensic Psychology, 16*(2), 5–15. Discusses ethical & legal implications of management of countertransference in therapeutic relationship, therapists working with patients with PTSD.

Walton, D. T. (1997). Vicarious traumatization of therapists working with trauma survivors: An investigation of the traumatization process including therapists' empathy style, cognitive schemas and the role of protective factors. *Dissertation Abstracts International Section B: Sciences & Engineering, 58*(3–B), 1552.

White, G. D. (1998). Trauma treatment training for Bosnian and Croatian mental health workers. *American Journal of Orthopsychiatry, 68*(1), 58–62. Describes 2 training programs carried out in 1995 in the former Yugoslavia. The goals of these programs were to 1) train indigenous mental health workers, and 2) evaluate and treat secondary posttraumatic stress, and 3) develop regularly scheduled peer supervision/consultation groups.

Williams, M. B. & Gindlesperger, S. (1996). Developing and maintaining a psycho-educational group for persons diagnosed as DID/MPD/DDNOS. *Dissociation: Progress in the Dissociative Disorders, 9*(3), 210–220. Discusses treatment issues such as the effect on the therapist.

Yassen, J. (1995). Preventing secondary traumatic stress disorder. In C. R. Figley, (Ed.), *Compassion fatigue: Coping with secondary traumatic stress disorder in those who treat the traumatized.* New York: Brunner/Mazel. This chapter presents an understanding of the concept of prevention and offers an ecological model as a framework for planning for the impact of secondary traumatic stress (STS). It assumes that unless we prepare, plan, or attend to the effects of STS, we can cause harm to ourselves, to those who are close to us, or to those who are in our professional care.

Exposure Due to Research Work

Armstrong, J. G. (1996). Emotional issues and ethical aspects of trauma research. In E. Carlson, (Ed.), *Trauma research methodology.* Lutherville, Maryland: Sidran Press. The author contends that it is important that a researcher's subjective responses to studying the catastrophic reactions of victims of traumatic events be part of his research methodology because trauma is contagious. Some general ethical issues likely to be encountered during trauma research are discussed.

Derry, P. & Baum, A. (1994). The role of the experimenter in field studies of distressed populations. *Journal of Traumatic Stress,* 7(4), 625–635. This paper reports on issues identified in a graduate seminar for nonclinically trained health psychology researchers, and describes the program of training provided. Paradoxically, adhering to a more detached, noninfluential style of interaction requires adapting a flexible, rather than a rote, behavioral style. Relevant skills include explicating values, developing relational and communications skills, and training in post-traumatic stress syndromes. By thus redefining the experimenter's role, ethical and practical considerations introduced in field studies of distressed populations can be balanced with laboratory values.

Pickett, M., Brennan, A. M. W., Greenberg, H. S., Licht, L., & Worrell, J. D. (1994). Use of debriefing techniques to prevent compassion fatigue in research teams. *Nursing Research,* 43(4), 250–252. Nurses often study subjects who have experienced traumatic events involving intense and emotionally charged consequences. This paper describes how the process of crisis debriefing can be used to mitigate the concerns of interviewers who collect data from such subjects.

Exposure Due to Teaching & Training

Danieli, Y. (1994). Countertransference, trauma, and training. In J. P. Wilson & J. D. Lindy (Eds.), *Countertransference in the treatment of PTSD.* New York: Guilford Press. The author presents a training model for mental health professionals who work with PTSD. This chapter contains step-by-step instructions on how to identify and manage countertransference reactions

Felman, S. (1991). Education and crisis, or the vicissitudes of teaching. *American Imago*, *48*(1), 13–73. The first of two special issues on "Psychoanalysis, culture and trauma." An account of a graduate seminar on "Literature and Testimony," taught by the author at Yale, in which students read works by Albert Camus, Fyodor Dostoevsky, Sigmund Freud, Stephane Mallarme, and Paul Celan, and saw life accounts from the Video Archive for Holocaust Testimonies at Yale.

McCammon, S. L. (1995). Painful pedagogy: Teaching about trauma in academic and training settings. In B. H. Stamm (Ed.), *Secondary traumatic stress: Self-care issues for clinicians, researchers, and educators*. Lutherville, MD: Sidran Press.

Exposure Due to Occupations other than Emergency Services or Health Care Service, Research & Training

Bricker, P. L. & Fleischer, C. G. (1993). Social support as experienced by Roman Catholic priests: The influence of vocationally imposed network restrictions. *Issues in Mental Health Nursing*, *14*(2), 219–234. This qualitative descriptive study explored the experience of social support as perceived by four Roman Catholic priests who are community caregivers subject to role-related stressors and who have vocational limitations placed on their social support networks.

Carr, K. F. (1997). Crisis intervention for missionaries. *Evangelical Missions Quarterly*, *33*(4), 450–458. Discusses interventions for direct and indirect traumatic exposure among missionaries.

Farmer, R., Tranah, T., O'Donnell, I., & Catalan, J. (1992). Railway suicide: The psychological effects on drivers. *Psychological Medicine*, *22*(2), 407–414. The research reported in this paper was designed to characterize the range of responses of drivers to the experiences of killing or injuring members of the public during the course of their daily work. It was found that 16.3 percent of the drivers involved in incidents did develop PTSD and that other diagnoses, e.g. depression and phobic states, were present in 39.5 percent of drivers when interviewed one month after the incident.

Freinkel, A., Koopman, C., & Spiegel, D. (1994). Dissociative symptoms in media eyewitnesses of an execution. *American Journal of Psychiatry*, *151*(9), 1335–1339. The first execution in California since 1976 took place recently in the San Quentin Prison gas chamber. 18 journalists were invited as media eyewitnesses. The authors postulated that witnessing this execution was psychologically traumatic and that dissociative and anxiety symptoms would be experienced by the journalists.

Hafemeister, T. L. (1993). Juror stress. *Violence and Victims* , 8(2), 177–186. This article explores the intense pressures and stress jurors may undergo in cases where the evidence is particularly graphic and gruesome.

Janik, J. (1995). Correctional compassion fatigue: Overwhelmed corrections workers can seek therapy. *Corrections Today*, 57, 162–63.

McCarroll, J. E., Blank, A. S., & Hill, K. (1995). Working with traumatic material: Effects on Holocaust Memorial Museum staff. *American Journal of Orthopsychiatry*, 65(1), 66–75. This article describes the process of psychological consultation and the interventions designed to lower distress among museum workers and volunteers of United States Holocaust Memorial Museum who faced potentially disturbing personal artifacts of Holocaust victims and other reminders of the horrors of the Holocaust.

Contributors

Lyndra J. Bills, M.D.
The Sanctuary Unit at
  Northwestern Institute of
  Psychiatry and The Alliance
  for Creative Development
Quakertown, PA

Sandra L. Bloom, M.D.
The Sanctuary Unit at
  Northwestern Institute of
  Psychiatry and The Alliance
  for Creative Development
Quakertown, PA

Don R. Catherall, Ph.D.
The Phoenix Institute, Ltd.
Chicago, IL

Kelly R. Chrestman, Ph.D.
Dept. of Veterans Affairs
  Medical Center
National Center for PTSD
Boston, MA

Charles R. Figley, Ph.D.
Psychosocial Stress Research and
  Treatment Program
Florida State University
Tallahassee, FL

Chrys J. Harris, Ph.D.
Linder, Waddell and Harris, PA
Greenville, SC

Nancy Kassam-Adams, Ph.D.
Philadelphia Child
  Guidance Center
Philadelphia, PA

Jon G. Linder, M.E.
Linder, Waddell and Harris, PA
Greenville, SC

Susan L. McCammon, Ph.D.
Dept. of Psychology
East Carolina University
Greenville, NC

James F. Munroe, Ed.D.
National Center for PTSD
Dept. of Veterans Affairs
    Outpatient Clinic
Veterns Improvement
    Program (VIP)
Boston, MA

Laurie Anne Pearlman, Ph.D.
Traumatic Stress Institute
South Windsor, CT

Anne C. Pratt, Ph.D.
Traumatic Stress Institute
South Windsor, CT

Dena J. Rosenbloom, Ph.D.
Traumatic Stress Institute
South Windsor, CT

Jonathan Shay, M.D., Ph.D.
Dept. of Veterans Affairs
    Outpatient Clinic and
    Dept. of Psychiatry,
    Tufts University
Boston, MA

John F. Sommer, Jr.
The American Legion
Washington, DC

B. Hudnall Stamm, Ph.D.
Institute of Rural
    Health Studies
Idaho State University
Pocatello, ID

Michael J. Terry, R.N., A.N.P.
Trauma Support Program
Norton Sound Health
    Corporation
Nome, AK

Mary Beth Williams, Ph.D.
Trauma Recovery Education
    Counseling Center
Warrenton, VA

Index

Family members
secondary reactions in, 6–7, 212
Family support
for Community Health Aides, 158–59
as peer support model, 83–85
skills and variables (Figley), 83–85
for therapists, xxv–xxvii, 22, 32, 54, 55, 56
Fathers
secondary reactions in, 6
Feminist theory
and moral dimension of trauma work,
xli–xlii, 257–67
Fetal Alcohol Effect/Syndrome
in Alaska Natives, 162–63
Figley, Charles R.
family support skills/variables, 83–85
Fiscal policy. see Human capital
Flaming (electronic mail practice), 199–200
Flannery, Raymond B.
social support component list, 82–84
Florida State University Psychosocial Stress
Research Program, xlvi
Folie a deux, 6–7
Frame of reference disruption, 53–54,
56–57, 68–69
Free speech, 198

Gay-bashing
as classroom topic, 111, 115
Gender
and secondary PTSD risk, 43–45
and self-selection into trauma work, 45
Genocide
Alaska Native, 160–61
Rwandan, xlviii–li
Germ theory of trauma, xlii, 257–74
vs. individual model of treatment,
259–60, 265, 273
Global/Detailed sort (Densky & Reese;
Harris & Linder), 100
Global village. see Internet
Goodness (philosophical concept), 249–50
Government policies. see Policy analysis;
Policymakers
Grace (Christian doctrine), 250
Group supervision. see Peer support
Guilt, l, 84, 265
Gynecological symptoms
and trauma history, in primary care pa-
tients, 124–25

Health Aides. see Community Health Aides,
Alaska

Health and Human Services Dept. (U.S.)
Office for the Advancement of Tele-
health website, 203
Health care delivery
policy development, 281–89
rural, 151–60, 166–75, 187, 203–5
Health care policy. see Health care delivery
Health insurance. see Medicare; Mental
health benefits (employment)
Health insurance plans, 78
Healthy Protocol for primary care patients,
128
Herman, Judith Lewis
moral dimension of trauma work, 257,
266–67
treatment theory, 234
Historical trauma
Alaska Natives, 160–61
Holocaust survivors
testimonies, in classroom, 111
Homicide, 161
Homophobia
as classroom topic, 111, 115
HTML (Hypertext Markup Language), 182
Human capital
concept, in business/government,
277–78, 280
maximization policy, 280–89
Humor, 59
Husbands
secondary reactions in, 6–7
Hypertext, 182

Identity disruption, 53–54, 68, 69
Impairment. see Disability; Secondary
traumatic stress risk; Worker value
Incest. see Childhood trauma history; Sexual
abuse; Sexual trauma history
Income
as stress mediator, 31, 214
Indian Health Service, 152, 171
Indirect vs. direct traumatization, xxii–xxiii,
160–64
Individuality principle of post traumatic
therapy (Ochberg), 86
Individual model of treatment, 259–60,
265, 273
Infection theory of trauma. see Germ theory
of trauma
Informatics, 181–83, 200–203
Information superhighway. see Internet
Information use
by policymakers, 279–80

Psychobiology of PTSD (van der Kolk),
163–64
Psychological needs
disruption, 60–61, 70–75
Psychosocial Stress Research Program,
Florida State University, *xlvi*
PTSD
as classroom topic, 117
in Community Health Aides, 163–66
as disability, 165–66
DSM criteria for, *xxxvi–xxxix,* 4–6, 123,
213, 249
measurement techniques, 35
paradigm, changing, *xxxv–xxxix,* 9–10
psychobiology of (van der Kolk), 163–64
public education and, 244
renamed "Primary Traumatic Stress
Disorder," 11
and STS/STSD, compared, *xix–xx, xxiv,*
xxxvii–xxxviii, 12
treatment research, *xlv*
and vicarious traumatization,
compared, 67
PTSD risk, 5–7. *see also* Secondary traumatic
stress risk
in Community Health Aides, 162,
163–66
in therapists, 20–21, 30–34, 41–46,
212–13
gender factor, 43–45
and trauma history, 43–46
Public health programs. *see* Epidemics;
Health care delivery
Public safety officers. *see* Emergency service
providers

Radiology, 193
Random/Sequential Sort (Densky & Reese;
Harris & Linder), 102
Rape
as classroom topic, 113, 115–17
Reframing of trauma, 84
Relational trauma
in peer support group, 87
Relaxation therapy, *xlv*
Republic (Plato), 250
Requests for Proposals, electronic, 190
Research activities
as STS risk factor, *xxviii*
vs. clinical work, as stress mediator, 34,
62, 78
Retraumatization, 236
RFPs, electronic, 190

Ricoeur, Paul
ethical philosophy, 248
Rural areas
health care delivery in, 151–60, 166–75,
187–88, 205
isolation in, 149–50, 186–88, 205, 241
telehealth in, 171–72, 186–88, 203–5
trauma disorders in, 149–50, 160–66
Rural-Care online professional forum,
187–88, 204–5
Rwandan genocide, *xlvii–li*

Safety
schema disruption, 32, 60, 70–71,
106–7, 241
self-care and, 60–61, 241
supervision and, 60–61, 77
Safety Protocol for primary care
patients, 128
Salary costs. *see* Human capital
Sameness/Difference Sort (Densky &
Reese; Harris & Linder), 101
Saskatchewan
Prairie and Northern Critical Incident
Group, 174
Secondary catastrophic stress reactions, 6–7
Secondary Traumatic Stress literature,
xxi–xxiii, xxxiv–xxxv. see also
Trauma research
in policy development, 286
Secondary-Traumatic-Stress online
professional forum, 205
Secondary Traumatic Stress phenomenon
(STS/STSD)
classification, *xxiv, xxxv–xxix*
defined, 10–11
naming of, *xx–xxi,* 17, 20
and PTSD, *xix–xx, xxiv, xxxv–xxxix,*
10–11, 12
and related concepts, compared, 11–13,
17, 20
Secondary Traumatic Stress risk, 5–7
in Community Health Aides, Alaska,
162, 163–66
in emergency service providers, *xxi–xxiii,*
xxxiv
and human capital, 278, 280, 281–89
minimization, policy agenda, 284–89
in primary care providers, 122
in researchers, *xxviii*
in teachers, 106–8
in therapists, 20–21, 30–34, 41–46,
75–76, 212–13, 277–89

Traumatic stress reaction
  defined, *xxxvii*
Traumatized children. *see* Children,
  traumatized
TRAUMATOLOGYe (online journal), *xlvi*
Traumatology Institute Certification
  Program, *xlvi*
Travel
  as stress mediator, 57
Trust
  schema disruption, 60–61, 71–72, 241
  self-care and, 60–61, 241

University of Maine
  Training for Health Care for Rural Areas
    project, 186–87
U.S. Advisory Board on Child Abuse and
  Neglect, 269
U.S. Dept. of Health and Human Services
  Office for the Advancement of Tele-
  health website, 203
Usenet groups, 184. *see also* Online profes-
  sional forums
Utilitarian ethics, 253

Vacations
  policy recommendations, 284, 286,
    287–88
  as stress mediators, 54, 55, 56, 78, 284,
    286, 287–88
Value pattern, professional, 251–52
van der Kolk, Bessel A.
  psychobiology of PTSD, 163–64
Vicarious traumatization concept, *xlvii–li*
  clinician reactions to, *xx*
  defined, 7–8, 52, 67–68
  development of, *xxxiii, xlvii–xlviii*
  and PTSD, compared, 67
Victim blaming
  of therapist, in peer group, 86–91,
    216–17, 223–24, 272–73
  of trauma survivors, 266–67

Village Response Teams, Alaska, 172–73
Violence
  as classroom topic, 111, 115
  collusion of therapist in, 264–67, 273
  cycle interruption, 270–71
  as epidemic, 261–63
Virtual community. *see* Internet; Telehealth
Virtue, 249–50
Visual sense
  as core sense in communication, 96–99
Vulnerability. *see* Safety

Walker, Lenore E.A.
  survivor therapy, 234
Websites, 182, 200–205
Wetmore, Ann A.
  classroom CISD model, 116
Williams, Mary Beth
  post traumatic treatment theory, 234
Women
  trauma history, and PTSD risk, 43–45
Worker value, 277–78. *see also* Human
  capital
  cost-benefit analysis, 282–83
  mental health benefits and, 280
Working conditions
  for Community Health Aides, Alaska,
    154–55, 164–65
  policy recommendations, 284–89
  STS risk and, *xxiv, xxvi, xxxix–xl,* 76–78,
    154–55, 164–65, 216–17, 284–89
  at Traumatic Stress Institute, *xl,* 76–78
World view
  Alaska Native, 158, 168–69
  disruption, 54, 57, 68–69
World Wide Web, 182, 200–205

Yoga, 55, 57, 58

Zuk, Rhoda J.
  classroom CISD model, 116